The Federalist

THE
Federalist

Design for a Constitutional Republic

GEORGE W. CAREY

University of Illinois Press : *Urbana & Chicago*

Publication of this work was supported in part by a grant
from the Earhart Foundation.

Illini Books edition, 1994
© 1989 by the Board of Trustees of the University of Illinois
Manufactured in the United States of America
P 5 4 3 2

This book is printed on acid-free paper.

Library of Congress Cataloging-in-Publication Data

Carey, George Wescott, 1933–
    The Federalist : design for a constitutional republic.

    Bibliography: p.
    Includes index.
    1. Federalist. I. Title.
JK155.C37   1989   342.73'029   88-26100
                         347.30229
ISBN 0-252-06449-6 (alk. paper)

Previously published in a cloth edition (ISBN 0-252-01609-2)
by the University of Illinois Press.

To the memory of Charles S. Hyneman—may this work prove worthy of his inspiration.

ACKNOWLEDGMENTS

I wish to thank the officers of the Liberty Fund and the Earhart Foundation. Generous grants from these institutions enabled me to take time away from my university and teaching duties to complete this book.

Thanks are also due Pamela Sullivan, Alex Aichinger, and Dale Kuehne, present students of mine, for their helpful comments and criticisms. I am particularly indebted to James B. Williams and Michael Jackson, two of my former students, for their painstaking efforts to make this a better book.

Contents

Introduction

$\mathcal{T}$HE FEDERALIST comprises eighty-five essays written by Alexander Hamilton, James Madison, and John Jay between October, 1787, and May, 1788, under the pseudonym "Publius" to help secure ratification of the proposed Constitution in New York state.[1]

But its status today as one of the three or four basic documents of our founding period—the others by common consent being the Declaration of Independence, the Constitution, and the Bill of Rights—derives from considerations that far transcend the immediate purpose of its authors.[2] Indeed, some have gone so far as to rank it among the great classics of political thought because of its realistic analysis of and approach to the perennial problems associated with popular self-government.[3] What is beyond question, however, is its place in the American political tradition as the single most authoritative source for understanding the character of our constitutional system.

The reasons for its lofty status in our political tradition are multiple and interrelated. Clearly the prestige of its authors, their prominence during the founding era, and especially the fact that one of them, James Madison, has come to be regarded as the father of the Constitution, have lent both respectability and authenticity to this work. Quite apart from the stature of its authors, however, its prominent position among our founding documents would still be secure. It is, to begin with, the most systematic and comprehensive treatment of this era that we have concerning the proposed Constitution. To be sure, it is an avowedly sympathetic treatment, one that puts the best possible light on the Framers' handiwork. But for this reason it is all the more invaluable. Precisely because Publius is obliged to acknowledge and refute the principal objections posed by the critics of the new system, he must go well beyond simply explaining the provisions of the proposed Constitution and their interrelationship. He is also obliged to delve into the whys and wherefores of its main features; to articulate and defend in the strongest terms possible the principles upon which they rest. What is more, in this enterprise he cannot avoid presenting us with a hierarchy of values and sense of priorities relative to its goals and operations which are not readily comprehended, if at all, from reading the Constitution with an innocent eye.

The Federalist, we may go so far as to say, provides us with what can appropriately be termed a "constitutional morality" which, of course, represents another reason for its centrality in our political tradition. That is, concomitant with its effort to render the proposed Constitution a coherent whole, it urges upon the rulers and ruled alike standards of behavior conducive to maintaining and perpetuating this coherence—e.g., the public's tranquility ought not be disturbed and its confidence in the regime undermined by unnecessarily submitting constitutional questions to it for resolution; the people should not tolerate representatives who exempt themselves from the operations of the laws they pass; the courts should exercise "judgment," not "will," which is the prerogative of the legislature. Sometimes this morality is presented more obliquely in the form of assumptions or presumptions central to key aspects of Publius's argument—e.g., that given the opportunity, the people's votes will center on "fit" characters; that sympathetic bonds between representatives and their constituents will serve to deter the representatives from betraying the public trust.

Because it does provide us with a constitutional morality, we have come to look upon *The Federalist,* with exceptions here or there, as revealing the intentions and motives of the Founding Fathers. It is not uncommon to find justices of the Supreme Court appealing to its authority in disputes over constitutional questions ranging from the prerogatives and responsibilities of the respective departments of government to the proper relationship between national and state authorities.[4] Such is clearly the case, too, among students of the

American political tradition, who have, since the turn of the twentieth century, increasingly come to look upon it as the most authoritative source for understanding the theory and "spirit" behind our constitutional order—a theory and spirit which many, if not most, would contend still prevails in the operations of the system.

Major Problem Areas

While there is no gainsaying the central role of *The Federalist* for an understanding of the American political tradition, serious differences do arise over the character and substance of its teachings— differences so basic and substantial as to raise the question of whether we can ever understand our political tradition, much less the nature of the regime that the Founders sought to establish. This concern may be put as follows: In recent decades, *The Federalist* has come to be viewed by students of the American political tradition as embracing mutually inconsistent positions and values. These inconsistencies, it is further contended, not only reveal a good deal about Publius's real motives and ends, but those of the Founding Fathers as well. From their perspective, more concretely, *The Federalist* represents an ambitious but futile effort to wrap the mantle of republicanism around a regime designed to protect minorities of various descriptions of wealth and status from the leveling demands of popular majorities.[5]

In their earliest and crudest form, the essential outlines of the picture most frequently drawn by these critics ran roughly as follows: contrary to what he writes at various places in *The Federalist,* Publius shared the Framers' conviction that the democratic and egalitarian impulses fed by the rhetoric of the Declaration and unleashed by the Revolution had to be restrained.[6] His positions reveal that he shared the Founders' distrust of the people and their low estimate of man's inherent nature. So much, it is contended, is evident from his defense of the separation of powers, which would allow the Senate and president, both elected through processes designed to insure their allegiance to the privileged classes, to block the democratic impulses of the House of Representatives. What is more, so this line of attack runs, if these institutions should fail, or if, perchance, they were to join the House in common cause, the Supreme Court, whose members are selected through a process that virtually insures a "conservative" outlook and loyalty to entrenched interests, with its power of judicial review would pose the final and impassable barricade to truly popular government.

The more modern and sophisticated versions of this theme take the form of arguing that Publius, more clearly than even the Framers, could see that the government of an extended union such as that envisioned under the proposed system would be relatively inert and largely immune to majority pressures. At the very least, the extensiveness of the union, coupled with the multiplicity and variety of interests it embraces, would render the formation of ruling majority coalitions very difficult. Moreover, even if such coalitions were to form, the separation of powers would afford opposing interests or coalitions ample opportunity to block the will of the majority. By this account, then, Publius's legacy is a system which, to a great extent, incorporates Calhoun's "concurrent majority" or "concurrent consent" principle,[7] wherein, on any given measure, powerful groups can exercise a veto over laws affecting their interests or, short of this, can secure important modifications and changes in such laws to make them more palatable. As a consequence, so this critique runs, our national government is not only most attentive to the better organized and more affluent interests (which belies its presumably republican character), it is also frequently paralyzed by these interests. This paralysis, in turn, renders it incapable of comprehensively meeting and dealing with the long-term and deep-seated social and economic problems confronting the nation[8]—a deplorable and dangerous state of affairs exacerbated by the federal character of the system which further disperses authority and power.[9]

This, in brief, constitutes the essentials of the modern liberal critique of *The Federalist*, which, since the turn of the twentieth century, has gained currency in academic circles. But, astonishingly enough, many conservative commentators have come to accept Publius's legacy in similar terms, albeit with one highly significant difference: they look upon these presumed undemocratic features with an approving eye.[10] *The Federalist*, in their view, articulates the Framers' belief in the sanctity of the rights of private property, rights which constitute the foundation for securing and perpetuating a truly free society. They see the separation of powers as designed to curb the democratic excesses, particularly the insatiable demand for greater equality, which would adversely affect these rights. Thus, in their view, one of the chief functions of the Senate and the president is to temporize or thwart these destructive and egalitarian impulses that might find expression in the popularly elected House. But if these institutions should prove unequal to the task, the conservatives conceive the Supreme Court as specially designed or constructed to thwart infringements on inviolable property rights.[11]

Nor, unlike their liberal counterparts, are modern conservatives particularly concerned about the dispersion of authority inherent in the constitutional design. On the whole they consider federalism a vital principle, not only for preventing a dangerous concentration of powers in the hands of the national government, but also for reinforcing and perpetuating the traditions of self-government by allowing for meaningful grass roots political participation at the state and local levels. Consequently, of special concern to conservatives in recent decades has been the nationalization of the Bill of Rights by the Supreme Court—a process wherein, they hold, the Court has abandoned its intended role as an impartial arbiter between the state and national governments by intruding upon the sovereign prerogatives of the states.

Leaving to one side the normative dimensions of the conservative-liberal perspectives and their views concerning the changes that have occurred, we see that both share very similar views relative to the nature of the Constitution and its intended functions. Moreover, as we have said, in no small measure their views are derived from their readings of *The Federalist*. Yet what cannot help but strike even a casual reader of *The Federalist* is that it conveys an almost entirely different picture of the character of the Constitution and its place in our tradition. For instance, the clear message of the appeal in the last paragraph of Federalist 14 is that the movement toward the new system represents a progression quite in keeping with the spirit and principles of the Revolution, as well as with the political developments that followed in its wake. "They [the American people] accomplished a revolution, which has no parallel in the annals of human society. They reared the fabrics of governments which have no model on the face of the globe. They formed the design of a great Confederacy, which it is incumbent on their successors to improve and perpetuate" (104–5).[12] And, in this regard, as Publius makes clear at various junctures in *The Federalist*, the proposed system is designed to correct the potentially fatal defects of the Articles. From his per-

spective, at least, the proposed Constitution is an effort to improve
and perpetuate the union that grew out of the Revolution.

Indeed, the very first paragraph of *The Federalist* poses the question of whether the abiding principles of the Declaration of Independence can be realized in practice. That is, in raising the concern
of whether "societies of men are really capable or not of establishing
good government from reflection and choice, or whether they are
forever destined to depend for their political constitutions on ac-
cident and force" (33), Publius is also asking, in effect, whether the
people are really capable of exercising in practice that fundamental
right proclaimed in the Declaration, namely, "to institute new Government, laying its Foundation on such Principles, and organizing
its Powers in such Form, as to them shall seem most likely to effect
their Safety and Happiness." Moreover, like the Declaration, Publius's enterprise is predicated on the proposition that there is an
obligation to show the reasons and need for change: that fundamental changes in the constitutional order are not to be undertaken
for "light and transient causes." In other words, there is no incompatibility between Publius's overriding purpose and the basic values
of the Declaration. On the contrary, his goal and mode of procedure
are precisely those we should expect from one who has accepted the
fundamental principles of the Declaration.

But it is not only with regard to the relationship of the Constitution
to the Declaration that we find a discrepancy between what Publius
writes and the conservative-liberal interpretation. Publius, as we shall
see, has no doubts that the deliberate sense of the community will
prevail under the forms of the proposed Constitution (e.g., 63:384).
While he is concerned about rule by unjust majorities (majority factions), he sees the futility of providing against "this evil . . . by creating a will in the community independent of the majority" (51:323).
The solution to this problem provided by the proposed system he
regards as faithful to "the spirit and the form of popular government" (10:80). In fact, he boldly asserts that "a republican remedy
for the diseases [majority factions] most incident to republican government" is to be found "in the extent and proper structure of the
Union" (10:84).

Equally important, he seems to pride himself on the fact that the
proposed system is an "unmixed" republic, i.e., one whose foundations are "wholly popular" (14:100–101). There are, he writes, "no

qualifications of wealth, of birth, of religious faith, or of civil profession" for elective office under the proposed system. The path to elective office, as he puts it, is open to "every citizen whose merit may recommend him to the esteem and confidence of his country." Likewise, the electorate for members of the House, as he sees it, is to be "the great body of the people of the United States" comprised of those who are eligible to vote for members of the lower chambers in the states—"not the rich, more than the poor; not the learned more than the ignorant; not the haughty heirs of distinguished names, more than the humble sons of obscure and unpropitious fortune" (57:351).

Nor is it fair to say that Publius rationalizes a system built upon the Calhounian "concurrent majority" principle. On the contrary, he is critical of the rules governing the voting in the Congress of the Articles for reasons that go beyond the equal suffrage of the states—a provision which, we cannot help but note in passing, he regarded as contrary to "that fundamental maxim of republican government, which requires that the sense of the majority should prevail." What seemed to bother him more, however, was the requirement of an extra-majority—two-thirds of the states—for passing laws, a requirement which, due to the "non-attendance of a few States," he remarks, has "frequently" put the Congress "in the situation of a Polish diet, where a single veto has been sufficient to put a stop to all their movements." And his comments that follow in this context are most revealing in light of the modern critiques: "The necessity of unanimity in public bodies, or of something approaching towards it," he writes, "has been founded upon a supposition that it would contribute to security." "But," he continues,

> its real operation is to embarrass the administration, to destroy the energy of the government, and to substitute the pleasures, caprice, or artifices of an insignificant, turbulent, or corrupt junto to the regular deliberations and decisions of a respectable majority. In those emergencies of a nation in which the goodness or badness, the weakness or strength, of its government is of the greatest importance, there is commonly a necessity for action. The public business must in some way or other go forward. If a pertinacious minority can control the opinion of a majority, respecting the best mode of conducting it, the majority in order that something may be done must conform to the views of the minority; and thus the sense of the smaller number will overrule that of the greater and give a tone to the national proceedings.

Hence, tedious delays; continual negotiation and intrigue; contempt-
ible compromises of the public good.

To this he is quick to add that sometimes even such compromises
are impossible when there is no room for "accommodation" or when,
as is "often" the case, the majority is simply incapable of "obtaining
the concurrence of the necessary number of votes" for positive action. In any event, he concludes, such a system is inherently weak,
sometimes bordering "upon anarchy" (22:146-48).

Beyond any question, there is a wide discrepancy between what
Publius writes in *The Federalist* and what his friends and critics, alike,
maintain he is up to. Of course, as some of his critics would have
it, these discrepancies can be explained away because Publius was
out to put one over on the ordinary reader. But in trying to interpret
The Federalist, such an explanation puts us in the difficult, if not
impossible, position of judging which of its arguments or positions
are to be taken at face value and which are not—a difficulty which
Publius's critics have not faced, much less resolved. Or, by way of
explanation, we might say—contrary to what most of his modern-
day students hold—that he was simply unaware of what the principles
of the proposed Constitution, taken as a whole, amounted to: that
he did not see or comprehend the extent to which the underlying
constitutional principles—e.g., separation of powers, federalism—
were incompatible with republicanism or how they would operate
to thwart effective and positive majority rule. But clearly, these and
similar explanations are uncharitable because they bring either his
intellectual honesty or capacities into serious question.

The fact is, to go no further, that these conservative-liberal interpretations simply do not present us with a coherent account of
The Federalist's teachings. Not only are crucial aspects of these interpretations frequently at odds with one another, they cannot explain why—assuming that Publius was bent upon achieving the goals
and conditions which they attribute to him—he proceeds as he does.
For instance, to turn to an obvious difficulty, it is clear that Publius
and the Founders wanted a more energetic government. So much
is admitted on all sides to be among their chief goals. Why, then,
do we find Publius defending those principles and institutions which,
according to his liberal critics, serve to render the government virtually inert? How is it, for example, that he can maintain that separation of powers is indispensably necessary while, at the same time,

stressing the need for a far more energetic government? Or, to illustrate how his teachings seem to be at variance with the goals ascribed to him, if he believed that the Supreme Court was designed to play a vital role in protecting the social and economic elites by thwarting proletarian majorities, why is it that he does not describe the Court as the institution particularly well suited to invalidate legislation contrary to the spirit of the Constitution? Why, instead, does he picture the Court's role in relatively narrow terms? And, perhaps most telling, why does he oppose a bill of rights, which could and has served to expand the authority of the courts? Why does he do so, moreover, using a line of argument that not only questions the efficacy of a bill of rights, but its compatibility with popular government as well?

There are other major aspects of Publius's teachings and commentary that run counter to what has become accepted wisdom in some quarters. Conservatives, for instance, who have come to regard federalism as one of the main pillars of our freedoms will find little support for this notion in *The Federalist*. Nor will those liberals who believe that Publius wanted a system that would allow vested economic interests a free reign. But these and related concerns are best discussed later in another and broader context.

Reasons for Misunderstandings

What accounts for these interpretations, which, despite Publius's repeated professions to the contrary, render him hostile to republicanism? While there can be no definitive answer to this question, we can mark out certain of the more plausible ones, which also have a bearing on our concern with and approach to *The Federalist*.

Certainly a major reason might be termed "perspectives of the times." In this regard it is generally agreed that the origins of the modern critiques of our constitutional system and the Founders, the general outlines of which we have set forth above, are to be found in the writings of the populists and progressives during the first two decades of this century. Significantly, they came after an extended period during which the national government had assumed a laissez-faire posture toward the economy and business, particularly in those areas where progressive and populists had championed the cause of change and reform. In retrospect it is understandable how those

whose interests were ill served by this laissez-faire policy could come
to believe that its roots were to be found in the constitutional design,
the more so as the Supreme Court—the presumed bastion of unfettered property rights—gave birth to and perpetuated such a view
for a considerable period. The unresponsiveness of the system, in
other words, could readily be attributed to the inherently "undemocratic" character of the Constitution. From this position, it was
but a small step to the proposition—still very much with us—that the
Framers abandoned the democratic principles and ideals of the Declaration of Independence.

Moreover, for one so disposed, *The Federalist* can be read—albeit
in a highly selective manner—to support these views. Publius, simply
put, was far from being an uncritical admirer of republicanism. The
history of republics, he informs us at one point, can scarcely be
encouraging for the patrons of free government and civil liberty
because of their demonstrated incapacity to control the violence of
faction. He evidences alarm at the situation within the states where
the very conditions that had doomed earlier republics were beginning to manifest themselves. In this connection, he writes of the
"prevailing and increasing distrust of public engagements and alarm
for the private rights which are echoed from one end of the continent
to the other" (10:77–78). He even goes so far as to contend that
"pure democracies" can never be anything other than "spectacles
of turbulence and contention" (10:81).

In addition, underlying Publius's concern about popular government was, as we might expect, an equally hardheaded appraisal of
human nature, one cast largely in terms of human motivation.[13] Men,
he tells us, have a pronounced propensity to pursue their immediate
self-interest even at the expense of the long-term common good. So
strong is this propensity, according to Publius, that majorities formed
around the immediate self-interest of their members will often pursue their ends, no matter how unjust or wicked they might be, even
in the face of religious or moral appeals. Nor does he believe that
the rulers, without adequate precautions, can be trusted; they, too,
will use their authority and power to advance their interests and
those of their family and friends at the expense of the ruled. Consequently, when impulse and opportunity coincided, Publius did not
look primarily to reason, virtue, morality, or religion to stay the

hands of either the majorities or of the rulers from acting oppres- |
sively in the pursuit of their immediate self-interest.

In holding to and expressing such beliefs, Publius can be viewed
as providing the theoretical linkage between the Constitution and
the behavior of the institutions it creates—the linkage which, as both
the populists and more recent critics of the system are wont to
contend, reveals the real motives of the Framers. But, as we have
already intimated, drawing this connection relies upon selectively
extracting quotes from *The Federalist* without regard to Publius's
broader perspective or the assumptions upon which he operates. For
instance, to take perhaps the most basic issue, we cannot justifiably
consider his observations concerning republican government or his
related assumptions concerning the nature of man as presumptive
evidence of hostility on his part toward popular government. On the
contrary, his critical remarks follow directly from what he regards
as givens. Revealing in this respect are his comments on the proposition, advanced by some opponents of the proposed Constitution,
that if the union were to break up into smaller parts there would
be little cause for concern because "commercial republics" would
not be "disposed to waste themselves in ruinous contentions with
each other" (6:56). While he maintains that experience does not
bear out this proposition, his more fundamental point is that this is
but another of "those idle theories which have amused us with promises of an exemption from the imperfection, the weaknesses, and the
evils incident to society in every shape." He asks rhetorically, "Is it
not time to awake from the deceitful dream of a golden age and to
adopt as a practical maxim for the direction of our political conduct
that we, as well as the other inhabitants of the globe, are yet remote
from the happy empire of perfect wisdom and perfect virtue?" (6:59).
In short, his remarks about republicanism are conditioned by an
assumption that republics will not be free from vices and wickedness,
the lot of imperfect man. For him, the imperfections of man are a\
reality which the proponents of republican government, himself in- |
cluded, must recognize and make due allowance for. Viewed in this/
light, Publius—by recognizing the weaknesses inherent in republican
government and by pointing to factors that promise to mitigate these
weaknesses—emerges as a true friend of popular government.

The critics' failure to view the problems associated with the realization of republican government from Publius's perspective is only

a manifestation of a more profound difficulty: Publius and his critics are, so to speak, proceeding on two different tracks or levels that are of such a qualitatively different nature that the concerns and principles of one are frequently meaningless or irrelevant for the other. Concretely, Publius is obliged to confront reality by taking into account givens of the nature of man and republics alluded to above. In contrast, however, his critics have been more preoccupied with abstract or theoretical concerns, the most significant of which have, either implicitly or explicitly, turned out to be the standards or requirements of a model democracy.[14]

Those models that have formed the basis for the critiques of *The Federalist*, as well as of the Founders and their handiwork, are similar in certain salient respects. They seek, above all, to maximize political equality, the underlying value for the principle of majority rule. Moreover, they embody the requirement of the "pure" or classical conception of democracy wherein these majorities are to be vested with the capacity and means to translate their preferences immediately into laws.[15] Consequently, the majority-rule principle in this sense becomes a critical standard against which Publius's teachings are measured.

These aspects of the critics' models are alone sufficient to indicate the wide gulf that separates them from Publius's approach and the realm in which he necessarily had to operate. To begin with, Publius's conception of republicanism, particularly as it relates to the proper role of the people and the functions of the representatives, differs in salient respects from that of his critics. Perhaps the most important of these is that Publius did not evaluate republican institutions and processes by the degree to which they would enable the people to translate their particular policy preferences directly into law through electoral processes. On the contrary, we have every reason to believe that he would have found serious fault with this brand of republicanism.

Beyond this, of course, Publius had to deal with a variety of concerns about which the modern models are largely silent or whose principles yield little by way of instruction. Chief among these would be how to structure the machinery of government—e.g., what does republicanism require in establishing the judicial branch and fixing its role? What provisions, consonant with republicanism, can be taken to insure that judges will possess the requisite knowledge and experience for their responsibilities? Nor do the models address other obvious problems of another, but equally important, order. For instance, it seems evident that stability and order are prerequisites for decent and effective popular government. But, again, the models can tell us nothing about what institutions or procedures are necessary for this stability and order, much less how they are to be rendered compatible with republican principles. Nor, at another level, are such models suited to realistically appraising the prospect that representatives might betray the people's trust and thereby endanger the very existence of the regime. In sum, to put this somewhat differently, models are models: they are limited in their relevance and applicability to the real world by what their builders put into them.

We need not dwell on the inherent limitations of the models by which Publius's republicanism has been measured and found wanting to see their inappropriateness for this purpose. In sum, they are both limited and rigid, incapable of recognizing, much less of placing in proper context, the values and concerns uppermost in Publius's mind. However, it is the effort to squeeze Publius's thoughts into these narrow parameters that has served to distort his commitment to popular government. For without recognizing the purposes or concerns which stand behind the principles Publius advances, it is all too easy to conclude that he wanted to pose unnecessary obstacles to popular control of government. Such, as we shall see later, is clearly the case with respect to the prevailing view concerning the purpose of the separation of powers—a view which, as we have remarked, is crucial to both the liberal and conservative conceptions of our constitutional order.

These observations, we believe, bring us to what is the most basic reason of all for the general misunderstanding that surrounds Publius's teachings: a propensity on the part of his critics to take a truncated or partial view of *The Federalist*, to concentrate on one or a few aspects of the work without an overall view of Publius's concerns or approach. Thus, it is hardly surprising to find that certain elements of his thought have been isolated and emphasized without regard to their contextual relationship with other significant principles of his teachings. Nor, lacking an overall conception of his task, is it difficult to see why *The Federalist* has been unfairly judged by inappropriate standards or principles.

Toward an Understanding: Plan of Approach

While the liberal-conservative interpretations illustrate the felt need for a systematic and comprehensive understanding of *The Federalist*, they also point out the path by which we can gain such an understanding. Broadly speaking, Publius's posture toward republicanism is at the heart of the major controversies surrounding the underlying character of our constitutional system. This by itself would suggest that using his conception of republicanism as a point of departure might be worthwhile, at least from the vantage point of correcting major misapprehensions concerning his thought. But more significantly, as our remarks to this point would indicate, Publius clearly felt obliged to show the compatibility between the republicanism provided for in the Constitution and other highly valued conditions or ends associated with decent, orderly, and effective government. Publius alludes to this concern when, in Federalist 37, he remarks on "the difficulties encountered by the convention . . . in combining the requisite stability and energy in government with the inviolable attention due to liberty and to the republican form" (226). Yet Publius's task had to go well beyond showing that stability, energy, and republicanism were mixed together in their proper proportions. Beyond this he had also to show how the system would simultaneously allow for popular control, avoid the evils long associated with republican government, and provide for the public good.

We may profitably view Publius's concerns from still another angle. His conception of good government can be seen to embody two partially overlapping functions: the protective and the positive. Without going into great detail at this point, we may say that the protective function is intimately linked to the "justice" he conceived to be "the end of government" and "of civil society" as well: that is, security for individual and minority rights and liberties against unjustified or arbitrary invasions by popular majorities or the government (51:324). The positive function of government is associated with the "public good" and involves fulfilling its delegated responsibilities in an orderly, effective, and deliberative manner consonant with "the real welfare of the great body of the people" (45:289). In these terms, his task was to show how the proposed system was designed to achieve these primary ends in conformity with the republican principle.

To put this otherwise, Publius was acutely aware of the republican genius of the American people—an awareness that tacitly provides the perspective for much of what he has to say about the proposed Constitution. Nevertheless he was also fully aware that republicanism had to be fashioned in light of other concerns and values that superseded even this yearning for republican government. For instance, he writes of the "transcendent law of nature and of nature's God, which declares that the safety and happiness of society are the objects at which all institutions aim and to which all institutions must be sacrificed" (43:279). Consequently, he is obliged to explain how the republicanism he advances and defends conforms with this "transcendent law." Or, as will be evident, his commitment to liberty (as well, we may assume, as that of the people whom he was addressing) was more deeply held than even his desire for republican government. Thus, he has to show that under the proposed system the two were compatible, that republican government can coexist with ordered liberty. Indeed, in our view, one of Publius's most enduring and significant contributions to the practice of self-government resides in the degree to which he was able to show how and why republicanism could be reconciled with the complex and interrelated elements of constitutionalism broadly defined. By this synthesis, he redeemed the republican principle that had fallen into disrepute.

In the chapters that follow we endeavor to set forth the main elements of Publius's synthesis by examining his position and views toward what are commonly acknowledged to be the four leading principles of our constitutional order: republicanism, the separation of powers, federalism, and limited government. We are fully aware that in concentrating on these principles we are superimposing a framework of analysis on *The Federalist*, a framework that in important respects is different from that which Publius sets forth in Federalist 1 and which, for the most part, he follows in describing and justifying the proposed Constitution.[16] But there are, we believe, excellent reasons for departing from Publius's outline. For instance, a good deal of what Publius is obliged to dwell on—e.g., the *"insufficiency of the present confederation,"* the *"necessity of a government at least equally energetic with the one proposed"*—is of significance today principally as it relates to his thinking about the powers, structures, and processes of government; that is, to the basic principles which form the nucleus of our approach. In other words, our approach does not ignore the major areas that Publius discusses. Rather, it relates these areas to the fundamental principles of the system and the major concerns that thread though the essays. In an important sense, then, we are doing little more than superimposing a comprehensive approach on *The Federalist* that embraces the basic elements of Publius's thought—an approach which, we believe, in no way distorts his positions, but rather lends an added coherence to them.

Quite apart from this consideration, there are other sound reasons for examining the nature of Publius's synthesis by using these principles as our focal points. In the first place, each of these principles relates to a fundamental aspect of government. Those who set out to found a political regime, for example, must at some point answer certain basic questions: who is to have the final say in the system? How is authority to be distributed? Should there be limits on the powers of government? These basic questions clearly bear a direct relationship to our focal principles: republicanism means that the people are sovereign; separation of powers tells us that there is a horizontal division of authority in the national government; federalism signifies that there is, presumably, a vertical division of authority or functions between the national government and the states; and limited government indicates that there are certain limitations on the authority or powers of government.

Each of these principles, of course, stands in need of considerable elaboration. Republicanism, as we have already intimated, can take different forms, even though in the last analysis all of them embody the notion of popular sovereignty. Likewise, it is clear, the principles of federalism and separation of powers do not, by themselves, tell us how the powers and authority are divided, nor does limited government inform us about the substance and nature of the limitations. Moreover, we need to know what provisions have been made for the implementation, perpetuation, and enforcement of these principles—not an insignificant matter, because without some means to insure compliance with their terms, the Constitution itself would become a dead letter.

While this, of course, brings us back to one of the reasons which justifies a careful reading of *The Federalist*, the elaboration of these principles in the sense indicated above also renders Publius's conception of our constitutional system a coherent whole which, in turn, allows us to see the relationship of these principles to one another. For instance, though these principles may be seen as analytically distinct, there is, as we shall see in the following chapters, an interesting overlap between them in the functions they perform and their contributions to the ends of good government. With a more comprehensive view we also come to see why and where Publius is less than clear and, at times, even contradictory in his account of how the system is designed to operate.

Still another reason for using these principles as focal points comes down to the fact that the debate over the nature of our constitutional system as described by Publius has been conducted in a framework in which these principles are key elements. This is to say that those who, for whatever reason, maintain that the system, far from being republican in character, is designed to protect or promote the interests of privileged and entrenched minorities base their arguments to a great extent on the fact that these basic principles do not keep house with one another: that separation of powers and limited government, for example, are incompatible with republicanism. This contention, and hence the conception of the Constitution to which it leads, is most effectively answered, we believe, by showing that these principles are, to a great degree, not only compatible but supportive of one another. In other words, our analysis at least promises to point out the misunderstandings that have led to the conservative-liberal interpretations that we have surveyed.

But our analysis goes well beyond correcting the misconceptions fostered by these liberal-conservative interpretations. What emerges, we believe, is a new way of looking at how the system was designed to secure multiple ends such as republicanism, individual liberty, order, and the rule of law. We say "new way" because, as the following chapters will reveal, many, if not most, who admire our constitutional system—i.e., those who look with favor upon separation of powers, federalism, and judicial review—do not fully comprehend the interrelationship of these principles and how Publius envisioned they would operate to secure the desired ends.

Mode of Procedure

Our survey and analysis of Publius's synthesis begins with the principle of republicanism, which involves an examination of his extended republic theory. Here one of our chief concerns is to point up how, consonant with the republican principle, the conditions associated with the extensive republic will operate to overcome the chief difficulties he perceives at the state level: the dominant interests judging their own cause. In this endeavor we provide an answer for a critical question posed by his critics: why would the extended republic pose formidable obstacles to majorities bent upon factious policies and not to nonfactious majorities as well? This question embodies what has long been regarded by Publius's critics as the fatal flaw in his extended republic theory.

We next examine, in Chapter 2, Publius's version of the separation of powers. In many ways this principle stands at the heart of Publius's synthesis. On the one hand, it serves a vitally important protective function by preventing a concentration of legislative, executive, and judicial powers that would constitute tyranny or a permanent state of oppression by the rulers. On the other, it is indispensable for the fulfillment of positive functions. Without it, for example, the national government could not be trusted with the powers necessary for the fulfillment of its objectives. The separation of powers provides for the rule of law, stability, continuity, and deliberation, all of which are essential not only for republicanism, but also for the public good. But it is, as we shall note, a misconception of the purposes of the separation of powers that has led Publius's critics to view it as an indispensable element of his solution to the problem of majority factions and incompatible with the republican principle.

We move next to federalism, in many ways the most complex principle. Publius, it would appear, wanted to picture the proposed system as occupying a middle ground between one organized on confederate principles and one constituted on unitary or national principles. Yet with the experiences of the Articles burned in his mind, he was keenly conscious that the national government must possess unfettered authority to pursue the objects entrusted to its care. Publius is understandably ambiguous about this middle-ground position and what portions of sovereignty are reserved to the states. What is perhaps less understandable is his ambiguity surrounding the question of who should decide when there is a conflict between the two jurisdictions. In any event, as our discussion will indicate, federalism (understood in the modern sense as the middle-ground position Publius sought to establish between the unitary and confederate forms) was largely tangential to his synthesis and not, as many have contended, vital to the preservation of liberty.

Finally, we turn to limited government. This involves an analysis of Publius's argument that the Constitution represents the fundamental law—or the constituent will of the people—which is superior to ordinary law. Integral to this position is another which we also examine: that it is within the special province of the courts to enforce the constitutional limitations against the Congress. This, of course, raises a number of questions particularly in light of those interpretations which, from a variety of perspectives, stress the key role of the courts with respect to the protective function. In our view, for reasons we set forth, a decisive factor in understanding what Publius conceived the courts' proper role to be—an understanding quite at variance with what is often attributed to him—is to be found in his arguments against a bill of rights.

Throughout this work, we feel constrained to add, we treat Publius as one person, not three. That *The Federalist* was intended to be read and understood as the product of one pen is sufficient justification for this. However, we do so because in the most relevant sense Publius was a single individual. His three components, that is, had to set aside their pet notions about what form the new government should take and set themselves to the task of explaining and defending the Constitution as it emerged from the Philadelphia Convention. What is more, in order to insure the success of their collaborative effort, each of the authors in writing his contributions was obliged to take into account the beliefs and sensibilities of his co-authors. As a consequence, Publius takes on a character different from any of his parts: he articulates the common ground or consensus of his components regarding the nature of and need for the Constitution.

This "oneness" of Publius is reflected in the positions of Hamilton and Madison (as well as Jay in his far more limited contributions) on virtually all the salient principles of the proposed Constitution, particularly those we are to examine. The agreement between them extended to such crucial concerns as the compelling need for a stronger union with sufficient powers to achieve its primary objects, the benefits to be derived from an extensive republic (their contributions in this respect complementing one another), the nature of the division of powers between state and national government, the purposes of and need for the separation of powers, the fear of legislative aggrandizement, the status of the Constitution as fundamental law, unalterable through the ordinary political processes, and, *inter alia,* the dangers of state encroachment on national powers. As we shall see, the reasons for the few and minor tensions or seeming contradictions we find between them clearly arise from "problems endemic to the Constitution or inherent to republicanism."[17]

Finally, before proceeding, we should remark that, consonant with treating Publius as one individual, we confine the analysis and commentary which follows to the text of *The Federalist.* That is, we resist the temptation to go outside of *The Federalist* to the works of Madison, Hamilton, or Jay to stress or reinforce this or that point or position. The reasons for this forbearance are multiple but they stem from a desire to present Publius's thoughts in their purest form: to confront the text, as best we can, in a manner and on terms the author intended. Moreover, the first logical step in any endeavor that seeks to integrate the individual thoughts of Hamilton, Madison, or Jay with those of Publius—or, for that matter, to show the influence of other political philosophers on Publius's thinking, an increasingly popular undertaking—is first to gain a clear understanding of Publius's thought. This is the task to which we now turn.

NOTES

1. For a thorough treatment of when and where the essays first appeared see Jacob E. Cooke's Introduction to *The Federalist* (Middletown, Conn.: Wesleyan University Press, 1961). Bibliographic appendices to *The Federalist Papers* (2d Ed: Baltimore: John Hopkins University Press, 1981), selected and edited by Roy P. Fairchild, provide a listing of the various editions of *The Federalist* that have appeared.

2. To this point Clinton Rossiter writes: "It would not be stretching the truth more than a few inches to say that *The Federalist* stands third only to the Declaration of Independence and the Constitution itself among the sacred writings of American political history." Introduction to *The Federalist Papers* (New York: New American Library, 1961), p. vii. Jacob E. Cooke is even more emphatic: "The United States has produced three historic documents of major importance: The Declaration of Independence, the Constitution, and *The Federalist.*" *The Federalist Papers,* p. ix.

3. Jefferson went so far as to describe it as "the best commentary on the principles of government ever written." Letter to Madison, 18 Nov. 1788, in Julian F. Boyd, ed., *The Papers of Thomas Jefferson* (Princeton: Princeton University Press, 1958), XIV, 188. Charles A. Beard, interestingly enough in light of his economic interpretations of the Founders' motives, was lavish in his praise

of *The Federalist*, ranking it "first in the world's literature of political science." *The Enduring Federalist* (New York: Doubleday, 1948), p. 10. For the laudatory comments of others such as John Marshall, Chancellor Kent, John Quincy Adams, and Woodrow Wilson see Gottfried Dietze, *The Federalist* (Baltimore: John Hopkins University Press, 1960), chap. 1. See also Fairfield's Introduction to *The Federalist Papers*.

4. James G. Wilson, "The Most Sacred Text: The Supreme Court's Use of *The Federalist* Papers," *Brigham Young University Law Review* 1 (1985).

5. Robert Dahl in his *Preface to Democratic Theory* (Chicago: University of Chicago Press, 1956) writes that "the Madisonian style of thinking has led to a rather tortuous political theory" (p. 30), that "as political science rather than as ideology the Madisonian system is clearly inadequate" (p. 31). What Madison had sought, according to Dahl, was to provide "a satisfying, persuasive, and protective ideology for the minorities of wealth, status, and power who distrusted and feared their bitter enemies—the artisans and farmers of inferior wealth, status, and power, who they [the Framers] thought constituted the 'popular majority'" (p. 30). Because this ideology appeals to Americans, most of whom are members of one minority or another that could potentially be threatened by majorities, Dahl believes it is "the most prevalent and deeply rooted of all the styles of thought that might properly be labeled 'American'" (pp. 30–31).

6. The first of the modern critiques is generally acknowledged to be James Allen Smith's *The Spirit of American Government* (New York: Macmillan, 1907). Cushing Strout in his Introduction to the Harvard University Press edition (1975) writes: "In the first decade of the twentieth century a generation of reformers began to question [the heritage of the Founders]. The Founding Fathers had become the idols of the established powers in business and politics, and the reformers began to seek elsewhere for the democratic wisdom to deal with the corruption, monopoly, and exploitation which characterized urban and industrial life. Perhaps the saving wisdom had somehow been lost—lost ever since it had first been glimpsed by the American rebels of 1776. It might even be that the Founding Fathers and their Constitution were themselves at the root of the evils. This twist of thought in a country whose people and heroes had long venerated the framers of the Constitution was a somersault of perspective that enthralled a powerful group of Progressive reformers and still survives in the writings of some influential historians." And Strout continues: "The original prophet of this new political vision was James Allen Smith," whose work "illustrated the reversal of perspective in 1907" (pp. xiiv–xiv).

There are numerous works, significant in their own right, written from the same or very similar perspectives that expand on or emphasize one or more of Smith's charges against the Framers and the constitutional system. Among these would be Charles A. Beard, *An Economic Interpretation of the Constitution* (New York: Macmillan, 1913); Vernon L. Parrington, *Main Currents in American Thought*, 3 vols. (New York: Harcourt Brace, 1927–30); Richard Hofstadter, *The American Political Tradition* (New York: Vintage Books, 1948); E. E. Schattschneider, *Party Government* (New York: Farrar and Rhinehart, 1942) and *The Semisovereign People*

(New York: Holt, Rinehart and Winston, 1960); James McGregor Burns, *The Deadlock of Democracy* (Englewood Cliffs, N.J.: Prentice-Hall, 1963) and *Uncommon Sense* (New York: Harper and Row, 1972); and Robert Dahl's *Preface*, which Gary Wills in his *Explaining America* (Garden City, N.Y.: Doubleday, 1981) regards as the "most important and devastating" critique of the principles underlying the Constitution produced in modern times.

The basic elements of the modern critique are manifest in historical works dealing with the founding era. For instance, those who hold that the Constitution represents a "reaction" to the democratic ideals of the Declaration echo, in various and subtle ways, Smith's original charge along these lines. Among others, see Gordon S. Wood, *The Creation of the American Republic* (Chapel Hill: University of North Carolina Press, 1969); Merrill Jensen, *The Articles of Confederation* (Madison: University of Wisconsin Press, 1940) and *The New Nation* (New York: Alfred A. Knopf, 1950); and J. Franklin Jameson, *The American Revolution Considered as a Social Movement* (Princeton: Princeton University Press, 1923). Douglass Adair indicates the widespread acceptance of this view regarding the relationship between the Declaration and the Constitution in his "The Tenth Federalist Revisited," in Trevor Colbourn, ed., *Fame and the Founding Fathers* (New York: W. W. Norton, 1974).

7. As Dahl puts this in his analysis of *The Federalist:* "The concept of 'minority veto' or 'concurrent majorities' is not, strictly speaking, of Madison's creation. This view associated with the name of John C. Calhoun nevertheless seems to have become a fundamental element in the American ideology, and it is frequently defended in essentially Madisonian language." *Preface*, p. 29.

8. As James McGregor Burns writes: "It [the political system] discriminates cruelly against the unorganized or ill-represented masses of people. It is always too late; hence social malaise breeds and proliferates for years before action is taken. And the system makes for crisis, which serves only as a temporary catharsis; conditions fester until there is a dramatic breakdown, national attention rivets on the crisis . . . a solution becomes, for a time, the first priority for all concerned; actions are piecemeal, with little attention to long term need or effects; the crisis seems to be resolved; the brokers turn back to business as usual—and the underlying ills persist." *Uncommon Sense*, p. 118. In this vein, a customary defense of a form of judicial activism which embraces legislative action by the courts stresses the presumed failure of political institutions to take "needed" action.

9. Herbert Croly, in many ways the intellectual father of the New Deal, was among the first of the early critics to see that federalism was an obstacle to centralized, national planning necessary for the realization of "progressive" goals. Croly's views stand apart from the earlier critiques of the system because he praises Hamilton for at least seeing the need for a stronger union. And, on these grounds, he finds fault with Jefferson. See his *The Promise of American Life* (New York: Macmillan, 1911).

10. For a discussion and analysis of this point see Martin Diamond, "Conservatives, Liberals, and the Constitution," in *Left, Right, and Center*, Robert A. Goldwin, ed. (Chicago: Rand McNally, 1966). Diamond notes that "the more

liberal or conservative the writer, the likelier and fuller the agreement" between them regarding "the original intention of the Constitution and the nature of the original institutions it established." As he remarks, "one tends to deplore and the other to applaud" the principles of the Constitution such as the separation of powers (pp. 60–61).

11. Dietze's *The Federalist* is the locus classicus for this position. "From among those values [those embodied in the Constitution], the freedom of the individual is considered to be of paramount importance. As a matter of fact, Hamilton's exposition of the doctrine of judicial review in the seventy-eighth essay amounts largely to an advocacy of the preservation of individual freedom from the progressivism of popular majorities and their infringements upon life, liberty, and property. The protection of these rights is in good hands because the judges, due to the nature of their profession, are likely to be conservatives" (p. 278).

12. All citations to *The Federalist* in the text are to *The Federalist Papers*, Clinton Rossiter, ed. (New York: New American Library, 1961). When the number of the essay is apparent from the text, the numbers in parentheses will be only to the page numbers. Otherwise the citations will be to the essay number followed by the page numbers.

13. For an examination of Publius's conception of human nature from this perspective see James P. Scanlan, "*The Federalist* and Human Nature," *Review of Politics* 21 (Oct., 1959).

14. Perhaps the best known and most sophisticated of these models in Dahl's "polyarchy," which is recognizably a refinement of the majoritarian model set forth by Austin Ranney and Willmoore Kendall in their *Democracy and the American Party System* (New York: Harcourt Brace, 1956). The conditions of Dahl's polyarchy are set forth and discussed in chap. 3 of his *Preface*.

15. For example, many works in the political science literature that advocate responsible, disciplined, and programmatic political parties as a means of overcoming the "undemocratic" character of the Constitution also accept the major premises of the modern critique. Moreover, the advocates of party reform share the vision of the classical model of democracy and seek to provide the means through which majorities can enact their preferences into law. Yet little thought has been given to the consequences that might flow from such a "reform" in terms of other cherished values embodied in our system. On this matter see Evron M. Kirkpatrick, "Toward a More Responsible Two-Party System: Political Science, Policy Science, or Pseudo-science?" *American Political Science Review* 65 (Dec., 1971).

16. Publius writes in Federalist 1: "I propose, in a series of papers, to discuss the following interesting particulars: —*The utility of the* UNION *to your political prosperity —The insufficiency of the present Confederation to preserve that Union — The necessity of a government at least equally energetic with the one proposed, to the attainment of this object —The conformity of the proposed Constitution to the true principles of republican government —Its analogy to your own State constitution —*and lastly, *The additional security which its adoption will afford to the preservation of that species of government, to liberty, and to property*" (36).

17. For a full development of these and other points see George W. Carey, "Publius—a Split Personality," *Review of Politics* 46 (Jan., 1984).

The Federalist

1

·

Republicanism

> To secure the public good and private rights
> against the danger of [majority factions], and at
> the same time to preserve the spirit and form of
> popular government, is then the great object to
> which our inquiries are directed [10:80].

*A*NY NUMBER OF places in *The Federalist* could be used as a suitable point of departure for an analysis of Publius's conception of republicanism. The very first essay, aside from being a logical starting point, suits our purposes very well. Here we find listed among the subjects to be covered in the subsequent papers *"The conformity of the proposed Constitution to the true principles of republican government"* (36). The word *true* in this context suggests that the proposed Constitution already has been measured against standards of republicanism that were not "true"; or that, at the very least, there were principles of republicanism abroad which were not valid. These suppositions are borne out in the first section of Federalist 39, wherein Publius endeavors to show that the "general form and aspect of the government" does conform with republicanism rightly understood. In the course of this essay, Publius notes that the characteristics and principles of republicanism are not to be derived by examining the governments of those nations and states (Holland, Venice, England, and Poland) which "political writers" are wont to call republics. He observes that there are no principles or elements common to these regimes, a fact which, taken together with their deviations from "genuine" republican principles, he offers as evidence of "the extreme inaccuracy with which the term has been used in political disquisitions" (240–41).

What are these "genuine" principles to which Publius refers? Averting to principles that serve to differentiate forms of govern-

3

ment, principally those relating to the derivation and exercise of power, he defines a republican government as one "which derives all its powers directly or indirectly from the great body of the people, and is administered by persons holding their offices during pleasure for a limited period, or during good behavior." For a government to be truly republican, he holds, "it is *essential* . . . that it be derived from the great body of the society, not from an inconsiderable proportion or favored class of it." "Otherwise," he remarks, "a handful of tyrannical nobles, exercising their oppressions by a delegation of their powers, might aspire to the rank of republicans and claim for their government the honorable title of republic." As for the exercise or administration of powers, "it is *sufficient*" that the officeholders "be appointed, either directly or indirectly, by the people" either for a "limited period, or during good behavior" (241).

What we see from this is that the proposed Constitution fits very nicely into Publius's conception of republicanism—so nicely, in fact, that skeptics might argue, not without reason, that he has formulated or tailored his conception of republicanism to fit the proposed system. Clearly, his discussion does suggest that his formulation of republicanism was conditioned by the constitutional structures and processes of the existing state governments. Be that as it may, Publius is certainly intent on driving home the point that "mixed" regimes which recognize and institutionalize the claims and interests of "favored" classes—e.g., the "hereditary aristocracy and monarchy" in England—simply do not fit into the republican category.[1] This "repudiation" of mixed government is highly significant because, as we have remarked, the major criticisms directed at both Publius and the Founding Fathers have centered on their presumed intention to establish an American equivalent of a mixed regime with an elaborate system of separation of powers that would protect the wealthy and socially privileged from the ravages of majority rule.[2] We will have occasion to examine this particular misconception in greater detail when we analyze Publius's views on separation of powers. Suffice it to note at this point that any such intention would clearly have contravened what Publius professes to be an "essential" element of republicanism.

Closely related to this matter, we also see that Publius presents us with what can be termed a "laid-back" or "passive" conception of republicanism in marked contrast to the "active" or "positive" conceptions embodied in the strict majoritarian models to which we have referred. Put otherwise, Publius's republicanism does not call for either immediate or direct rule by the people; it is enough, according to Publius, that those who govern are ultimately accountable, directly or indirectly, to the people. In this respect, he seems to believe that if provision is made for the exercise of popular sovereignty in the sense described above, the system will, sooner or later, move in the direction desired by the greater number. Indeed, as we shall see in due course, one fundamental and recurring proposition in Publius's thought is that persistent and determined majorities simply cannot be denied under the forms of the proposed Constitution; that, off at the end, all the institutions, even those indirectly accountable to the people, would follow suit. Aside from the obvious threat of eventual political sanctions or reprisals on officeholders by majorities, we can only speculate about the reasons why he anticipated such responsiveness. High among them would certainly be his conviction that the republican "genius" of the American people would make it difficult, if not impossible, for institutions to block indefinitely the legitimate will of the people.

With Publius's definition of republican government before us, we are prepared to examine other dimensions of his thoughts on republicanism which have, over the decades, generated controversy. Precisely because he was convinced that the system would move, to borrow Locke's phrase, "whither the greater force carries it," he was concerned to point out how the proposed union under the forms of the Constitution would curb and control the excesses of popular government. A good deal of *The Federalist*, therefore, is devoted to a pathology of popular self-government, particularly pure democracies and small republics. Publius, that is, did not suffer from the delusion that republican governments, because of their popular foundations, were immune from the arbitrariness, injustice, and disorders that had plagued other forms of government. On the contrary, a central concern that permeates these essays is how to deal with the evils and shortcomings peculiar to republican government— a fact which, as we have remarked, has been construed by some as evidence of Publius's animosity toward popular government and his distrust of the "masses."

After examining Federalist essays 9 and 10 to see why Publius believed that the proposed system could overcome the fatal short-

comings of previous republics, our attention will turn to questions
that have arisen over the adequacy of Publius's solutions. In this
regard, we will examine the major charge that has been leveled against
Publius, namely, what he views as a remedy for the diseases of republican government involves processes and conditions that render
it virtually impossible for majorities, either good or bad, to rule.
Such charges, as we will show in the sections that follow, arise from
a conception of republicanism foreign to Publius's thought. In our
view, only by examining Publius's conception of republicanism in
the context of the extended republic proposed by the Constitution
can we see clearly the basis for his assertion at the end of Federalist
10 that "In the extent and proper structure of the Union . . . we
behold a republican remedy for the diseases most incident to republican government" (84).

Federalist 9 and the New and Improved Principles of Political Science

The depth, nature, and scope of Publius's concern about the feas-
iblity of republican government is clearly evidenced at the outset of
Federalist 9, an essay which in important particulars sets the stage
for the more widely read and highly crucial Tenth Federalist. Here
Publius writes that "the history of the petty republics of Greece and
Italy" can only evoke "horror and disgust," plagued as they were
by unremitting internal convulsions. He pictures them as having
existed "in a state of perpetual vibration between the extremes of
tyranny and anarchy." To be sure, he admits, there were "occasional
calms" when "intervals of felicity open[ed] to view," but these were
inevitably swept away by, as he puts it, "tempestuous waves of se-
dition and party rage." Indeed, he continues, the record of republics
is so bad that if "models of a more perfect structure" had not been
devised, "the enlightened friends to liberty would have been obliged
to abandon the cause of that species of government [republican] as
indefensible" (71–72). The refined models to which he refers are the
outgrowth of the "great improvements" he perceives in the "science
of politics." In this vein, he writes of the "efficacy of various principles now well understood, which were either not known at all, or
imperfectly known to the ancients," principles that provide "very
powerful means . . . by which the excellencies of republican govern-

ment may be retained and its imperfections lessened or avoided" (72–73).

These new and improved principles to which Publius refers would scarcely seem to constitute, as some commentators would have it, a "new political science."[3] To begin with, they do not comprise a coherent and systematic body of interrelated axioms and principles that a term like "new science" normally brings to mind. Rather, two of them relate directly to the separation of powers and its maintenance ("the regular distribution of power into distinct departments; the introduction of legislative balances and checks"), to which a third, "the institution of courts composed of judges holding their offices during good behavior," is also connected. The fourth principle, "the representation of the people in the legislature by deputies of their own election," bears more directly upon the republican principle. And the fifth and last principle, "ENLARGEMENT OF THE ORBIT," is not exactly collateral with the previous four since it does not involve constitutional arrangements or provisions (72–73).

Beyond this, neither the principles nor Publius's discussion of them embrace or advance new assumptions or perspectives for the study of politics that would characterize the foundations of a "new political science." Indeed, at this juncture, we can say that Publius is confronted with a very traditional concern: how to control the excesses of popular governments. And he holds out the prospect that through the proper combination and application of these new and improved principles—the efficacy of which has been revealed through experience, not through deduction or a new science of politics—"the excellencies of republican government may be retained and its imperfections lessened or avoided" (72–73).

As the principles which Publius advances indicate, his concern in Federalist 9 is not confined solely to the matter of republican government. But, in at least two significant ways, Federalist 9 sets the stage for Federalist 10 and the extended republic theory. First, in discussing the new and improved principles, Publius focuses his attention almost exclusively on how enlargement of the orbit will serve to ameliorate the evils associated with republican government. In so doing, he directly challenges the traditional and accepted wisdom to the effect that republican government is suitable only for a small, homogeneous population within a limited territorial expanse.[4] His

CATO

basic line of attack is to argue that the leading authority in support of this proposition, Montesquieu, is not at all unambiguous about this matter, that, in fact, he can be read to support the concept of a "CONFEDERATE REPUBLIC as the expedient for extending the sphere of popular government and reconciling the advantages of monarchy with those of republicanism" (74). In this regard, Publius stresses the benefits of such a confederation in providing for the common defense of its members, policing relations between them, and quelling insurrections that may arise within any of its members—benefits relative to a range of concerns that are not central to the approach used in Federalist 10 but which, nevertheless, serve to complement and bolster the arguments for the feasibility and desirability of an extended republic. In sum, Federalist 9 begins the process of completely inverting the traditional wisdom with regard to the conditions necessary for republican government. This inversion, in its final form, holds that an orderly, decent, and stable republican regime with the capacity to defend itself against foreign and domestic enemies is possible only over an extensive territory that embraces varied and multiple interests and that, conversely, the small republics incorporating the ideals of traditional theory are destined to vibrate perpetually "between the extremes of tyranny and anarchy" (71).[5]

A second and less obvious way in which Federalist 9 anticipates the extended republic argument that follows can be seen in the high priority accorded liberty. As we have remarked, on his reading of the historical record Publius is willing to concede that there is an apparent incompatibility between republicanism and liberty. Indeed, he leaves little doubt that, if it were not for the fact that the new and improved principles of political science promise a remedy for the evils associated with republicanism, he would abandon it for a "species of government" more hospitable to liberty (72). And, while he does not specify in any detail the constituents of this liberty, we are not without clues as to its essential character. It is a liberty that is not stifled by tyranny, a condition or state of affairs wherein, *inter alia*, the citizen lives in constant uncertainty and anxiety over how the laws will be interpreted and applied from one day to the next. On the other hand, the liberty to which he refers is clearly not to be found in a condition of anarchy wherein the individual is completely unrestrained by law. In short, what little he does say at this point conforms very well with what is commonly referred to as "ordered liberty."

Federalist 10 and the Problem of Factions

The foregoing considerations, logically enough, bring us to Federalist 10, whose theoretical richness is attested to not only by the numerous and intensive analyses to which it has been subjected, but also by the variety of interpretations that have emerged which purport to give us a deeper insight into the foundations of our political system and the motives of the Framers. Perhaps, even, the essay has been overburdened in these endeavors. If we place it in context of our preceding discussion, however, we cannot help but view it as a systematic effort to explain why the extensive republic under the proposed Constitution will not suffer the same fatal vibrations as the "petty republics of Greece and Italy." As such, this particular aspect of Publius's teachings is crucial to his arguments on behalf of the proposed system. To put this another way, the presumed benefits of an extended republic, such as those described in Federalist 9, could only be realized if the internal convolutions associated with popular rule could be avoided or somehow controlled. Failing this, of course, the entire system would soon collapse, either through an incapacity to act in a resolute manner or by a usurpation of powers. But Publius had to go beyond even this concern, as critical as it was, in making his case for the proposed system: he also had to show how the extended republic could simultaneously protect or provide for a number of primary goals and values such as liberty, justice, and the common good, without compromising republican principles.

As we might expect, Publius begins his analysis in Federalist 10 by amplifying on the nature of the "mortal diseases under which popular governments have everywhere perished" and "from which the adversaries to liberty derive their most specious declamations." In this endeavor, he focuses his attention exclusively on the conditions which he and others perceive in the existing states. He notes that, despite the "valuable improvements made by the American constitutions on the popular models, both ancient and modern," "complaints" are still forthcoming "from our most considerate and virtuous citizens, equally the friends of public and private faith and of public and personal liberty" about the instability of these governments, their disregard for the "public good" in the resolution of political conflicts, as well as their abandonment of the "rules of justice" and the "rights of the minor party" to the "superior force of an interested and overbearing majority." These complaints and the "prevailing and increasing distrust of public engagements and alarm for private rights which are echoed from one end of the continent to the other" are, he argues, "chiefly, if not wholly," the "effects of the unsteadiness and injustice with which a factious spirit has tainted our public administration" (77–78).

At this point Publius sets forth his now famous definition of factions: "By a faction I understand a number of citizens, whether amounting to a majority or minority of the whole, who are united and actuated by some common impulse of passion, or of interest, adverse to the rights of other citizens, or to the permanent and aggregate interests of the community" (78). Factions are, as he puts it at the end of this essay, the "diseases most incident to republican government" and as such the principal threats to a limited or constitutional republic (84). For this reason, Publius's observations concerning their nature and how to handle the problems they pose merit our close attention.

This definition of faction informs us that Publius must be read and understood as an "objectivist," that is, as one for whom such concepts as "the permanent and aggregate interests of the community," "the rights of other citizens," and, as we will see later, "justice" have an existence and meaning quite apart from that which any majority or minority may assign to them at any given point in time. Otherwise there would be no standards, principles, or norms for determining whether or not any given group is factious or not. Later, and in other contexts, he remarks in greater detail on the standards or principles he would seem to have in mind for determining what constitutes a faction. At this juncture, we must simply note that many modern commentators have generally shown an unwillingness to enter his objectivist framework in analyzing his extended republic theory. Indeed, in their analyses, many of them impose a positivism on *The Federalist* altogether foreign to its authors and to the Founders in general.[6] Such a perspective leads one to forget about Publius's purposes and to treat Federalist 10—as a goodly number of modern political scientists, most notably the pluralists, are wont to do—as simply providing a reasonably accurate explanatory/descriptive account of why and how our system operates as it does.[7]

A related observation flows from this: while "passion" and "interest" are at the core of factions, clearly not all groups based on "passion" or "interest" are factions. What distinguishes a faction, as the definition makes clear, is the oppressive or socially destructive end which it seeks. Again, modern analysts, given their relativistic perspectives, do not distinguish between factions and interest groups. As a result, pluralists often describe the dynamics of American politics in terms of factions fighting factions, a process which, they suggest, tends to moderate the positions or demands of the competing factions. This process of moderation, in turn, they have come to look upon as Publius's solution to the problem of factions. This conclusion, however, is both partial and misleading.[8] True enough, in some conflicts, particularly those involving interest-based factions—i.e., those which center on economic policies and issues—moderation and compromise can produce nonfactious results. Indeed, so much is suggested in some of the examples of interest conflict at the state level that Publius cites—e.g., creditor-debtor, landed-manufacturing—where he laments their onesided and factious resolution due, in part, to the fact that the "rights of the minor party" were not taken into account (77). Other types of conflict, however, particularly those stemming from principle, are simply not amenable to resolution through the processes of give and take.

The character of factious strife and its resolution may profitably be viewed from still another, slightly different, perspective. There are certainly groups whose ends or purposes render them inherently factious according to Publius's definition. Their announced goals may be to deprive other citizens of their rights, or their allegiances to foreign countries unfriendly to the United States may lead them to back measures contrary to long-term interests of the nation. Any compromise with such factions is highly unlikely to produce an outcome that contributes to the public good. On the other hand, creditors, debtors, farmers, and merchants—the kinds of interests with which Publius is primarily concerned—are not inherently factious. If we are to believe Publius, however, they can and will act factiously when given the opportunity to do so. That is, they become factious, albeit retrospectively, when they take advantage of the opportunity to judge of their own cause and advance their partial interests to the exclusion of all others. The factiousness of these groups, unlike those inherently factious, can be removed through the processes of moderation that result from compromise with opposing interests. But "can" is the operative word; in this context, compromise is a necessary, but not sufficient condition to prevent the passage of a factious measure. The manner in which Publius anticipated compromise operating to eliminate "factiousness" is a matter to which we will return in due course.

We learn a good deal more about the nature of factions by turning our attention to Publius's main concern in this essay, namely, "curing" their "mischiefs." He briefly considers the alternative of "removing the causes" of faction—an alternative which, he contends, would involve either "destroying the liberty which is essential to its existence" or "giving to every citizen the same opinions, the same passions, and the same interests." Publius rejects both solutions; the first he deems "worse than the disease" and the second, "impracticable" (78).

It is in his brief discussion of the impracticability of reducing individuals to the same opinions, passions, and interests that we gain some insight into the enormity and complexity of what can be termed the problem of factions. In two sentences Publius draws an involved relationship between reason, opinion, and passion which can be put roughly as follows. So long as man "is at liberty to exercise" his fallible reason "different opinions will be formed." Beyond this, there is a "reciprocal influence" between opinions and passions: passions will attach themselves to opinions "as long as the connection subsists between" an individual's "reason and his self-love"; passions may influence opinion, particularly as individuals attempt to justify their passions; or opinions could well serve to direct the passions (78).

Whatever the precise relationship between opinion and passion—Publius does not spell it out in any detail—we can see the virtual impossibility of "reducing" men to the same opinions and passions, the more so as it seems that reasoning itself, quite apart from passion, is capable of generating different opinions to which passions will attach themselves.[9] His treatment of opinions and passions, moreover, leads us to wonder whether—contrary to what he intimates—the destruction or abolition of liberty which fuels faction is even possible. To put this another way, leaving to one side the oppressiveness that would be necessary in any effort designed to squelch liberty, would it even be possible to extinguish the "liberty" to reason? Short of this, or somehow rendering man's reason infallible, there would appear to be no way to eliminate factions.[10]

As for giving men the same "interest," Publius writes that an "obstacle" no less "insuperable" than those encountered with regard to opinions and passions is "the diversity in the faculties of men, from which the rights of property originate." His discussion, though brief, would suggest, however, that this obstacle is not insuperable, not at least in the same sense as those encountered with "giving" individuals the same opinions and passions. So much we may infer because he goes on to write immediately after making this point that "the protection of these [diverse] faculties is the first object of government." Whereas there would seem to be inherent obstacles (e.g., fallible reason) to uniformity of opinion, the diversity that leads to different interests seems to require the protective shield of government, because, we may reasonably surmise, it can be more easily destroyed or eliminated. In any event, Publius does recognize that "the protection of different and unequal faculties of acquiring property" leads to the "possession of different degrees and kinds of property," which, in turn, conditions the "sentiments and views of their respective proprietors," thereby dividing "society into different interests and parties" (78).

We see from his discussion of opinions, passions, and interests that Publius, far from advocating measures that would inhibit factions, actually nourishes the roots from which they spring by urging the protection of the diverse faculties that spawn interest-based factions. We also come to see from his analysis just how highly he values liberty. While he recognizes its potential dangers ("liberty is to faction what air is to fire"), he regards liberty as "essential to political life" in a republican regime (78). In the last analysis, then, the way is open for factions to flourish by availing themselves of this liberty.

The nature and scope of the problem of factions is reflected only partially in Publius's remark that the "latent causes of faction are thus sown in the nature of man" (79). Publius compounds and exacerbates the problem by, in effect, holding that those measures which would serve to remove their root causes are themselves factious. Certainly, we may say, this is how he would look upon any effort to destroy liberty or to insure a uniformity of opinion, passion, or interest among individuals.

Before turning to his cure for the "mischiefs of faction," which does, indeed, avoid this difficulty, Publius presents us with relatively specific examples of factionalism. In so doing, he presents the reader with an understanding of the nature of the problems that have caused so much concern among the "considerate and virtuous citizens" about the stability of the state governments (77).[1] "The latent causes of faction," he remarks, are "everywhere brought into different degrees of activity, according to the different circumstances of civil society." In this respect, he notes the "zeal for different opinions concerning religion, concerning government, and many other points, as well of speculation as of practice." More, he sees passion-based factions growing up around "different leaders ambitiously contending for pre-eminence and power; or to persons of other descriptions whose fortunes have been interesting to the human passions." He laments that all of this has produced animosities and rivalries rather than cooperation in pursuit of the "common good," but he is under no illusions about there ever being a factionless society: "so strong is this propensity of mankind to fall into mutual animosities that where no substantial occasion presents itself the most frivolous and fanciful distinctions have been sufficient to kindle their unfriendly passions and excite their most violent conflicts" (79).

This aspect of Publius's presentation merits our attention because of the numerous misinterpretations of his outlook and strategy in approaching the problem of factions; misinterpretations which, we should note in passing, have also provided a basis for attributing ulterior motives to Publius and the Founders. These passages, when read in context, are unexceptional; they more or less follow from what Publius has said to this point in the essay. Yet they are usually ignored or subordinated by those who seize upon the sentences which immediately follow in an effort to show that Publius was an economic determinist or a pre-Marxian Marxist. In these sentences, Publius acknowledges that the "most common and durable source of factions has been the various and unequal distribution of property" and that "those who hold and those who are without property have ever formed distinct interests in society" (79).

Read in isolation, these passages do lend credence to the thesis that Publius was, indeed, an economic determinist who viewed political conflict from a Marxist perspective as a struggle between the haves and have-nots. But, as we have noted, the passages in question are part of a larger paragraph, the begining portions of which, quoted above, point to opinion and passion as sources of conflict and faction. For this reason alone, Publius can hardly be charged with having the tunnel vision characteristic of an economic determinist.

Equally important, we should note that when Publius does discuss interest-based factions, which do form around the "various and unequal distribution of property," he speaks not only of "horizontal" cleavages between the haves and have-nots but, significantly, of "vertical" cleavages as well: "A landed interest, a manufacturing interest, a mercantile interest, a moneyed interest, with many lesser interests, grow up of necessity in civilized nations, and divide them into different classes, actuated by different sentiments and views" (79).[12] Thus, from Publius's perspective, the cleavages, animosities, rivalries, and the like which do surround interest factions may be said to run in helter-skelter patterns over time, both among and within these various interests.

Other analysts and critics, far from ignoring those passages relating to opinion and passion-based factions, deem them critical for understanding Publius's grand strategy for avoiding the fatal consequences of faction. They suggest that Publius, consonant with the teachings of David Hume, recognized that factions based on opinion and passion could be the most vicious and intractable. Factions united, for example, on principle and consumed with a feeling of self-righteousness cannot, as we have intimated above, be easily handled, a concern which is manifested in contemporary times by those who caution against the intrusion of potentially explosive social issues— e.g., abortion or prayer in the public schools—into the political arena. On the other hand, according to this interpretation, Publius did believe factions based on interest to be far less dangerous; that is, their differences could more easily be resolved through compromise without endangering the order and stability of the system. Consequently, so this line of analysis runs, Publius's strategy was to encourage divisions based on economic interests: if divisions could be channeled along these lines and away from opinions and passions, the proposed political system would be able to avoid fatal "vibrations."[13]

What we do know from the text is that Publius does believe that
the "principal task of modern legislation"—the matter with which
he is concerned—is, in fact, the "regulation of these various and
interfering [economic] interests" (79). We can, with reason, speculate that Publius uses the word modern to indicate that the principal
task of legislation was different in times past. From his conception
of the role of government and the chief function of the legislature,
we may also say that he writes from the vantage point of one who
firmly embraces a distinction between government and society. Such
a distinction, it would appear, was probably so much a part of the
generally accepted political ethos that he simply takes it for granted
that the proposed system will not have to face up to the full scope
and intensity of the kind of factious strife which proved too much
for the "petty republics" of the past.

We can readily adduce other, not entirely unrelated, reasons why
Publius believed that the proposed system would be able to withstand
the effects of the more destructive factions. The proposed national
government, he points out by way of arguing against a bill of rights,
"is merely intended to regulate the general political interests of the
nation" (84:513). As a consequence, he may well have anticipated
that the states would constitute the principal arena of conflict between passion-based factions—a view supported by his observations
regarding the division between state and national concerns which
we will examine in Chapter 4. Moreover, he did see extensiveness
operating to diffuse potentially factious issues so that they might
never reach the national political arena. For instance, he writes toward
the end of Federalist 10: "A religious sect may degenerate into a
political faction in a part of the Confederacy; but the variety of sects
dispersed over the entire face of it must secure the national councils
against any danger from that source" (84).

There are at least three interrelated difficulties in attributing to
Publius a strategy of narrowing or channeling politics to conflicts
over interests in order to moderate the effects of faction at the
national level. First, the text would suggest, as we have indicated,
that he believed the national government will, to a significant degree,
be insulated or sheltered from disputes involving passion-based factions. Second, interjecting the notion of channeling conflict is foreign to Publius's approach to the problem of factions, which does
not involve manipulation. Put another way, the essay, far from being

prescriptive, is primarily descriptive and explanatory in nature. That is, he endeavors to show how the factors associated with an extensive republic will operate naturally to create a political environment which will serve to control the effects of faction. And third, a related point, from Publius's perspective, conflict along interest lines already predominates in the political arena at the state level, and he obviously assumes that the resolution of such conflicts will be the "principal task" of the national legislature as well. Moreover, in writing that property interests are "the most common and durable sources of faction," he is suggesting that such conflicts are natural to man, scarcely in need of any artificial stimulation.

The fact is that Publius's attention focuses on the problems associated with the regulation of "various and interfering interests." The crucial difficulty which he identifies centers on the fact that "the spirit of party and faction" is "involve[d] . . . in the necessary and ordinary operations of government." It is precisely this situation—unavoidable, of course, in a society which places a high premium on liberty—that has resulted in the instability and injustice at the *state* level, because, as he observes, the parties or interests to a dispute have in many instances also been the judges of that dispute. And this state of affairs clearly violates a maxim central to his conception of justice: "no man [should be] a judge in his own cause." Otherwise, he contends, "his interest would certainly bias his judgment, and, not improbably, corrupt his integrity" (79).

In illustrating his point, Publius conceives of the legislature operating in a judicial capacity: its "most important acts," he maintains, constitute "judicial determinations . . . concerning the rights of large bodies of citizens." Yet, very much unlike the judicial setting, he sees the "different classes of legislators" as both "advocates and parties to the causes which they determine." As we should expect, he draws his examples from the economic sphere: creditors and debtors divide over the laws relating to "private debts"; the landed and manufacturing interests differ over whether "domestic manufacturers" should be encouraged and to what degree "foreign manufacturers" ought to be restricted; and the "apportionment of taxes on the various descriptions of property" pits the wealthy against the not so wealthy. Although, Publius writes, "justice ought to hold the balance between them," this is far from being the case. Instead, because "the parties are, and must be, themselves the judges . . . the most numerous party, or in other words, the most powerful faction must be expected to prevail" without regard to either "justice" or "the public good." And, consonant with what he is to argue later, Publius leaves little doubt that when "opportunity and temptation are given to a predominant party," it will "trample on the rules of justice" (79–80).

Controlling the Effects of Faction and the Extended Republic

With this we have come full circle in Publius's statement of the problem of factions: after having explored in some depth the scope and nature of factions, he brings us back to his point of departure, to the conditions which have stirred "complaints" about the "spirit of faction" in the existing governments. To this he adds, as if to close off the last remaining out to this dilemma, that "it is vain to say that enlightened statesmen will be able to adjust the clashing interests and render them all subservient to the public good." Such "statesmen," he points out, "will not always be at the helm," and, what is more, such adjustments will frequently involve taking "indirect and remote considerations" into account, considerations that "rarely prevail over the immediate interests which one party may find in disregarding the rights of another or the good of the whole" (80). Thus we are led to believe that, even if enlightened statesmen were at the helm, their capacity to resolve conflicts consistent with the general welfare would be severely limited by the propensity of interests to pursue their immediate self-gratification at the expense of the long-term common good.

Publius's remarks on this score strongly suggest that he believed enlightened statesmen, whether at the helm or not, would, at best, normally constitute a minority in the legislative assemblies. From the context in which he introduces and discusses the role of enlightened statesmen, it seems clear that one of their chief attributes is the ability and willingness to subordinate partial, short-term self-interest to the long-range common good. Consequently, if he believed that they would with some frequency comprise a majority, he could not very well write as he does that "indirect and remote considerations . . . will rarely prevail over . . . immediate interests." In other words, the chief limitation on the statesmen's ability to "render" the "clashing [and partial] interests . . . subservient to the public good" simply would not exist if statesmen constituted a majority. This, in turn, means—to follow through with this line of reasoning—that when Publius writes of statesmen being "at the helm" he means something akin to their being in positions of leadership, not as constituting a numerical majority (80).

The "inference" that Publius draws from his analysis to this point in the essay is that the "*causes* of faction cannot be removed and that relief is only to be sought in the means of controlling its *effects*" (80).

Publius makes it abundantly clear at the outset in presenting his "cure" for the "mischiefs" of faction that he is concerned almost exclusively with the "mischiefs" of majority factions. A minority faction, he writes, "may clog the administration . . . may convulse the society; but it will be unable to execute and mask its violence under the forms of the Constitution" because "the republican principle . . . enables the majority to defeat its sinister views by regular vote" (80). With only two sentences, he dismisses the problem of minority factions. In so doing he highlights a very perplexing problem that arises within his objectivist framework: what can be done when a majority is included in a faction? What is to prevent it from sacrificing "both the public good and the rights of other citizens" to its "ruling passion"? (80).

Publius does not shrink from acknowledging this difficulty. In one of the most critical sentences of this essay, he declares: "To secure the public good and private rights against the danger of such a faction, and at the same time to preserve the spirit and the form of popular government, is then the great object to which our inquiries are directed." To this he immediately adds that this "great object" is also "the great desideratum by which alone this form of government can be rescued from the opprobrium under which it has so long labored and be recommended to the esteem and adoption of mankind" (80–81). In sum, this is the central concern for Publius; a concern which must be continually borne in mind in analyzing his solution.

We must jump ahead a bit in our analysis to understand the full significance of this matter. Publius claims in the last paragraph of the essay to have discovered a "republican remedy for the diseases most incident to republican government" (84). No doubt he regarded this as his crowning achievement and principal contribution to the theory and practice of republican government since it provided a means for rendering this species of government compatible with other highly cherished values such as liberty, order, and justice— a compatibility, as he suggests both in essays 9 and 10, heretofore thought virtually impossible for any extended period of time. However, modern critics have questioned whether he does, in fact, realize his "great desideratum"—whether, for example, he really provides a *republican* remedy for the problem of majority factions. And still another area of dispute surrounds the interrelationship and relative significance of the elements of his solution, the core of which constitutes his extended republic theory. These concerns, with which we will deal later, rank high among those that have arisen regarding the adequacy of his remedy.

Publius sees but two means for the attainment of his principal objective, i.e., controlling the effects of majority factions: "Either the existence of the same passion or interest in a majority at the same time must be prevented, or the majority, having such coexistent passion or interest, must be rendered, by their number and local situation, unable to concert and carry into effect schemes of oppression" (81). In this regard, he stresses a proposition which is central to his theoretical approach both in this essay and elsewhere: nothing can be relied upon to restrain majorities from pursuing their goals "if the impulse and the opportunity be suffered to coincide." He remarks that "neither moral nor religious motives" have proved to be an "adequate control" on the "injustice and violence of individuals" and that they "lose their efficacy in proportion to the number combined together, that is, in proportion as their efficacy becomes needful" (81).

Publius drives the foregoing points home regarding the need to prevent the coincidence of "impulse and opportunity" by showing why in a "pure democracy"—that is, a "society" small enough so that the people can "assemble and administer the government in person" —there can be "no cure for the mischiefs of faction." Simply put, there are no obstacles or barriers to prevent the same passion or interest from overcoming a majority, nor are there any impediments which prevent such majorities from executing their will as soon as the common passion or interest is felt. This he holds is why "such democracies have ever been spectacles of turbulence and contention; have ever been found incompatible with personal security or the rights of property; and have in general been as short in their lives as they have been violent in their deaths." In his eyes these conditions are simply inherent to this "form of government" contrary to the teachings of "theoretic politicians" who, as he puts it, "have erroneously supposed that by reducing mankind to a perfect equality in their political rights, they would at the same time be perfectly equalized in their possessions, their opinions, and their passions" (81). In short, according to Publius, factions are not only inevitable in pure democracies, they are also highly volatile.

Publius's analysis of pure democracy provides the necessary introduction for the elaboration of his extended republic theory. What he is bent on showing is that a republic, "a government in which the scheme of representation takes place," holds out the prospect for "the cure for which we are seeking." To this end, he compares a republic to a pure democracy to "examine the points" of difference in order to show "the nature of the cure and the efficacy which it must derive from the Union" (81). What becomes clear as he proceeds is that what he really wants to show are the advantages of a large over a small republic in order to illustrate, we may assume, the advantages the proposed national system will enjoy over the individual states. Throughout he seems to assume that small republics will exhibit the same weaknesses as pure democracies—weaknesses to which more extensive republics are far less prone.

At no point, we should note in passing, does he delve into the matter of an optimal size, though in Federalist 14 he tells us that the proposed union is not too large. In this determination practical concerns such as transportation and communication seem to be uppermost in his mind. At the very end of Federalist 51, he writes that, despite opinions to the contrary, "the larger the society, provided it be within a practicable sphere, the more duly capable it will be of self-government" (325). What is somewhat remarkable is that Publius seems oblivious to the arguments of the Antifederalists, based upon traditional republican theory, that extensiveness could be carried too far by embracing interests that simply cannot be peacefully accommodated under one political roof. Certainly he does not think this to be the case with the proposed union, for he writes of the people of the states as "members of the same family" bound together by "cords of affection" (14:103; see also 2:38–39).

Publius develops his case for the extended republic around the "two great points of difference" he perceives between a pure democracy and a republic. The first of these is representation. At the outset of his discussion on this point, he leads his readers to believe that "it may well happen that the public voice, pronounced by the representatives of the people, will be more consonant to the public good than if pronounced by the people themselves, convened for the purpose." Certainly this would result if the representatives were to possess the abilities and character he attributes to them at this point in his presentation: they will, he writes, "refine and enlarge the public views"; their collective "wisdom" will enable them to "best discern the true interest of their country," and their "patriotism and love of justice will be least likely to sacrifice it to temporary or partial considerations." But, quite abruptly, he switches perspectives by observing that "the effect" [of representation] "might be inverted": "Men of factious tempers, of local prejudices, or of sinister designs, may, by intrigue, by corruption, or by other means, first obtain the suffrages, and then betray the interests of the people." Since he cannot compare the likelihood of these outcomes in a large republic against a pure democracy, the question for him now becomes "whether small or extensive republics are most favorable to the election of proper guardians of the public weal" (82).

Publius sees two reasons to believe that a finer quality of representative will emerge in the large rather than in the small republic. The first of these relates to the fact that for both large and small republics the legislatures must be small enough "to guard against the confusion of a multitude"; that is, that there is an upper limit to legislative size no matter how big the republic (82). This upper limit—he intimates (55:343) that it might be 400—means that the proportion of fit characters to representative seats will be higher in the large than in the small republic, thereby allowing the voters of the large republic more fit characters from which to chose their representatives. In terms of Publius's broader argument, this advantage rests on the unarticulated assumptions that fit characters will seek office and that the voters will elect them.

The second advantage that a large republic enjoys over the small, as Publius sees it, relates to the size of the electorate. With a "greater number of citizens," he writes, "it will be more difficult for unworthy candidates to practise with success the vicious arts by which elections are too often carried." Thus, he believes, the "suffrages of the people" will be freer and "more likely to center on men who possess the most attractive merit and the most diffusive and established characters" (82–83). Publius does not tell us what he means by "vicious arts" so that we are left to speculate what they might be in this context. Certainly bribery and intimidation by a dominant faction would be rendered less likely with a more extensive electorate (see 57:354).

Federalism comes into play when Publius acknowledges that if the electorate is too extensive, the representative will lack a familiarity with "local circumstances and lesser interests," whereas, if it is too confined, he will be too attached to local interests and "too little fit to comprehend and pursue great and national objects." This difficulty is overcome by the proposed "federal Constitution," which "forms a happy combination in this respect" by referring "the great and aggregate interests" to the national government and "the local and particular to the State legislatures" (83).

The second "great" point of difference between a republic and a democracy for Publius comes down to "the greater number of citizens and extent of territory" that the republican form can embrace. Indeed, it is of some significance to note that he believes "it is this circumstance principally which renders factious combinations less to be dreaded" in republics than democracies. To show this, he stresses the conditions that render the coincidence of impulse and opportunity far more likely in smaller societies: "the fewer the distinct parties and interests, the more frequently will a majority be found of the same party; and the smaller the number of individuals composing a majority, and the smaller the compass within which they are placed, the more easily will they concert and execute their plans of oppression." On the other hand, he points out, in the extended republic, with its multiplicity and diversity of "parties and interests," it is "less probable that a majority of the whole will have a common motive to invade the rights of other citizens." Moreover, even if such a common motive did exist, he continues, "it will be more difficult for all who feel it to discover their own strength and act in unison with each other."

At this point he refers to "other impediments" to the formation of factious majorities, but cites only one: that communication among those bent upon "unjust and dishonorable purposes" will be inhibited by a "distrust in the proportion to the number whose concurrence is necessary." This impediment, he recognizes, depends on the "consciousness" of the participants that the ends they seek are "unjust and dishonorable"—a condition that raises problems best examined in another context (83).

In the latter part of essay 51, Publius echoes and amplifies this aspect of his extended republic theory. Here he examines two possible solutions to the problem of majority factions: the first "creating a will in the community independent of the majority"; the second, "comprehending in the society" so many interests "as will render an unjust combination of the whole very improbable, if not impracticable" (323–24). The first method he regards as a "precarious security" because there is no guarantee that such an independent body will protect minorities from unjust majorities or even turn "against both parties." The second method is obviously that embodied in the proposed system: authority is "derived from and dependent on the society," but the society will contain "so many parts, interests and classes of citizens" that minorities "will be in little danger from interested combinations of the majority." In this regard, he writes, "the security for civil rights must be the same as that for religious rights . . . in the one case in the multiplicity of interests, and in the other the multiplicity of sects." But Publius sees this diversity and multiplicity of interest as providing for more than just protection against factious majorities. Given the "great variety of interests, parties, and sects" within the proposed system, he holds that "a coalition of a majority of the whole society could seldom take place on any other principles than those of justice and the general good" (325).

There are other aspects of his discussion in Federalist 51 that are noteworthy because they either emphasize points made in the tenth essay or they introduce a new dimension to his theory. The extended republic, we see more clearly, is not an iron-clad guarantee that majority factions will not rule. Publius's claims in this regard are put in probabilistic terms: the chances of their "combining" are "very improbable" (324); minorities are in "little danger" (324) from majority factions; majorities will "seldom" (325) form on principles other than justice and the general good.

We also see that he holds out a prospect for controlling the effects of faction that is somewhat at odds with his views that the remedy must be found in preventing the coincidence of impulse and opportunity and that short-term self-interest will usually prevail over long-term common interests. Noting that "justice is the end of government . . . [and] of civil society" and that "it ever has been and ever will be pursued until it be obtained, or until liberty be lost in the pursuit," he goes on to compare those societies in which the "stronger faction" oppresses the weaker to "a state of nature" wherein the "weaker individual is not secured against the violence of the stronger." And, he reasons, just as "stronger individuals . . . prompted by the uncertainty of their condition" saw fit "to submit to a government which may protect the weak as well as themselves," so too might the "more powerful factions or parties be gradually induced, by a like motive," to accept a government that will protect both the weaker and stronger factions (324–25). Thus, he opens up the possibility that long-term calculations of self-interest may operate to prevent the fluctuations between anarchy and tyranny so common to the republican form. Moreover, it would seem to follow that the initial motivation would be reinforced once these interests perceived the benefits of such a government. Over time their obedience might well become a matter of habit.

A notable absence in Federalist 51 is any discussion of the role of representation in controlling the effects of faction. Although we must speculate why this so, there would seem to be at least two probable reasons. First, as we saw in Federalist 10, Publius believes that the multiplicity and diversity of interest is the major obstacle to the formation of majority factions. The role that representatives can play would relate largely to preventing the enactment or execution of a factious will, a matter discussed in various contexts at other places in the essays. Second, Federalist 51 marks the last of a brace of five essays concerned with maintaining the separation of powers. Publius's primary concern in these essays is to show how the system will operate to prevent the legislature from drawing all powers into its "imperious vortex" (48:309), and, in the course of this, he has some very unkind words to say about representative assemblies. As a consequence, he may very well have thought it totally inappropriate to reiterate his position in Federalist 10 concerning their capacity to "refine and enlarge" the public views.[14] Be that as it may, essays 10 and 51, taken in conjunction, would indicate that he regarded multiplicity and diversity of interests, not representation, as the principal factor in curing the evils of faction. Shortly we will deal with the relationship between representation and the diversity of interests to indicate how both combine to control the effects of faction.

In both Federalist 10 and 51, he emphasizes that the states are highly vulnerable to the assaults of faction. Toward the end of number 10 he writes, for instance, that individual states may succumb to "a rage for paper money, for an abolition of debts, for an equal division of property, or for any other improper or wicked project" (84). Likewise, in both essays, he stresses the advantages of a proposed union in controlling the effects of factions. In Federalist 51, he goes so far as to predict that Rhode Island, "left by itself" outside of the "Confederacy," would suffer the full ravages of factions "under [its] popular form of government within such narrow limits" (325). In the same essay he remarks that if instead of union the states go their own way or form a number of confederacies, the primary protections against factious majorities will diminish. And, in concluding 10, he details the advantages which the large republic enjoys over the small. In sum, he holds, the "whole body of the Union" is less vulnerable to factions "than a particular member of it, in the same proportion as such a malady is more likely to taint a particular county or district than an entire State" (84).

With this we have before us the basic elements of Publius's cure for the evils of majority faction. The primary ingredient of this cure, we should take care to note, is the multiplicity and diversity of interests that are concomitant with extensiveness. As such it is, for the most part, a "natural," as opposed to man-made, remedy. Once, that is, extensiveness is provided for—this constitutes man's primary input—the remedy follows as a matter of course; the mere existence of multiple and diverse interests serves to control the effects of factions. Even the benefits that flow from representation are the result of extensiveness and this multiplicity and diversity of interests. To put this still another way, Publius does not rely upon the formal institutions and procedures spelled out in the proposed Constitution to channel, direct, thwart, or otherwise control factions. Nor do we find reference to separation of powers, checks and balances, judicial review, or a bill of rights as playing any role in providing a remedy. And when Publius does get around to discussing the role of institutions and procedures in curbing factions, we will see that their role is distinctly secondary to that provided by the extended republic. In this respect, his teaching is markedly different from our conventional wisdom today, which holds that our constitutional institutions and processes along with the Bill of Rights provide the primary protections against the excesses of majorities.

A Republican Remedy?

Any critical assessment of the extended republic theory must eventually come up against the question we have already alluded to: does Publius's solution constitute a *republican* remedy for the problem of factions? Almost from the moment scholarly attention focused on Federalist 10—that is, since shortly after the turn of the century—the answer to this question has taken various forms. But many, if not most, scholars come to the same conclusion: no; for good or ill, the system was designed to protect or advantage certain minorities against majorities in a manner contrary to the republican principle. We need not examine these appraisals in great detail because they are either misleading as to what Publius does say or they go well beyond the confines of the extended republic theory to make their case.

Both these charges can be readily illustrated. The authors who focus on the political-economic dimensions, for instance, are prone to read Publius as saying that the "first object of government" is the protection of property per se, rather than, as he states it, the protection of "the diversity in the faculties of men, from which the rights of property originate." Suffice it to say there is a good deal of difference between the two, the more so as Publius goes on to say that the "principal task" of government is the "regulation" of property-based interests. Or, as we have remarked in the Introduction, Publius's depiction of the nature and dimensions of factious conflict are sometimes misrepresented by his critics to fit their preconceived theories regarding his motivations. We also see that many analysts step outside Publius's theoretical framework to link his subsequent discussions of the separation of powers and judicial review to the extended republic theory set forth in Federalist 10—a linkage usually, but not always, intended to confute Publius's contention that the extended republic provides a republican remedy for the disease of faction.

Nevertheless, there are valid reasons to question the republican credentials of Publius's extended republic solution. To begin with, on the basis of his discussion it certainly seems safe to assume that majority factions will seldom be able to feel their strength and effectuate their policies in the extended republic. But, having said this, we come up against the "filter" problem: why will the impediments associated with pluralism filter out only factious majorities? Why won't the same impediments or obstacles that prevent factions from ruling also serve to prevent nonfactious or just majorities from ruling?[15] While this issue arises logically from Publius's analysis, at no point does he address it directly, so that we are obliged to deduce an answer to it from what he writes about other relevant concerns and issues.

We do not have to look beyond Federalists 10 and 51 to find ready, but ultimately unsatisfactory, answers to this filter problem. For instance, Publius contends that "consciousness" of "unjust and dishonorable purposes" will serve to inhibit factions, thereby diminishing their ability to garner majority support. But no such inhibitions operate upon nonfactious groups, so that, following Publius's line of reasoning, we would have every reason to believe that these groups would be able to withstand the scrutiny to which they would be subjected in the process of gaining majority support.

Yet the efficacy of this phenomenon as an impediment to majority factions is highly questionable. To begin with, Publius seems to presume that the individuals comprising factions will have the "consciousness" he describes. But even if this is the case, this consciousness can only be effective as an inhibitor in circumstances where there is already a well-developed and deeply held sense of morality, public spiritedness, or virtue. In short, either the faction possesses a sense of shame sufficient to inhibit communication or the faction realizes that its package simply will not sell in the public marketplace. In either case, Publius's remedy is in fact largely irrelevant to curbing factions. In the former case, internal restraints, perhaps acquired from social indoctrination, would be the real impediment; in the latter, the moral sense and virtue of the people. What is more—and this is a phenomenon that Publius never deals with—it is quite possible, even probable, that those who constitute a faction will not perceive it as such: they may well believe, for example, that they are simply asking for their just due. Certainly, on Publius's showing, they are not fit judges of their own cause. Then, too, there is good reason to suppose that individuals inclined to factious action will put a moral gloss on their positions or find ingenious ways to rationalize them, thereby sheltering themselves from any "consciousness of unjust or dishonorable purposes."

Publius writes of "other impediments" that extensiveness poses for the formation of majority factions, but he does not spell them out. Among them, however, would be the difficulty of communicating, of establishing a network or organization that would work toward the common goal, of formulating strategies and tactics that would be appropriate for the different situations and contexts in various parts of the republic. But these impediments, taken by themselves, hold out no prospects of filtering out factions. That is, they operate on both nonfactious and factious groups with equal force. And if these factors are sufficient to curb factious majority, it is a very legitimate question whether extensiveness and the factors associated with it operate not so much as a filter, but as a barrier to formation of majorities, factious or not.[16]

Nevertheless, Publius certainly does believe that nonfactious majorities can overcome the obstacles posed by extensiveness. He argues that the multiplicity of interests resulting from extensiveness assures that such majorities will not be factious, that, quite to the contrary, they will be based on principles of "justice" and the "general good." We can discern at least one major reason for this belief by recurring to his discussion in Federalist 51 wherein he holds that "multiplicity of interests" will serve the same function in preserving "civil rights" as "multiplicity of sects" does in guaranteeing "religious rights." Here his emphasis is clearly on the difficulties of forming coalitions among 'competitive' sects and his reasoning would seem to take the following form: if we find that there is general agreement among the sects on a given measure or course of action, then we can be reasonably sure that the measure or action conforms with or advances the common interests of the sects. If on the other hand an objective is sought by one sect to the detriment of others, we would not expect any action. And we can go further with this parallel: if substantial questions are raised about the merits or impact of a particular proposal, we should expect a degree of fragmentation that would at least serve to prevent the precipitous actions that plague the pure democracies. That Publius anticipates a similar process taking place among competing interests seems clear enough; that such a process tends to promote the realization of the common good, if not justice, also seems evident.

Now this represents a very rigorous and stringent filtering process, and we can certainly see why Publius was so confident that majority factions would seldom work their will in the extended republic. On the other hand, while the difficulty of forming coalitions does not necessarily block nonfactious interests, it does pose serious obstacles for them, particularly when the goals they seek would have a negative impact on other interests. The process, in sum, is biased against measures that call for a significant departure from what is perceived to be the shared interests of the groups necessary for a majority coalition.

We do not mean to suggest that Publius subscribed to the doctrine of "concurrent consent" later articulated by Calhoun in his *Disquisition*. But what is clear, whether one accepts the general outlines of the process set forth above or not, is that forging a popular majority, factious or not, from the great variety of interests in the extended republic would be an extremely difficult task. At best Publius only indicates this task might be less arduous for nonfactious interests because a "consciousness of unjust or dishonorable purpose" would not haunt their efforts. Setting aside our severe reservations about the effectiveness of this barrier, it scarcely constitutes an advantage sufficient to "solve" the filter problem. Thus, those critics of the extended republic theory who assert that factors associated with the extended republic do serve to impede the formation of nonfactious majorities would appear to be substantially correct. Their case is strongest with regard to majority formation around objectives or policies that would significantly change the status quo, especially changes that would involve costs for established interests.

Republican Remedy: Another Approach

We should not conclude from our discussion to this point that Publius's solution contravenes republicanism. His remedy is found wanting principally because we have been analyzing it from the perspective of classical republicanism in which popular majorities play a decisive role in the deciding issues through the medium of their representatives.[17] In this conception, the republican process consists of popular majorities continually coalescing in support of or opposed to clearly defined issues and policies. But the conditions associated with extensiveness clearly render this form of republicanism inappropriate, if not unattainable. And what is evident from his definition of republicanism is that Publius conceived of republican institutions and processes in a manner fundamentally different from that of the classical model.

Publius's discussion of majority factions simply tells us that if popular majorities do coalesce in the extended republic, which will not be very often, seldom will they be factious. His focus on popular majorities, factious and otherwise, is to be understood in the context of showing why the extended republic will not suffer the same fate as pure democracies or even small republics where, as a matter of course, majorities could coalesce without facing any or very few impediments. However, we cannot read Publius to say that because the effects of majority factions can be controlled in the extended republic, the proposed system could or should operate in the same fashion as pure democracies or small republics. As Publius emphasizes, size renders the extended republic qualitatively different from both pure democracies and small republics by providing a new and fundamentally different political environment. And his answer to the filter problem—controlling the effects of majority factions in a fashion consonant with republican principles—is to be found in another conception of republican operations and processes which takes into account this altered political environment.

To comprehend the republican nature of Publius's solution involves conditions and elements that must be considered both independently and in relation to one another. Consequently, it is best that we return to and work outward in a systematic fashion from what he pictures to be the basic problem caused by factions at the state level, a problem that we have already canvassed. His concern in this respect focused on the state legislatures and the fact that in their operations "different classes of legislators" are both "advocates and parties to the causes which they determine." He pictures this difficulty, we should also recall, in terms of a bipolarity—creditors versus debtors, manufacturers versus farmers, tax payers versus tax consumers—in which, there being no mediating body between them, the most numerous party disregards the public good and the "rights of the minor" party in pursuit of its own interest. This factious behavior is very similar to that which he paints of majorities in the assemblies of pure democracies.

Certainly Publius did not think this factionalism would ever disappear from the states' legislatures, nor, for reasons we have discussed, would he approve of measures that would lead to their elimination. If, however, their effects could be nullified or neutralized, the problems caused by these factions, as he describes them at various points in essay 10, would no longer exist. By the same token, we can see that the solution to the problem of factions in the proposed republic consists of the Congress being able to operate without factions dominating as they have at the state level. Just as state legislatures are the problem at the state level, so the Congress is the key to the solution in the proposed system. And the reasons for its critical role in his solution are not hard to discern. Publius, as we see in numerous places in *The Federalist*, considers Congress to be the heart of the proposed system. It is by far the most powerful of the branches and no faction can work its will on the people for very long without the acquiescence of Congress. Or, put another way, if factions are able to dominate in Congress as they have the state legislatures, then the system is doomed. How then, we must ask, does the extended republic serve to prevent Congress from acting like a popular assembly or the state legislatures? Another and collateral question is this: in what ways do the conditions of the extended republic provide a solution to the filter problem?

A good deal of what Publius has to say about the virtues of the extended republic at various junctures in *The Federalist* is best understood as pointing out precisely why the Congress will not behave contrary to the permanent and aggregate interests of the community. The cure, so to speak, is to be found in the conditions associated with the extended republic. Consider, to begin with, his views on the proper size of the representative assembly, a matter to which he alludes in Federalist 10. In Federalist 58, he expands upon this matter: "the more numerous any assembly may be, of whatever characters composed, the greater is known to be the ascendancy of passion over reason." Nor is this by any means the only drawback of large assemblies. They will, he argues, contain a larger proportion of unfit characters ("members of limited information and weak capacities") who are highly susceptible to the "eloquence and address of the few." In this vein he remarks that in the assemblies of the "ancient republics . . . a single orator, or an artful statesman, was generally seen to rule with as complete a sway as if a scepter had been placed in his single hand." And he continues: "On the same principle, the more multitudinous a representative assembly may be rendered, the more it will partake of infirmities incident to collective meetings of the people. Ignorance will be the dupe of cunning, and passion the slave of sophistry and declamation" (360). And in one of the more widely quoted passages of these essays, he makes it abundantly clear that these consequences are unavoidable: "In all very numerous assemblies, of whatever characters composed, passion never fails to wrest the scepter from reason. Had every Athenian citizen been a Socrates, every Athenian assembly would still have been a mob" (55:342).

What Publius is also out to counter is the belief that increasing the number of representatives will necessarily "strengthen the barrier against the government of a few." By increasing the numbers beyond a certain point, he cautions, "the countenance of the government may become more democratic, but the soul that animates it will be more oligarchic" (58:360–61). On the other hand, he is equally aware of the dangers of an excessively small size. There should be, he writes, "*a sufficient number for the purposes of safety, of local information, and of diffusive sympathy with the whole society*" (58:360). In this respect, he offers some guides as to what the optimal size ought to be: "in all cases a certain number at least seems to be necessary to secure the benefits of free consultation and discussion, and to guard against too easy a combination for improper purposes" (55:342).

Federalist 10 points up still another way size relates to securing a representative assembly free from passions that inevitably overtake the assemblies in pure democracies: the extended republic will provide a sufficiently large number of "fit characters" from which to choose members for the assembly. We may assume from this that he believed the prospects of passion overwhelming reason through demagoguery and the like in Congress would be considerably reduced. We do know that he felt the people would avail themselves of the wider choice by electing individuals knowledgeable of the local circumstances within their states and possessed "of the necessary degree of intelligence to be able to communicate that information"

(36:218). He holds out the prospect, furthermore, that the elected representatives will have a receptive and inquiring mind so that, in the course of their service, they will come to know the conditions in other states relevant to advancing the "principal objects of federal legislation" (53:333). Though the bulk of his remarks are directed to members of the House, he sees every "reason to expect" that the state legislatures will employ "peculiar care and judgment" in electing senators—a process that holds out "promise" of insuring "greater knowledge and more comprehensive information in the national councils" (27:175).[18]

These qualities, of course, are necessary if the representatives are to "refine and enlarge the public views." But the qualities of a fit character go beyond them. The additional qualities involve a wisdom and virtue that will enable the representatives to comprehend and pursue the "common good of the society" (57:350), or, as he puts it in another context, to maintain "fidelity to the object of government, which is the happiness of the people" (62:380). This he believes is secured best through the free suffrages of the people: "as they [the representatives] will have been distinguished by the preference of their fellow-citizens, we are to presume that in general they will be somewhat distinguished also by those qualities which entitle them to it, and which promise a sincere and scrupulous regard to the nature of their engagements" (57:351).

Now Publius says a good deal more about representatives and their character. But we have enough before us to see that he believes the extensiveness of the republic combined with a Congress of appropriate size will serve to place individuals with wisdom, knowledge, intelligence, and a sense of civic duty superior to that of the ordinary citizen in control of the predominant branch of the proposed system. Moreover, we should note, he believes that the "elevated" character of the representatives can be had without deviating from republican principles. As far as the "electors" to the House of Representatives are concerned he writes that they are "not the rich, more than the poor; not the learned more than the ignorant; not the haughty heirs of distinguished names, more than the humble sons of obscure and unpropitious fortune." Likewise, concerning the eligibility of candidates, he notes that there is "no qualification of wealth, of birth, of religious faith, or of civil profession" for the office "to fetter the judgment or disappoint the inclinations of the people." "The objects of popular choice," he contends, will be "every citizen whose merit may recommend him to the esteem and confidence of his country" (57:351).

Our remarks to this point concerning the character of representatives and electors, it is crucial to note, bear upon only one element of Publius's solution to the filter problem. Likewise, they only partially answer the question of why Congress will not behave in the same unjust manner as the state legislatures. If the "fit characters" that Publius anticipates will comprise the bulk of both chambers of Congress were "statesmen," then both problems would be solved. But Publius makes no such claim. While he clearly believes they will possess the degree of virtue necessary for republican government—a degree of virtue "higher" than that required for other forms (55:346)—it is clear from his comments on multitudinous assemblies and in Federalist 10 that they are not immune from the impulses of passion or of interest that can lead to factious behavior. Even "fit characters" of the sort described by Publius situated in an deliberative assembly represent only a necessary, not a sufficient, condition for blocking majority factions while simultaneously allowing nonfactious majorities to work their will. To achieve this state of affairs requires not only fit characters but also the multiplicity and diversity of interest associated with extensiveness.

Diversity, Representation, and Distance

The solution to these concerns, to put this another way, involves an intricate interrelationship between the size of an assembly, securing fit characters, as well as the numerous and diverse interests of the extended republic. This relationship derives from the fact that, as we have intimated, even with fit characters in an assembly of optimal size, factious interests will be both represented and heard. In other words, Publius's solution, for reasons we have discussed in another context, does not call for the elimination of factions, so that even under the best of circumstances the cleavages between debtors and creditors, merchants and farmers, and so forth will still be reflected in the legislature. The effect of the multiplicity and diversity of interests is to distance, on any given issue that may come before the legislature, a significant proportion of the representatives from the conflict—a distance or a sufficient degree of detachment from the contending interests so that they can bring reason and impartial judgment to bear in the resolution of the issue at hand. In slightly different terms, while aware of the stakes involved in the conflict and the circumstances surrounding it, they are not intimately and immediately linked to the involved interest. And, because in this sense they stand sufficiently removed from the conflict, they are not easily overtaken by impulse.

By recurring to that portion of Federalist 10 where Publius writes about the salutary effects of representatives being "chosen by a greater number of citizens," we can appreciate one aspect of this interrelationship. The enlarged constituency means, of course, that there will be more "fit characters" and, as Publius remarks in another place, it also reduces the possibilities of the people being diverted from selecting a fit character "by the intrigues of the ambitious or the bribes of the rich" (57:354). By the same token, it is far less likely that the representatives from large constituencies will be beholden to one or a few dominant interests.[19]

But probably the one factor that is decisive in producing the requisite distancing at the national level is that the composition of the House of Representatives, due to limitations of size, simply cannot mirror the numerous distinct interests in the extended republic. Indeed, Publius points out the difficulties that would be involved in trying to represent the major categories of interest, e.g., labor, manufacturing, mercantile. Within these categories, he observes, there are other distinct interests which often find themselves in conflict with one another. "It is notorious," he writes in this connection, "that there are often as great rivalships between different branches of the mechanic or manufacturing arts as there are between any of the departments of labor and industry." Thus he concludes that even provision for the representation of the major categories of interest would render the "representative body . . . far more numerous than would be consistent with any idea of regularity or wisdom in its deliberations" (36:218).

Quite aside from this consideration, however, Publius remarks that when "the votes of the people [are] free" (35:215), "the natural operation of the different interests and views of the various classes of the community" (36:217) usually results in the election of "landholders, merchants, and men of the learned professions" (35:216).

Thus distancing, or detachment, comes about naturally through the ordinary processes of politics.

The "mechanics and manufacturers," he maintains, "will always be inclined, with few exceptions, to give their votes to merchants in preference to persons of their own professions or trades" (35:214). The "common interest" of landholders, both the largest and smallest, "to keep taxes on land as low as possible," he observes, will serve to unite them in electing individuals in whom they repose "most confidence; whether these happen to be men of large fortunes, or of moderate property, or of no property at all." But the "learned professions," he writes, "form no distinct interest in society." Thus, he writes, "according to their situation and talents" they "will be indiscriminately the objects of the confidence and choice of each other and of other parts of the community" (35:215).

In writing to the issue of the "judicious exercise of the power of taxation," Publius seems to sum up his vision of what the character of the representative body should be. Its members he informs us "should be acquainted with the general genius, habits, and modes of thinking of the people at large and with the resources of the country." "This," he maintains, "is all that can be reasonably meant by a knowledge of the interests and feelings of the people" (35:217).

From what we have surveyed to this point, at least two aspects of Publius's thinking are important in comprehending the nature of the remedy he provides for the disease of majority faction. First, because of this "natural" process of selection, there is an attenuation of the connection between interests and the representatives which enlarges the extent of detachment so that reason and objectivity can be brought to bear in assessing the merits of any particular program or policy. Or, to put this somewhat differently, certainly this process insures a greater 'distance' between the representative and the impulses of interests than would be the case if "all classes of citizens" were to have "some of their own number in the representative body." To be sure, Publius believes the three dominant classes in the legislature will represent "the interests and feelings of the different classes of citizens" (35:215–16). Yet it is clear they must do so from a wider, more comprehensive, perspective given the greater range of interests that they must accommodate even within their own realm.

And second, Publius sees members of the "learned profession" playing a significant role when conflict arises between "the different

branches of industry": "Will not the man of the learned profession,"
he asks rhetorically, "be likely to prove an impartial arbiter between
them, ready to promote either, so far as it shall appear to him conducive to the general interests of the society?" (35:216). With members of the "learned profession," in other words, we find a total
detachment or a distance sufficient to assure an impartiality in the
regulation of conflict between the major interests. What is more, he
suggests that the representatives of this profession might have sufficient strength to play a decisive role so that neither of the contending interests in the case he mentions will be able to enact its
will without their support.

But whether this is the case or not, it does seem clear that these
impartial representatives will have an impact on the deliberations
principally because the merchants and the landholders are sufficiently distanced from their clientele to entertain compromises and
accommodations that might be offered by disinterested parties. For
instance, Publius does not picture the merchant as a mere slave to
the interests of the "mechanic and manufacturing arts." Rather, he
portrays him as "disposed to cultivate" their interests "as far as may
be proper." Likewise, the landholder will be "prone to resist every
attempt to prejudice or encumber" landed property. In sum, for
Publius, inclination and propriety are key factors in determining the
representatives' behavior. He does believe that the representative
should be aware of his constituents' "disposition and inclinations"
and that, moreover, "he should be willing to allow them their proper
degree of influence upon his conduct" (35:216). While, of course,
"proper" is the key word here, Publius also believes the representative can make this determination without committing political su-
icide—without, that is, being forced to "descend to the level" from
which the people had "raised" him (57:352). But what this shows is
the degree to which the interrelated conditions associated with the
extended republic serve to liberate the representative from the factious impulses which overtake assemblies in pure democracies and
the legislatures of small republics.

Mediating Groups and the Filter Problem

We are now in a position to return to the questions posed at the
beginning of this line of analysis. We can readily see, for instance,

why Congress is not likely to succumb, as the state legislatures have, to factious impulses. This is not to say that such impulses might not find expression in the Congress. Indeed, as we have already indicated, there is little doubt that Publius felt they would. However, to win the day they would have to convince those who do not share the same attachment to their interests, a task made the more formidable, if not impossible, given the knowledge, intelligence, and character of these individuals and a setting or environment conducive to deliberation. In short, the representative assembly of the extended republic is well protected against the fatal infirmities that Publius identifies which have afflicted the pure democracies and the state legislatures.

Above all, then, what saves the representative assembly of the extended republic from the disastrous consequences of the bipolarity (creditor versus debtor, landed versus manufacturing interests) that Publius observes within the state legislatures is the existence of an impartial group of representatives that can mediate between conflicting interests.[20] The same bipolar interests will be found in the assembly of the large republic, but neither one will be able to dominate over the other; holding the balance between them will be what may be called an independent group acting, we may assume, very much in the fashion Publius believes the "learned professions" will act with regard to disputes between the "different branches of industry." Thus, the parties to the dispute—to return to another of Publius's concerns—will not be judges of their own cause. In this regard, we should add, the composition of this independent or mediating group is not stable or fixed. On the contrary, given Publius's description of the behavior of interests in the extended republic, it would vary from issue to issue depending on the parties involved.

That Publius saw the critical role of a mediating group providing relief from the factious strife which had overcome the state legislatures is most evident in his defense of the "national legislature to regulate, in the last resort, the election of its own members" (59:361). In the course of his argument he discusses the possibility of either the "landed men or merchants" using this power to advance their own partial interests. To this issue he writes: "I scruple not to affirm that it is infinitely less likely that either of them should gain an ascendant in the national councils; that the one or the other of them should predominate in all the local councils." And he elaborates on why this is so: representation at the national level will embody "a greater variety of interests, and in much more various proportions than are to be found in any single State." Consequently, he contends, the national legislature "will be much less apt to espouse either of them with a decided partiality than the representatives of any single State" (60:369).

The significance of a body of legislators sufficiently numerous to hold a balance of power, yet far enough removed from the involved interests to mediate between them dispassionately, goes well beyond merely curbing factions. In the first place, its mere existence affects the tenor and caliber of deliberations in the assembly. Conflicting interests, because they must sway this group, are forced to appeal to reason, not the passions. At some point in the deliberations, therefore, they must address central questions and issues regarding both the short- and long-term impact of their proposals on individuals and the nation as a whole. Here we come upon the essence of the solution to our second concern which launched this inquiry: how the conditions associated with the extended republic provide a solution to the filter problem, or why, to rephrase this in light of the foregoing discussion, the national legislature with an independent or mediating group, while thwarting factious proposals, will not at the same time impede nonfactious proposals.

The answer takes roughly the following form: far more so than any other group of individuals in the country, the impartial representatives are in a unique position to make a determination of whether a given proposal is, indeed, factious. And there is no reason to suppose that after intensive examination, in contrast to their probable reaction to a factious measure, they would act in any cohesive fashion to block a nonfactious measure. On the contrary, we should expect that their position would be consonant with the basic values, outlook, and orientation of their constituents in the fashion contemplated by Publius in Federalist 35 (see above).

To put this another way, the representatives of these independent or mediating groups, while they are not enlightened statesmen, are in a position to act as if they were. Having no immediate self-interest in the resolution of the issue at hand, they are in a position to contemplate what would be best for the long-term collective interests of the nation. Viewed in this light, we can see why Publius in Federalist 10 can maintain that the bulk of the representatives will not be enlightened statesmen, while simultaneously holding that, collectively speaking, their "patriotism and love of justice" will allow them to "discern the true interests of their country." The pivotal role played by these mediating or independent groups enables the representative assembly to render statesmanlike decisions along the lines he suggests.

That Publius viewed the Congress as a jury, in the sense of a mediator as we have described it above, is borne out not only by his own words in Federalist 10, but also in what he writes about other highly related aspects of the system. When he tells us, for instance, that manufacturers and mechanics will normally vote for merchants, his reasons revolve around the adversarial character of legislative proceedings. The merchants will be sympathetic to the interests of the manufacturers and mechanics, which is to say, merchants will plead their case with conviction and sincerity. But, more important, merchants have demonstrated a capacity to defend and promote their interests "more effectively" than the mechanics and manufacturers who lack "those acquired endowments, without which in a deliberative assembly the greatest natural abilities are for the most part useless." Their need, as Publius goes on to say, is a representative "more equal to a contest with any" hostile or "unfriendly" "spirit" that "might infuse itself into the public councils" (35:214–15). In other words, what these interests want and need are able and articulate advocates to promote and defend their interests in adversarial proceedings.

What the assembly also needs, if it is to perform its function well, is knowledge and information. In the "great theater of the United States," Publius remarks, there is such a diversity of circumstances, conditions, and laws that a knowledge of them "can with great difficulty be correctly learned in any other place than in the central councils, to which a knowledge of them will be brought by the representatives of every part of the empire." He observes that those concerns of the national government which require uniformity—e.g., foreign trade, taxation, regulations for the militia, interstate commerce—point up "most forcibly the extensive information which the representative ought to acquire." But, as difficult as this task may be, it is, according to Publius, facilitated by the fact that the representatives, aside from having a knowledge of local circumstances and state laws, "will probably in all cases have been members . . . of

the State legislature, where all the local information and interests
of the State are assembled, and from whence they may easily be
conveyed by a very few hands into the legislature of the United
States" (56:348). Because of this, the legislature is more than just a
jury; as an institution it is well equipped to "refine and enlarge the
public views" by moderating, altering, or even initiating proposals
in light of circumstances in the "great theater" about which it, far
more than the other branches, possesses a comprehensive knowledge.

This capacity of the Congress to judge, refine, and enlarge—which
simultaneously goes a long way toward protecting against factious
rule and, on the more positive side, insuring carefully wrought legislation to promote the common interest—is at the heart of Publius's
solution to the filter problem. This capacity, as we have seen, is the
result of an interplay of various factors, all directly or indirectly
related to extensiveness. It cannot be obtained simply by allowing
each of the interests, insofar as possible, to "have some of their own
number" in the legislature because, among other things, this would
not be conducive to providing either detachment or the comprehensive view needed for refinement and enlargement. Nor, at another level, can we view Publius's solution as depending on the various and interfering interests in the society somehow canceling each
other or achieving a compromise among themselves. Such a process
might well result in factious policies. Moreover, any refinement or
enlargement of the public views that might come about through such
a process would be purely accidental.

The Role of Majorities

In setting forth the elements of Publius's solution to what we have
dubbed the filter problem, we have concentrated almost exclusively
on the legislative branch and its role. Having done so puts us in a
better position to appreciate Publius's position toward popular majorities in the context of the normal operations of his system.

We have already remarked that in Publius's solution, for reasons
spelled out in Federalist 10, popular majorities would seldom form.
And from what we know, Publius considered this to be all to the
good. He did not want "decisive" popular majorities[21]—i.e., majorities demanding specific policies or actions—hovering over the shoul-

ders of the representatives. If such a state of affairs were to become common practice, his system would be seriously endangered because the representatives' role would be proportionally diminished with a corresponding diminishment in the role of an impartial or independent force. The system would then begin to partake of the character of a plebiscitary democracy with many of the major evils of pure democracy or the small republic. Nevertheless, Publius was aware that popular majorities, and factious ones at that, would occasionally form to impress their will on the legislature. "The people," he observes, "stimulated by some irregular passion, or some illicit advantage, or misled by the artful misrepresentations of interested men," may be induced to back factious measures (63:384). While the legislature may delay such majorities, Publius holds out little prospect for thwarting them if they are sufficiently persistent.[22]

As our analysis of Federalists 10 and 51 indicates, Publius did not believe that decisive popular majorities would play much of a role in regulating the "various and interfering interests." However, it is clear that he thought the representatives would and should be bound by generally accepted norms and values of the community. In formulating and setting down taxation policy, for instance—a matter which Publius regards as one of the more challenging—he writes of the need for the representatives to be "acquainted with the general genius, habits, and modes of thinking of the people at large" (35:217). We may assume that he envisioned the normal operations of his system taking place in the context of what can be appropriately termed "permissive" majorities, that is, majorities which grant a wide latitude to representatives both in selecting what issues to deal with and how they are to be resolved—so long, that is, as the representatives do so within the boundaries set by the basic norms and values of the general society. This is one reason why, we may presume, he makes it clear in Federalist 57 and elsewhere that "duty, gratitude, interest, ambition itself, are the cords by which they [the representatives] will be bound to fidelity and sympathy with the great mass of the people" (353). He looked, in other words, to a strong "communion" between the representatives and their constituents to insure that the representatives will render decisions within these boundaries.

These observations bear upon the filter problem. We have an additional and substantial reason why Publius did not believe the

extended republic would serve to impede nonfactious causes or measures: in the context of permissive majorities where the representatives share the broad sentiments of the people, there is no need
for majorities to form around such causes to secure their enactment.
Certainly any such measure or policy with potentially broad support
would be championed by a large portion of the representatives themselves. Moreover, there is no reason to presume that such causes
would not gain a sympathetic hearing in the legislative councils.[23]
But the same cannot be said of factious proposals: lacking a popular
majority in order to force the issue, they would fall by the wayside
in the assembly. Put another way, factions—normally lacking widespread support in the legislative chamber—are obliged to go the long
route in order to get their way: to go through the process of mus-
tering popular majorities which requires them to hurdle the obstacles
of the extended republic.

With this we see another dimension of the critical role which the
representative assembly plays in providing a republican solution for
the problem of majority factions. The matter to which we must turn
our attention now is how to control the legislature. Its members are
not immune from the impulses that lead to faction and, given its
central role in the system and the bonds which unite it to the people,
the opportunity for them to act on these impulses to advance their
own interests is ever present. It is to this concern we turn our attention by way of examining Publius's version of the separation of
powers.

NOTES

1. That the "unmixed" feature of the proposed system was important to
Publius is also indicated in Federalist 14 where he writes: "If Europe has the
merit of discovering this great mechanical power in government [representa-
tion], by the simple agency of which the will of the largest political body may
be concentrated and its force directed to any object which the public good
requires, America can claim the merit of making the discovery the basis of
unmixed and extensive republics" (100–101).

2. While James Allen Smith was again the first to set forth this thesis, in one
fashion or another the works of Beard, Parrington, Hofstadter, Dahl, and Burns
cited above accept and enlarge upon this contention.

3. The Straussian school of political theorists uses this term to emphasize
that Publius's teachings are a part of modern, as opposed to classical, political
thought. It serves to link Publius with, among others, Machiavelli, Bacon, Hobbes,

and Locke. Strictly speaking, the term is not used by Publius. Nor, as we indicate below, does he offer up a "new political science."

4. This was a common argument used by the Antifederalists against the adoption of the Constitution. Typical is Cato's argument based on his understanding of Montesquieu's teachings: "The recital, or premises on which this new form of government is erected, declares a consolidation or union of all thirteen parts, or states, into one great whole. . . . But whoever seriously considers the immense extent of territory comprehended within the limits of the United States, together with the variety of its climates, productions, and commerce, the difference of extent, and number of inhabitants in all; the dissimilitude of interest, morals, and policies, in almost every one, will receive it as an intuitive truth, that a consolidated republican form of government therein, can never *form a perfect union, establish justice, insure domestic tranquility, promote the general welfare, and secure the blessings of liberty to you and your posterity*, for to these objects it must be directed: this unkindred legislature therefore, composed of interests opposite and dissimilar in their nature, will in its exercise, emphatically be, like a house divided against itself." Herbert J. Storing, ed., *The Complete Anti-federalist*, 7 vols. (Chicago: University of Chicago Press, 1981), II, 110.

5. This attack reaches its crescendo in Federalist 14 when Publius asks rhetorically: "But why is the experiment of an extended republic to be rejected merely because it may comprise what is new? Is it not the glory of the people of America that, whilst they have paid a decent regard to the opinions of former times and other nations, they have not suffered a blind veneration for antiquity, for custom, or for names, to overrule the suggestions of their own good sense, the knowledge of their own situation, and the lessons of their own experience?" (104). In this, however, Publius belies his argument in Federalist 9 by acknowledging the novelty of the proposed system.

6. Robert Dahl seems to articulate the feelings of most pluralists who have examined this aspect of Publius's theory when he describes the concept of faction as "meaningless." There is no way, he contends, by which we can "distinguish a 'number of citizens' who make up a 'faction' from any other number of citizens." The major difficulty according to Dahl is that "we do not know either the 'rights of other citizens' or the 'permanent and aggregate interests of the community.' " *Preface*, p. 24.

7. For a thorough treatment of how and why this came to pass see Paul F. Bourke, "The Pluralist Reading of James Madison's Tenth *Federalist*," *Perspectives in American History* 9 (1975).

8. In this connection, Karl A. Lamb writes: "The pluralist sees government policy as the outcome of a contest between organized groups, Madison's familiar 'factions.' As each group seeks its private interests, the bargaining and compromise between groups produces something akin to the public interest; the outcome need only by ratified by Congress." However, Lamb continues, rather than viewing factions as a "regrettable" (though unavoidable) "phenomenon," "the extreme pluralists invert Madison's emphasis by celebrating factionalism, and they see the role of government as one of accommodating, more than regulating, group activities." What is more, according to Lamb, "in this con-

ception . . . all interest groups are of equal significance and moral stature; there is no standard beyond the interest groups' contest that designates the public good." *The Guardians* (New York: W. W. Norton, 1982), pp. 77–78.

9. We can place Publius's thoughts in this regard into the implicit framework of thought-speech-action found in J. S. Mill's *On Liberty*. Publius would not touch the area of thought. His concerns center in the areas of speech-action.

10. It is of some interest to note that Publius, instead of pointing to the fallibility of reasoning as a source for different opinions from which factions arise, could simply have asserted that factions will arise so long as men reason differently. In putting the issue this way, he is asserting that there are objective standards by which to measure reasoning—how else would reference to "fallible" reasoning make sense?

We do not know how much Publius intended to place under the category of "reason." It may well be that we would overburden his conception of reason to argue that if man's reasoning were infallible, it would not constitute a source of faction. Whether it would or not depends on the extent to which we conceive of reason as a source of values and goals.

11. On this point, Publius follows very closely the general framework set forth by Hume in his analysis of factions and their causes. See "Of Parties in General" in *Hume's Political Essays* (New York: Liberal Arts Press, 1953). For an excellent discussion of the relationship between the thoughts of Hume and Madison on this matter see Douglass Adair's "That Politics May Be Reduced to a Science: David Hume, James Madison, and the Tenth Federalist" in Colbourn, ed., *Fame and the Founding Fathers*. For a critical view of Adair's analysis see James Conniff, "The Enlightenment and American Political Thought: A Study of the Origins of Madison's *Federalist* Number 10," *Political Theory* 8 (Aug., 1980).

12. Charles A. Beard quotes very extensively from Federalist 10 in an effort to show that Madison was an economic determinist, a pre-Marxian Marxist. However, in this endeavor he omits all those passages such as the one just quoted above which would indicate otherwise. Vernon Parrington is less obvious in his omissions but guilty of the same practice. In this regard, Benjamin Wright points out that Publius "uses the word 'class' only when dealing with . . . vertical divisions." Introduction to *The Federalist* (Cambridge: Harvard University Press, 1961), 36.

13. Martin Diamond, for example, holds that Madison felt "if Americans can be made to divide themselves according to their narrow and particularized economic interests, they will avoid the fatal factionalism that opinion and passion generate. By contrast, the relatively tranquil kind of factionalism resulting from economic interests makes possible a stable and decent democracy." Moreover, according to Diamond, "The American polity looks to replace this struggle over the *inequality* of property by causing to flourish a new kind of economic faction derived from the *variety* of property. It is on this basis that there can arise a tranquil, modern politics of interest groups, as distinct from a politics of class struggle." "Ethics and Politics: The American Way" in *The Moral Foundations of the American Republic*, Robert H. Horwitz, ed. (Charlottesville: University of Virginia Press, 1979), p. 54.

14. This is not to say that Publius is inconsistent in this position concerning the character of representatives. In discussing the separation of powers and the character of legislative assemblies, he is concerned with the representatives advancing their own interests *as* representatives to the detriment of society. However, when these interests do not come into play, he anticipates that the representatives, as a group, can normally be expected to decide impartially.

15. This question, to our knowledge, was first raised by Dahl in his *Preface*. He writes: "Whether or not the majority is factional is irrelevant to the operation of the restrictions imposed by the existence of a numerous, extended, and diverse electorate. Furthermore, so far as I am aware, no modern Madison has shown that the restraints on the effectiveness of majorities imposed by the facts of a pluralistic society operate only to curtail 'bad' majorities and not 'good' majorities; and I confess I see no way by which such an ingenious proposition could be satisfactorily established" (pp. 29–30). This problem nags Gary Wills, particularly in the final section of his *Explaining*. Wills, quite wrongly in our view, sees the answer in processes which assure that "enlightened statesmen" will be at the helm.

16. To what degree Publius felt that extensiveness in terms of area or mere territorial size would impede the formation of factious majorities is a matter of conjecture because he never clearly differentiates the effects of size in this sense from those that result as a consequence of the plurality of interests. Clearly, extensiveness per se is at least important up to a point. For instance, a small area—one in which it would be possible for the people to assemble—would not be suitable from Publius's point of view even if it did contain many interests. Distance by itself may serve to dissipate the effects of a single event or circumstance, the consequences of which might adversely affect smaller territories. Or distance may serve to shield the entire country from factious "fads" or "impulses" that have overtaken localities. Or, again, distance might serve to dissipate the passions. We can, in sum, contemplate any number of ways in which distance might be relevant to the problem of majority factions.

17. We should note that most critics of the system (see note 2) hold views of republicanism that correspond very closely with the classical conception. As such, to extrapolate from Joseph Schumpeter's analysis of democracy, they place a premium on arrangements which "vest the power of deciding political issues in the electorate." However, Publius—again to use Schumpeter's framework—reverses the priorities of the classical conception of democracy by subordinating "the deciding of issues by the electorate secondary to the election of the men who are to do the deciding." *Capitalism, Socialism, and Democracy* (New York: Harper and Row, 1950), p. 269.

18. In this regard, there is no question that Publius believed that the indirect election of the Senate and president would help to guarantee individuals of even "fitter" character than those in the House. For instance, he writes that the process of electing the president "affords a moral certainty that the office of president will seldom fall to the lot of any man who is not in an eminent degree endowed with the requisite qualifications. Talents for low intrigue, and the little arts of popularity, may alone suffice to elevate a man to the first honors

in a single State; but it will require other talents, and a different kind of merit, to establish him in the esteem and confidence of the whole Union" (68:414).

19. While the remarks which follow are directed to the character of the senators, they would obviously apply in some degree to members of the House as well. "And that on account of the extent of the country from which those [the senators] . . . will be drawn, they will be less apt to be tainted by the spirit of faction, and more out of the reach of those occasional ill-humors, or temporary prejudices and propensities, which in small societies frequently contaminate the public deliberations, beget injustice and oppression of a part of the community, and engender schemes which, though they gratify a momentary inclination of desire, terminate in general distress, dissatisfaction, and disgust" (27:175).

In this vein, Robert J. Morgan sees two general conclusions flowing from the extended republic theory: (a) "representatives chosen from large, heterogeneous districts are likely to be independent of any single interest"; and (b) "Congress would more probably be insulated from localized factional struggles normally occurring in the same districts." "Madison's Theory of Representation in the Tenth Federalist," *Journal of Politics* 37 (Nov., 1974), 861.

20. The idea of impartiality, as we have indicated, stems from Publius's deeply held conviction that "no man should be judge of his own cause." Wherever possible he tries to secure impartiality in decision-making. As we will see in the next section, he is opposed to appeals to the people in order to settle "boundary" disputes that might arise between the branches because he felt such an appeal would give an undue advantage to the legislature. One of his solutions to jurisdictional disputes between the states and national government is a "tribunal" (presumably the Supreme Court) whose "decision is to be impartially made, according to the rules of the Constitution" (39:245–46). At other points, he views the people as playing the role of an umpire between the states and the national government: "The people, by throwing themselves into either scale [state or national], will infallibly make it preponderate" (28:181). In writing of factional disputes within a state, he asks: "what better umpires could be desired by two violent factions, flying to arms and tearing a State to pieces, than the representatives of confederate States, not heated by the local flame?" They would, in his words, combine the "impartiality of judges" with the "affection of friends" (43:277). In defending the impeachment process, he asks rhetorically: "Where else than in the Senate could have been found a tribunal sufficiently dignified, or sufficiently independent? What other body would be likely to feel *confidence enough in its own situation* to preserve, unawed and uninfluenced, the necessary impartiality between an *individual* accused and the *representatives of the people, the accusers?*" (65:398). With regard to the role of the national judiciary, he remarks: "The reasonableness of the agency of the national courts in cases in which the State tribunals cannot be supposed to be impartial speaks for itself. No man ought certainly to be a judge of his own cause in respect to which he has the least interest or bias. This principle has no inconsiderable weight in designating the federal courts as the proper tribunals for the determination of controversies between different States and their citizens" (80:478).

21. Here we are using the terminology employed by V. O. Key in his *Public Opinion and American Democracy* (New York: Alfred A. Knopf, 1961). By way of summary, Key provides the following picture of the relationship between public opinion and decision makers: "Our explorations into the nature and form of mass opinion leaves no doubt that its directives tend toward generality rather than specificity. Even on broad issues on which opinion becomes fairly well crystallized room may remain for choice among a variety of specific actions. Furthermore, translation of opinion into actions of electoral punishment or reward is a tortuous and uncertain procedure. The predictability of electoral response to a particular action remains so uncertain that the avoidance of a sensible decision because it will lose votes is usually the work of a man whose anxieties outweigh his capacities of prediction" (pp. 557–58). This very closely resembles the kind of relationship which Publius thought the extended republic would provide.

22. At the very end of Federalist 63, after discussing the various roles the Senate should perform, Publius remarks: "Against the force of the immediate representatives of the people nothing will be able to maintain even the constitutional authority of the Senate, but such a display of enlightened policy, and attachment to the public good, as will divide with that branch of the legislature the affections and support of the entire body of the people themselves" (390).

23. Robert Dahl's "American Hybrid" can be viewed quite legitimately as describing precisely the conditions Publius thought would obtain in the representative assembly. After noting that the "majority rarely rules on matters of specific policy," Dahl writes, "nevertheless the specific policies selected by a process of 'minorities rule' probably lie most of the time within the bounds of consensus set by the important values of the politically active members of the society, of whom the voters are a key group . . . in this sense the majority (at least of the politically active) nearly always 'rules'. . . . For politicians subject to elections must operate within the limits set both by their own values, as indoctrinated members of the society, and by their expectations about what policies they can adopt and still be re-elected." *Preface*, p. 132.

2
·
The Separation of Powers

> The accumulation of all powers, legislative, ex-
> ecutive, and judiciary, in the same hands, whether
> of one, a few, or many, and whether hereditary,
> self-appointed, or elective, may justly be pro-
> nounced the very definition of tyranny [47:301].

*W*ITH ALL THE attention lavished
on Publius's extended republic theory, there has been a tendency
to overlook or to slight his solution to an equally important concern:
how to prevent the rulers from oppressing and abusing the ruled.
Indeed, some commentators treat Publius's solution, which involves
the separation of powers, as basically an extension of his remedy for
the problem of majority factions. Others view this constitutional
separation of powers as simply designed to thwart majorities, factious
or not.[1] It is crucial to note, however, that Publius takes great care
to differentiate between tyranny or oppression, which stems from
the abuses of government, and the injustice that majorities, on rare
occasions, may commit against minorities. In Federalist 51, for instance, he expressly draws a distinction between guarding "one part
of the society against the injustice of the other part" and guarding
"the society against the oppression of its rulers" (323). Here he
asserts, as he had in Federalist 10, that the extended republic he
contemplates will provide the remedy for factious popular majorities.
But what he also makes clear is that controlling government presents
a problem of an essentially different nature—a problem which, unlike
that posed by majority factions, does require carefully fashioned
constitutional structures and processes for its solution. In this endeavor, we find Publius actually applying certain of the new and
improved "principles" of the "science of politics" to which he refers
in Federalist 9.

In order to systematically examine and analyze Publius's solution to the problem of governmental oppression or tyranny, we can do no better than follow the leads provided by the first sentence of Federalist 51: "To what expedient, then, shall we finally resort, for maintaining in practice the necessary partition of power among the several departments as laid down in the Constitution?" (320). Clearly, he is about to offer a workable solution for maintaining "the necessary partition" between the branches. The words *then* and *finally* tell us that he has already examined other expedients to maintain this partition and found them wanting. In fact, Federalist 51 is the fifth and final essay in a cluster of essays (47–51) devoted to problems associated with the separation of powers, principally that of maintaining separation. The first of these essays begins with an examination of why the "partition of powers among the several departments" is necessary.

This brace of essays, then, promises to reveal three significant dimensions of Publius's thinking about the separation of powers: why it is necessary, the reasons for rejecting schemes designed for its maintenance, and his solution. These matters, as we shall see, are not entirely unrelated to one another or to other aspects of his theory. His solution, for instance, cannot be understood fully without reference to his rejection of alternative means for maintaining the separation. Moreover, these elements of his teachings are essential for comprehending the relationship between the separation of powers and his conception of republicanism, a matter which we take up in the final portions of this chapter.

The Need for Separation

In Federalist 47 we find one of the most frequently quoted passages of *The Federalist*: "No political truth is certainly of greater intrinsic value, or is stamped with the authority of more enlightened patrons of liberty than that . . . the accumulation of all powers, legislative, executive, and judiciary, in the same hands, whether of one, a few, or many, and whether hereditary, self-appointed, or elective, may justly be pronounced the very definition of tyranny." And, he remarks, if it be true, as certain Antifederalists contend, that the proposed Constitution does not make adequate provision for the separation of powers, "no further arguments would be necessary to inspire a universal reprobation of the system" (301).

We should note to begin with that this perceived need for separation was one of the principal reasons why the form or structure of the government established by the Articles could not merely be amended or altered, but rather had to be entirely scrapped. Once the decision was made that a more effective and energetic national government was necessary, a totally new constitutional framework was required because, as Publius argued, to allow a single assembly to exercise the new and invigorated powers was a sure path to tyranny. The Congress under the Articles, he observes, posed no real danger because of the "slender, or rather fettered, authorities, which have heretofore [been] delegated" to it. "But," he goes on to say, "it would be inconsistent with all the principles of good government to intrust it with those additional powers which even the moderate and more rational adversaries of the proposed Constitution admit ought to reside in the United States" (22:151). He sets forth what he perceives to be the likely scenarios if piecemeal or partial reforms and adjustments of the Articles were attempted: either the structure would collapse from its own "intrinsic feebleness" or, "by successive augmentations of its force and energy, as necessity might prompt, we shall finally accumulate in a single body all the most important prerogatives of sovereignty, and thus entail upon our posterity one of the most execrable forms of government that human infatuation ever contrived." In this vein, he concludes, the very "tyranny" which the "adversaries of the new Constitution" are so "solicitous to avert" would become a "reality" (22:152).[2]

Neither at this point nor elsewhere, we should note in passing, does Publius deal at any length with the questions and concerns raised by modern critics of his theory who argue that the mere concentration of powers does not by itself constitute tyranny; that, rather, tyranny involves the actual abuse or misuse of powers.[3] Publius's relative silence on these concerns is, in part, attributable to the fact that he looked upon tyranny in a fashion somewhat differently from his contemporary critics. For him, in an important respect, tyranny represented a state of affairs or permanent condition characterizing a regime. As he uses the term in Federalist 47, tyranny refers to a regime with an accumulation of powers such as he describes. In this sense, it is a classification of regimes based upon their organization of governmental powers and, as such, is independent of traditional standards used for such classifications that center on who rules. Thus, as he says, there may be a tyranny of the one, the few, or the many, because its existence does not depend on the number who exercise the accumulated powers.

From this we can see again how the problem addressed by separation of powers differs in nature from that posed by factions. Tyranny is not to be equated with the unjust or oppressive acts of majority factions. True enough, we can say that such majorities act tyrannically, but the regime cannot on this account be deemed a tyranny. The extended republic, Publius would have us believe, can survive those rare occasions when majority factions might act tyrannically. Conversely, from his perspective, tyranny represented an enduring state of affairs which rendered it impossible for the citizens to enjoy ordered liberty.

This is not to say that Publius is completely silent about what will result from an accumulation of powers. He quotes from Montesquieu to the effect that where there is a union or accumulation of any two powers in the same hands the liberty and well-being of the people is endangered. If there is a union of the legislative and executive powers " 'there can be no liberty, because apprehensions may arise lest *the same* monarch or senate should *enact* tyrannical laws to *execute* them in a tyrannical manner.' " If the judicial power is " 'joined with the legislative, the life and liberty of the subject would be exposed to arbitrary control, for *the judge* would then be *the legislator.*' " Finally, if the judicial and executive powers are combined, " '*the judge* might behave with all the violence of *an oppressor*' " (303).

Publius's basic concern, as we can adduce from this passage, is similar to that he expressed in Federalist 10 regarding parties in the legislature being the judges of their own cause. What we see this time around is that, in the absence of an adequate separation of powers, the governors are, to varying degrees, in essentially the same position. An accumulation of all powers in the same hands leaves the governors free to pass whatever laws they want. They can legislate to promote their own interests over those of the citizens, or they can pass oppressive legislation and then, in their executive capacity, exempt themselves from its provisions while strictly applying them to the general society. But if, perchance, they cannot avoid the application of the law, they can, acting in their capacity as judges, exempt themselves from its penalties. The union of either the judicial or executive power with the legislative carries with it the same potential, whereas a merging of the judicial and executive powers could very well lead to arbitrary and capricious rule or, if not this, then favoritism toward certain groups and individuals in the application and enforcement of the laws. Principally for these reasons, Publius believed that "where the *whole* power of one department is exercised by the same hands which possess the *whole* power of another department, the fundamental principles of a free constitution are subverted" (47:302–3).

Certainly one of the chief ends Publius sought through the separation of powers was to secure an impartial administration and adjudication of the laws so that no one, particularly the governors, would be above or beyond the laws. This called for the execution and adjudication of the laws by agencies separate from both the legislature and each other, which would play a role not totally dissimilar to that of the independent or detached legislators discussed in connection with the filter problem. Such a separation of powers or functions, he realized, would provide for the operation of the reflexive principle and the benefits that flowed from it. That is, more concretely, legislators would certainly not be inclined to pass oppressive laws knowing that through impartial application and adjudication such laws would also apply to them, their family, and their friends. To this point he writes that "one of the strongest bonds by which human policy can connect the rulers and the people together" stems from provision that members of the House "can make no law which will not have its full operation on themselves and their friends, as well as on the great mass of the society." This, he holds, "creates between them that communion of interests and sympathy of sentiments of which few governments have furnished examples; but without which every government degenerates into tyranny." But if, perchance, the members of the House should take to "making legal discriminations in favor of themselves" or "a particular class," Publius looks for redress to "the genius of the whole system; the nature of just and constitutional laws; and, above all, the vigilant and manly spirit which actuates the people . . . a spirit which nourishes freedom, and in return is nourished by it." He warns, however, that if this spirit "be so far debased as to tolerate a law not obligatory on the legislature, as well as on the people, the people will be prepared to tolerate anything but liberty" (57:352–53).

Publius's discussion reveals, above all, an acute awareness that the uniform, equal, and predictable application of the laws is necessary for liberty. In a regime where the powers are united there is, as he clearly intimates, a far greater chance of arbitrariness and capriciousness in the execution and the adjudication of the law than in those regimes with a separation of powers. Where, for example, there is a union of powers the rulers may reinterpret laws to suit their immediate interests or they may declare illegal on one day what was legal the day before. In such a situation, of course, the citizen cannot help but be apprehensive: because he can never be sure what the law permits or forbids, he can never know the boundaries of his liberty with any certainty.

Publius's brief treatment of the ends of separation of powers in Federalist 47 and elsewhere, particularly that which deals with the deleterious effects of the mutability of the laws in his discussion of the Senate, clearly indicate that he subscribed to a "rule of law" version of the separation of powers: that is, more precisely, a division of functions designed to insure that the lawmakers are subject to the laws they promulgate (the reflexive principle) and that the citizens are subject only to known and fixed laws applied impartially, i.e., uniformly, equally, and predictably.[4] From this perspective, and to go back to his definition of tyranny that has proved so troublesome for modern critics, he evidently felt that the distinguishing characteristic of a tyranny is "rule of man," not of law. Because the rulers, in the absence of a separation of powers, would not be subject and accountable to the laws was alone sufficient from Publius's perspective to render such rule tyrannical—just as we say slavery is wrong even though the master be enlightened.

As we have remarked, Publius spends relatively little time trying to justify the need for separation of powers, a fact that confirms what we already know: a consensus existed on all sides concerning the need for separation. But there was no consensus on precisely what the doctrine called for by way of implementation. It is understandable, therefore, that he would direct his attention to the charges of "respectable adversaries" of the proposed Constitution who contended that it "distributed and blended" powers "in such a manner as at once to destroy all symmetry and beauty of form, and to expose some of the essential parts of the edifice to the danger of being crushed by the disproportionate weight of other parts" (301).

He answers this charge on two levels. First, he has recourse to "the oracle who is always consulted and cited on this subject . . . the celebrated Montesquieu" (301). This ends up to be not so much an examination of Montesquieu's teachings but rather of the British Constitution, "the source from which the maxim was drawn" by Montesquieu. Publius has little difficulty in showing that "the legislative, executive, and judiciary departments" of the British system "are by no means totally separate and distinct from each other." He cites several instances of a blending of functions and powers to bolster the proposition that Montesquieu did not mean that the three departments "ought to have no *partial agency* in, or no *control* over, the acts of each other." What Montesquieu's "words import, and still more conclusively as illustrated by the example in his eye [the British Constitution]" is, according to Publius, that one department ought not to exercise the "*whole* power of another department." By this measure, he continues, the British Constitution would be deficient if, for example, "the king, who is the sole executive magistrate, had possessed also the complete legislative power, or the supreme administration of justice" (302–3).

His second level of response involves the use of what, for lack of a better term, can be called the "glass house" argument: a type of argument he employs at various places in *The Federalist* designed to show that the charges against the proposed Constitution could be leveled with far greater justification against the state constitutions and governments.[5] In this instance, he spends more than half of the essay surveying the constitutions of eleven states, after which he concludes: "It is but too obvious that in some instances the fundamental principle under consideration has been violated by too great a mixture, and even an actual consolidation of the different powers; and that, in no instance has a competent provision been made for maintaining in practice the separation delineated on paper" (307–8).

Maintaining the Necessary Partition

With this analysis, Publius has prepared the way for inquiring into expedients that might be used to maintain the necessary partition, an inquiry that represents perhaps the richest source we have concerning his views on the fundamental nature of the Constitution. At the outset of essay 48, he more or less brings the reader up to date by setting forth the rule "agreed" to "on all sides" regarding the permissible extent of blending, namely, "one of the departments ought not to be directly and completely administered by either of the other departments." Noting that "power is of an encroaching nature," he remarks that, after determining what powers belong to the respective branches, the "most difficult task is to provide some practical security against the invasion of the others." The question he poses is "what this security ought to be" (308).

In Federalist 48, the first of three essays devoted to exploring this question, he tells us that "parchment barriers" are not adequate "against the encroaching spirit of power." Given his belief in the insufficiency of moral or religious considerations in restraining factions expressed in Federalist 10, we can hardly be surprised at his conclusion regarding the inefficacy of parchment barriers in preserving the separation of powers. It seems evident that Publius could easily have dismissed this parchment barrier expedient with only brief comment. We may surmise that he did not do so because discussion of this expedient serves as an excellent opening for the major point he wanted to make concerning the problem at hand: the legislative branch poses the greatest threat to the separation of powers because it "is everywhere extending the sphere of its activity and drawing all power into its impetuous vortex." "It is," he warns, "against the enterprising ambition of this department [the legislature] that the people ought to indulge all their jealousy and exhaust all their precautions" (309). Most certainly this is his chief concern in this brace of essays (48–51) and in other essays as well (e.g., 71, 73, 78).

Publius presents his readers with reasons for this assessment, the first of which is that in republics, as distasteful as it may be for its friends to acknowledge, the legislature, being the most powerful branch, is also the most dangerous to liberty and the rule of law. (The judiciary, he is to tell us in '78, is the "weakest" and thus the "least dangerous.") Certainly, he admits, in a system "where numerous and extensive prerogatives are placed in the hands of an hereditary monarchy, the executive department" can rightfully be "regarded as the source of danger." "But," he points out, "in a representative republic where the executive magistracy is carefully limited, both in the extent and duration of its power," it is the legislative assembly that most bears watching. One of his concerns is that the legislative assembly will be "inspired by a supposed influence over the people with an intrepid confidence in its own strength" and, at the same time, it "will be sufficiently numerous to feel all the passions which actuate a multitude, yet not so numerous as to be incapable of pursuing the objects of its passions by means which reason prescribes" (309). This latter consideration, of course, brings to mind his remarks about pure democracy in Federalist 10: there is nothing to prevent the legislative assembly from acting like the popular majorities in pure democracies. In other words, lacking the natural barriers against the coincidence of impulse and opportunity which extensiveness provides, there is the ever-present danger that a majority of the assembly might use the legislative powers to advance its own interests.

Publius sees "other circumstances" which contribute to the "superiority" of the legislative department and why it is in a better position to encroach with success upon the other departments. Because its powers are broader "and less susceptible of precise limits" than either the executive or judicial powers, it is able to conceal its encroachments "under complicated and indirect measures." What is more, he notes that in some states the legislature has "full discretion . . . over the pecuniary reward of those who fill the other branches," a power which, for obvious reasons, facilitates encroachment (310).

With these observations, Publius again turns to the experiences of the states. While contending that "the records and archives of every State in the Union" would bear out his observations, he confines himself to the experiences of two states, Virginia and Pennsylvania, as recounted by "two unexceptionable authorities," Thomas Jefferson and the Pennsylvania Council of Censors. We need not summarize Publius's tale of horrors, a portion of which is taken from Jefferson's *Notes on the State of Virginia*, save to note that constitutionalism—in the sense of governance according to agreed-to, known, and specified procedures and rules—fell victim to the accumulation of powers in the legislatures. Such, for example, occurred in both states when the legislatures decided "cases belonging to the judiciary department" (312).

This account forms a fitting prelude to Federalist 49, in which Publius tackles in earnest the matter of how to maintain the necessary partition or, as he formulates it, of preventing one department, principally the legislature, from exercising the whole powers of the other departments. His point of departure is Jefferson's plan providing " 'that whenever any two of the three branches of government shall concur in opinion, each by the voices of two thirds of their whole number, that a convention is necessary for altering the Constitution, or *correcting breaches of it*, a convention shall be called for the purpose.' " Despite Publius's depiction of the plan as "original, comprehensive, and accurate," he proceeds to find fault with it on both practical and theoretical grounds.

The first of his objections relates to its workability and comes down to the fact that the legislature, the likely culprit, would find it relatively easy "to gain to its interest either of the others." Indeed, he points out, all the legislature would have to do is gain the support of one-third of the members of either department to clear the way for its usurpations. But his theoretical objections to popular appeals, implicit in Jefferson's scheme, involve some of the more profound and interesting aspects of his teachings.

At the outset of his argument, Publius makes certain concessions to the principles underlying Jefferson's solution. He acknowledges that "the people are the only legitimate fountain of power" and that "it is from them that the constitutional charter, under which the several branches of government hold their power, is derived." The departments so created, he goes on to say, are "perfectly co-ordinate by terms of their common commission" and, thus, no one of them "can pretend to an exclusive or superior right of settling the boundaries between their respective powers" should disputes arise.[6] Having granted so much, Publius must face the question of why the people, "the legitimate fountain of power," should not settle these disputes. Or, as he puts it, "how are the encroachments of the stronger to be prevented, or the wrongs of the weaker to be redressed, without an appeal to the people themselves, who, as the grantors of the commission, can alone declare its true meaning, and enforce its observance?" (313–14).

Publius grants that "it seems strictly consonant with republican theory to recur to the same original authority, not only whenever it may be necessary to enlarge, diminish, or new-model the powers of government, but also whenever any one of the departments may commit encroachments on the chartered authorities of the others" (49:314). What we see from this passage, as well as from the general context of his discussion, is that he evidently regards recourse to the people for the redress of encroachments to be the equivalent of a constituent act. Put somewhat differently, when Publius writes of recourse to the people for redress, he is not referring to people exercising their *political* will under the forms of the Constitution, a will which usually takes the form of legislation. Rather, he views the people as acting in their constituent capacity, not so much, as he makes clear at the outset of Federalist 50, from the perspective of altering the Constitution, but in authoritatively interpreting its provisions in order to prevent and correct infractions.

His remarks, to carry this matter one step further, presuppose the "fundamental law theory," which he first articulates in Federalist 53 and develops more fully in his argument for judicial review in Federalist 78. Briefly put, this theory holds the "Constitution established by the people" is "unalterable by the government" (53:331) and that the will of the people "declared in the Constitution" is "superior" to the "will of the legislature declared in its statutes" (78:468). Thus, the settlement of constitutional disputes concerning the proper domain of the departments would seem to require that the people act in the same capacity (i.e., constituent) as they did in adopting the Constitution. Under the terms of the proposed Constitution, this could only be done through the amendment process outlined in Article five.

While we will discuss the higher or fundamental law theory in detail when we turn to the matter of limited government, it is important to bear in mind Publius's view of what would be involved in such appeals to the people in order to understand and appreciate his opposition to this expedient. His first argument, for example, is that "as every appeal to the people would carry an implication of some defect in the government, frequent appeals would, in great measure, deprive the government of that veneration which time bestows on everything, and without which perhaps the wisest and freest governments would not possess the requisite stability." "If it be true," he argues, "that all governments rest on opinion, it is no less true that the strength of opinion in each individual" is, to some extent, a function of the "number which he supposes to have entertained the same opinion." In his view, "the reason of man, like man himself, is timid and cautious when let alone, and acquires firmness and confidence in proportion to the numbers with which it is associated." "When," he continues, "the examples which fortify opinion are *ancient* as well as *numerous*, they are known to have a double effect." Such he believes to be the realities of human exist- ence. If it were otherwise, if we were "a nation of philosophers," he concedes, we could count on a "reverence for the laws . . . suf- ficiently inculcated by the voice of reason." "But," he concludes, such a nation "is as little to be expected as the philosophical race of kings wished for by Plato" (49; 314–15).

An even "more serious" objection, not entirely unrelated to the foregoing, is that referring "constitutional questions to the decision of the whole society" will disturb "the public tranquillity by inter- esting too strongly the public passions." He acknowledges that "suc- cess . . . has attended the revisions of our established forms of gov- ernment." Yet he maintains that these "experiments are of too ticklish a nature to be unnecessarily multiplied." The present governments, he notes, were established "in the midst of a danger," wherein there was "an enthusiastic confidence of the people in their patriotic lead- ers" and a "universal ardor for new and opposite forms" fueled by a "resentment and indignation against the ancient government." All these factors, he points out, served to repress "passions," to stifle "the ordinary diversity of opinions on great national questions" so that "no spirit of party" was able "to mingle its leaven" in these revisions. And, as if to suggest that the conditions surrounding rat- ification also presented a favorable climate for constitutional change, he writes, "future situations in which we must expect to be usually placed do not present any equivalent security against the danger [the spirit of party or faction] which is apprehended" (315).

At other places in *The Federalist* Publius is even more emphatic in pointing out that the Philadelphia Convention met at a unique and propitious time—at a time when, so to speak, the constellation of forces would allow the participants to overcome factional differences and to think and act in terms of the long-range national interest. Moreover, he expresses serious doubts that once the system is set in motion, such favorable conditions would surround another act of founding. Of course, the first two paragraphs of the first essay sug- gest as much. But the strongest statement to this effect is to be found

 # 37

in Federalist 37 where, in comparing the success of the Philadelphia Convention with the efforts of other nations (particularly the United Netherlands) to reform their constitutions, he concludes that "the convention must have enjoyed, in a very singular degree, an exemption from the pestilential influence of party animosities." And, commenting on the proceedings of the Convention, he observes: "The real wonder is that so many difficulties should have been surmounted, and surmounted with a unanimity almost as unprecedented as it must have been unexpected. It is impossible for any man of candor to reflect on this circumstance without partaking of the astonishment" (230–31).[7]

With these objections Publius presents a constitutional morality as well, a morality reflected today in our belief that we should not trivialize the Constitution by overburdening it with amendments, that we should alter it only when a compelling case can be made. This is a morality which, he informs us, is highly important, if not vital, for the stability and well-being of the regime. It is also a conservative morality which many, over the decades, have come to view as one of the major obstacles to needed change in the constitutional order.

"The greatest objection of all" to such occasional appeals, he contends, is that they would not serve "the purpose of maintaining the constitutional equilibrium." By way of showing this he asks, in effect, what chance the judiciary or the executive would have in such appeals against the legislature, the most likely transgressor in republican regimes. And his answer is clear: The legislators are "numerous"; they have "connections of blood, of friendship, and of acquaintance" with a large segment of "the most influential part of society"; and their position, by itself, "implies a personal influence among the people, and that they are more immediately the confidential guardians of the rights and liberties of the people." On the other hand, those in the executive and judiciary departments "are few in number," and they are "personally known to a small part only of the people." What is more, the members of the judiciary, given their mode of appointment and the "nature and permanency of it, are too far removed from the people to share much in their prepossessions," while those in the executive branch "are generally the objects of jealousy and their administration is always liable to be discolored and rendered unpopular" (316).

But this is not all. The odds are, he writes, that the legislators would gain election to the conventions charged with the responsibility of resolving the disputes so that, more likely than not, "members of the department whose conduct was arraigned" would be the judges of the propriety of their own conduct—a clear violation of the maxim set forth in Federalist 10 that parties should not be judges of their own cause. But even if this were not the case, even if "appeals were made under circumstances less adverse to the executive and judiciary departments"—i.e., the legislative encroachment being "so flagrant and so sudden, as to admit of no specious coloring"—he believes the proceedings would still be dominated by "the spirit of pre-existing parties, or of parties springing out of the question itself." We would still find, he holds, parties forming around "persons of distinguished character and extensive influence" involved with the issue to be resolved. The decision, rather than being impartial, would again be made "by the men who had been agents in, or opponents of, the measures" in question. He concludes that "the *passions* . . . not the *reason,* of the public would sit in judgment." "But," he insists, "it is the reason, alone, of the public that ought to control and regulate the government," whereas the passions should "be controlled and regulated by the government" (317).

In Federalist 50, as we might expect, Publius also rejects the expedient of periodic appeals or appeals at fixed intervals. If the time between the alleged infraction and the appeal be a short one, he reasons that "the circumstances which tend to vitiate and pervert the result of occasional revisions" will be present. If the interval be a long one, he regards "a distant prospect of public censure . . . a very feeble restraint on power from those excesses to which it might be urged by the force of present motives." In rendering this assessment, Publius's operating assumptions regarding the powerful influence of immediate self-interest again come into play. This time around he tells us that an individual will normally pursue his immediate self-interest, not only to the detriment of the long-term general good, but of his own long-range interests as well. Thus, he cannot imagine that a "legislative assembly, consisting of a hundred or two hundred members, eagerly bent on some favorite object" and willing to break "through the restraints of the Constitution in pursuit of it, would be arrested in their career" by prospects of censure some "ten, fifteen, or twenty years" hence. To this he adds that if the interval between infraction and appeal is long, "the abuses would often have completed their mischievous effects before the remedial provisions would be applied," or, if not that, "they would be of long standing, would have taken deep root, and would not easily be extirpated" (318).

Finally, in this essay, Publius offers empirical evidence for the propositions he has advanced concerning the composition and nature of such periodic conventions. He notes that the Pennsylvania Council of Censors, authorized to determine " 'whether the Constitution had been violated and whether the legislative and executive departments had encroached on each other,' " was composed of active party members and that "active and leading members of the council had been active and influential members of the legislative and executive branches within the period to be reviewed." Moreover, the division in the Council along party lines clearly indicates to Publius that "*passion*, not *reason*" carried the day on virtually all issues. "When," he comments, in a manner consonant with his views set forth in Federalist 10, "men exercise their reason coolly and freely on a variety of distinct questions, they inevitably fall into different opinions on some of them." However, he observes, "when they are governed by a common passion, their opinions, if they are so to be called, will be the same" (318–19).

The difficulties encountered with the Pennsylvania Council, he asserts, cannot be explained away by arguing that Pennsylvania was at that time "violently heated and distracted by the rage of party." Neither Pennsylvania nor the other states, he argues, can expect to be free from the ravages of party for any length of time. Indeed, quite in keeping with views expressed in Federalist 10, the absence of parties is not, he holds, a condition to be desired. "An extinction of parties," he writes, "necessarily implies either a universal alarm for the public safety, or an absolute extinction of liberty." Nor, he points out, can the difficulties posed by parties be avoided by excluding from such councils those "concerned with the government within the given period." In his view, this would only mean that the councils' tasks would "devolve on men . . . with inferior capacities" who, in all probability, "would . . . have been involved in the parties connected with these measures and . . . elected under their auspices" (320).

The Solution

With the rejection of parchment barriers, occasional and periodic appeals, we come to Federalist 51, whose first sentence, as we have remarked, promises that a solution to the problem of maintaining a proper separation of powers will be forthcoming. And so it is. At the outset of the essay Publius informs us that "as all these exterior provisions are found to be inadequate the defect must be supplied, by so contriving the interior structure of the government as that its several constituent parts may, by their mutual relations, be the means of keeping each other in their proper places." Although he does not "undertake a full development of this important idea," he does set forth "general observations" concerning it which are invaluable for understanding both the forms of the Constitution and the views of human nature upon which they are predicated (320–21).

He turns first to the requirement that "each department should have a will of its own"—a requirement which, in his words, "is admitted on all hands to be essential to the preservation of liberty."[8] He is quite aware of the implications of this requirement if it were strictly observed: the member of one department "should have as little agency as possible in the appointment of the members of the others" and, though the members of each department "should be drawn from the same fountain of authority, the people," they should be selected through independent channels "having no communication whatever with one another." This, we might say, is what the pure doctrine would call for in light of the purposes of separation of powers.[9]

Publius's discussion of this point turns quickly to the "constitution of the judiciary department," which represents the principal deviation from the pure doctrine. That his attention should focus on this issue is hardly surprising in light of the fact that the theory and practice of separation of powers up to this point did not accord the judiciary the status of a coordinate branch, but rather regarded it as an offshoot of the executive authority. Consequently, the proposed Constitution itself was moving into largely uncharted territory in establishing an independent judiciary, and Publius felt obliged, so it would seem, to explain why "it might be," to use his words, "inexpedient to insist" that it be constituted according to the principles of the pure doctrine.

What Publius does, in fact, is offer two considerations which do justify a departure from the pure doctrine. The first of these, taken by itself, is unexceptional: the mode for the selection should be one that secures individuals with the "peculiar qualifications" necessary for the judiciary. While this, of course, does not necessarily mean that the president and the Senate should participate in the selection process as provided for in the Constitution, we may surmise that Publius felt it would be cumbersome or "inexpedient" to establish another institution for the specific purpose of naming judges—an institution which itself would have to be either directly or indirectly accountable to the people. Moreover, his second consideration, that the "permanent tenure" of the judges "must soon destroy all sense of dependence on the authority conferring them," obviates the need for a process of selection that is independent of the other branches.

In this same vein, Publius remarks that is it also necessary for the "members of each department" to be "as little dependent as possible on those of the other for the emoluments annexed to their offices." Otherwise, he maintains, the independence of the judges and executive from the legislature, the body which controls the purse, "would be merely nominal" (321).

The foregoing elements of Publius's solution involve constitutional provisions designed to insure that each department, particularly the judiciary and executive, will "have a will of its own." But, quite in keeping with his earlier analysis, he does not see this by itself as sufficient for the end of maintaining the necessary partition. He goes on to write that "the great security against a gradual concentration of the several powers in the same department consists in giving to those who administer each department the necessary constitutional means and personal motives to resist encroachments of others" (321–22). This security, in large part, involves what is commonly called the principle of "checks and balances."

These two elements of Publius's solution, personal motives and constitutional means, merit our attention. While the two are inseparable operationally speaking—the motive and constitutional means must conjoin for purposes of self-defense—they can be separated analytically. The constitutional means that he has in mind relate to specific formal provisions of the proposed Constitution, whereas the personal motives spring from his understanding of human nature.

As far as the constitutional provisions for defense are concerned, he believes they "must . . . be made commensurate to the danger of attack." And because, as he sees it, "it is not possible to give to each department an equal power of self-defense," the maintenance of the necessary partition of powers depends upon weakening the strong (the legislature) and strengthening the weak (the executive and judiciary). To the end of providing for self-defense, the most significant constitutional provision is the division of the legislature. Indeed, we learn from his discussion that the principal reason for the bicameralism in the proposed Constitution is to preserve the separation of powers. "In republican government," he writes, "the legislative authority necessarily predominates" and "the remedy for this inconveniency," as he sees it, involves not only dividing the legislature into two branches but also rendering these branches, "by different modes of election and different principles of action, as little connected with each other as their common functions and their common dependence on society will admit" (322).

But even this division is not enough for Publius: "As the weight of the legislative authority requires that it should be . . . divided, the weakness of the executive may require . . . that it should be fortified." In this connection, he does not deal unsympathetically with the notion of vesting the executive with an "absolute veto on the legislature." While noting that such a veto would appear to be "the natural defense," he goes on to remark that "perhaps it would be neither altogether safe nor alone sufficient," because "on ordinary occasions it might not be exerted with the requisite firmness, and on extraordinary occasions it might be perfidiously abused." But he asks rhetorically whether "this defect of an absolute negative" might not be overcome by "some qualified connection" between the executive and Senate which might lead the Senate, "without being too much detached from the rights of its own department," to back "the constitutional rights" of the executive (323). Though he does not elaborate on this point, it seems clear that he thought the Senate, in sharing the appointment and treaty-making powers with the executive, might be able to develop a more detached or impartial view toward his office and powers than the House.

What we see from the foregoing is that the constitutional provisions serve two interrelated purposes. Provisions such as those relating to judicial tenure and emoluments serve to build a wall or partition around the executive and judicial branches so that they can have a will of their own. Other provisions which serve to strengthen the weak and weaken the strong are designed to provide for self-defense, principally against legislative encroachments. But all of these provisions are for naught if there is not a will to resist legislative domination. What good does it do, for instance, to equip the president with a veto if he will not exercise it? Or what purpose is served by trying to provide each department with a will of its own, if it refuses to exercise that will when the occasion demands? For this reason, we cannot view the constitutional provisions apart from the "personal motives" to which Publius refers because the latter supply the force that will render the constitutional provisions effective.

We can readily see how the Constitution gives "those who administer each department" the "constitutional means" for resisting encroachments. But how it simultaneously supplies the necessary "personal motives" is not so readily perceived. Moreover, Publius does not directly address this specific matter. The unarticulated assumption underlying his discussion, it seems, is that "the interest" of the office holders *will* attach to or connect with (he writes "must be connected with") "the constitutional rights of the place" so that "ambition" *will* (again, he uses the imperative "must be made to") "counteract ambition." Such a view of Publius's position seems entirely warranted in light of the impulse-opportunity framework set forth in Federalist 10: officeholders are individuals who have succeeded in their quest for office and the powers that go with it; they are by nature individuals whose impulses will direct them to use the opportunities—i.e., the "constitutional means"—either to expand their turf or defend it against attack. In any event, as his observations in Federalists 48–50 indicate, the officeholder or political man Publius has in mind is an ambitious individual, one who scarcely needs much prodding to use the powers at his disposal to expand or protect his political domain. That he will do so with others similarly situated and, in effect, work through the institution in which he serves seems obvious enough. Certainly the institution to which he is attached provides the most logical and efficacious channel.[10] Such a presumption seems to underlie his entire discussion of the separation of powers.

Publius seems somewhat defensive about relying on ambition counteracting ambition by connecting the interest of the officeholder with the "constitutional rights of the place." In one of the most frequently cited passages of *The Federalist*, he writes: "It may be a reflection on human nature that such devices should be necessary to control the abuses of government. But what is government itself but the greatest of all reflections on human nature? If men were angels, no government would be necessary. If angels were to govern men, neither external nor internal controls on government would be necessary" (322). He continues in this vein by remarking that "in framing a government which is to be administered by men over men, the great difficulty" is enabling "the government to control the governed" and obliging government "to control itself." While he holds that "a dependence on the people is . . . the primary control on government," he notes that "experience has taught mankind the necessity of auxiliary precautions" such as those, we may assume, he has advanced in discussing the separation of powers (322). In any event, we should take care to note, the "auxiliary precautions" to which he refers are not meant to apply against factious majorities, but rather against the rulers. Moreover, they may be looked upon as necessary additions to the "primary control," "dependence on the people" which, consonant with his republican principles, would come down to the people acting in their political capacity through periodic elections. At the same time, however, these precautions would forestall the need for subsequent appeals to the people in their constituent capacity to settle disputes between the branches.

Publius believes that "this policy of supplying, by opposite and rival interests, the defect of better motives, might be traced through the whole system of human affairs, private as well as public." In this respect, he refers to "all the subordinate distributions of power" wherein the object has been to "divide and arrange the several offices" so that they may "check" each other, thereby providing "that the private interest of every individual may be a sentinel over the public rights." "These inventions of prudence," as he dubs them, he regards as no "less requisite in the distribution of the supreme powers of the State" (322).

The Solution: A Wider Perspective

Publius's endorsement of the policy of supplying opposite and rival interests constitutes a convenient point of departure for viewing his solution in a broader theoretical context. What we see at once is that this policy, designed to secure the constitutional separation of powers, differs in a fundamental way from the solution to the problem of majority factions provided by the extended republic. The strategy for maintaining partition is to let the contending parties have at it after providing the weaker parties with adequate protection or means of self-defense. The presumption on Publius's part would seem to be that the outcome of these confrontations will keep the system on an even keel: that they will, in other words, serve to perpetuate a government of laws. On the other hand, the key to controlling the effects of majority factions, as we have seen, is the existence of mediating groups—referees of sorts—between the contending parties. Indeed, as we can readily see from Publius's discussion of the situation within the states, it is the head-to-head confrontation between contending parties that produces the injustice of which he writes. Without, as he puts it, "justice . . . to hold the balance between them," the dominant party judges of its own cause. And while the confrontational strategy can be made to work in preserving the separation of powers by weakening the strong and strengthening the weak, an equivalent strategy with respect to factions—e.g., restraining majorities or protecting minorities—would necessarily have to depart from republican principles.

With regard to Publius's solution for preventing the abuses of government, unlike the solution he perceives to the problem of majority factions, we may appropriately speak in terms of strategy because the separation of powers does rest upon shaping institutions consonant with his assumptions regarding the likely behavior of officeholders—assumptions that, in turn, rest upon even broader assumptions concerning the nature of man.[11] And certain elements of this strategy merit our attention, particularly in light of some of the modern critiques of our system of separation of powers. In the first place, as we have seen, Publius does not rely only upon formal constitutional institutions and procedures to maintain the necessary partition. They are a necessary but not a sufficient condition for this end. As we have remarked, if the interest of the officeholder does not attach to the office and the "constitutional rights of the place," or if "personal motives" are not sufficient to impel the use of the weapons of self-defense, then constitutional provisions would be dead letters. Evidently Publius believed the formal constitutional arrangements would themselves provide officeholders with the motives and opportunity to do what comes naturally to them. Or, to put this another way, rather than attempting to drive a wedge between impulse and opportunity—a key to the solution of the problem of majority factions, which Publius perceived to be inherent in the conditions of the extended republic—he looks upon their union as the means to the desired end. In one important respect, however, this strategy parallels the remedy for controlling the effects of faction: both depend upon properly motivated individuals in strategic positions. Specifically, just as controlling the effects of factions depends on sufficiently disinterested representatives mediating conflict in the legislature, maintaining separation depends on the interested parties, the officeholders, willing to use the powers at their command to protect the prerogatives of their office.

Noting this similarity points to other significant dimensions of Publius's teachings. On his showing, the representatives would seem to possess Jekyll and Hyde characteristics. In Federalist 10 and elsewhere he leads us to believe that they are "fit characters," but throughout his discussion of separation of powers they are pictured in a far from flattering light. In what sense, then, can it be said that Publius is consistent? On what basis, that is, can he have it both ways? The answer is found in a distinction that seems to underlie Publius's analysis. He is not overly concerned about trusting representatives with powers that are reflexive in character—powers that operate alike on the representatives and the people. So much is evident, as we will see most clearly in the next chapter, from his insistence that the new national government should possess all the powers necessary to achieve its constitutional objectives. For reasons we have already spelled out, the separation of powers renders it unlikely that powers of this nature would be abused by the representatives.

Publius's distrust of legislators stems from the power they possess relative to the other branches—to powers of a distinctly nonreflexive character. Put another way, the representatives will, on his showing, possess an institutional interest quite apart from any shared by the general society, an interest they could only advance by consolidating the powers of the coordinate branches. He was aware that if the representatives were to assume the total powers of just one other branch, the reflexive principle—the principal restraint on the abusive exercise of the delegated powers of the national government—would no longer be operative: laws could then be executed or adjudicated without much difficulty to benefit representatives, their families and their friends, at the expense of the general society.

In sum, Publius did not regard the representatives as being above the pursuit of their own institutional self-interest distinct and apart from interests shared by the general society—a self-interest which, if not checked, will assume the form of legislative aggrandizement of the coordinate branches. So long, however, as the necessary partition of powers is maintained, this particular self-interest can be controlled. Controlling this self-interest, in turn, guarantees the operation of the reflexive principle that insures that representatives will not abuse the nonreflexive powers delegated to them by the Constitution.

In this connection, many have seized upon the fact that Publius depicts men, including representatives, as less than angelic to mean that he subscribed to a Hobbesian view of human nature. Why this particular passage is singled out to support this view is surprising because, in contrast to what he has to say about the nature of man in other essays (e.g., Federalist 6), his assertion in Federalist 51 that men are not angels is a rather charitable assessment to say the least. Nevertheless, if we view this assessment in a wider context, it seems clear that Publius is asserting nothing more than what he has already said about the nature of man in other places. It merely reflects his assumptions about man, which support his conclusions about the need for a more energetic government, as well as the need to control that government.

Such a perspective helps us to account for the fact that only four essays after his famous "angels" statement he writes, in the context of dismissing the possibilities of collusion among the departments of government through bribery, that there are some "qualities in human nature which justify a certain portion of esteem and confidence," and that, moreover, "republican government presupposes the existence of these qualities in a higher degree than any other form" (55:346). We can also come to understand why, when discounting the possibilities of a president bending the Senate to his will through use of the appointment power, he can write: "The supposition of universal venality in human nature is little less an error in political reasoning than the supposition of universal rectitude" (76:458). While he does not spell out these qualities in any detail, we may infer from the context of his remarks that they would certainly include a fidelity to the public trust that would strongly militate against betraying the confidence of the people for temporary private gain.

These observations lead us back, via another route, to our original point concerning the differences between the solution for the problem of faction and that for maintaining the necessary partition of powers between the branches. Looking at his solution for maintaining the partition of powers, there are those who picture Publius's theory as built entirely on force against force, ambition counteracting ambition, and conflict between "opposite and rival interests." Yet leaving aside those considerations we have already pointed out that militate against such an interpretation, this view ignores those qualities of man that do "justify a certain portion of esteem and confidence" that must exist for maintaining separation, as well as for controlling the effects of faction. This is no small matter because, as Publius contends, a republic depends upon these qualities to a "higher degree than any other form" (55:346).

Still another matter related to his solution involves the widely held view that he sought to establish a balance or equilibrium between the branches. Such a view would certainly suggest that he had some model or ideal in mind against which the degree of equilibrium or balance could be compared or measured, if only to inform us when the institutions were out of balance or equilibrium. But there is no such model to be derived from his teachings, save in the sense that he wanted each branch secure in its sphere from capture by another. One reason he does not go much beyond this notion of equilibrium we may adduce from a remark he makes in a philosophical discussion in Federalist 37 concerning the problems that confronted the Convention arising from the inherent difficulties of classifying, defining, and delineating the objects, functions, and powers of government: "Experience has instructed us that no skill in the science of government has yet been able to discriminate and define, with sufficient certainty, its three great provinces—the legislative, executive, and judiciary; or even the privileges and powers of the different legislative branches. Questions daily occur in the course of practice which prove the obscurity which reigns in these subjects, and which puzzle the greatest adepts in political science" (228).

Moreover, to think of separation of powers in terms of equilibrium or balance, at least in the sense that these concepts are normally employed in connection with the separation of powers, is both inappropriate and potentially misleading. To begin with, because each of the departments performs essentially different functions, it is difficult to see how they could be compared with one another in any meaningful sense. These terms, to be sure, would have meaning in the context of a mixed regime. Such is the case, for instance, where the institutions of government, like those of Great Britain at the time of our founding period, represent the predominant social classes, each equipped with a veto over the proposals of the other. In this context, each branch can be said to have had an equal power in the process of making the laws. In this process, one can even speak of a balanced or moderated government, since its policies would necessarily have to be accommodated to these dominant, and often antagonistic, interests.

But this is a far cry from what Publius had in mind. In the first place, as we see from his discussion of republicanism, he rejects this notion of mixed government as inconsistent with the republican "genius" of the people. He argues as well that true republicanism requires that all the branches of government should be anchored, directly or indirectly, on popular foundations—not on specific interests or social classes. The balance or moderation of policies would come about as a result of the extended republic with its diversity of interests through processes we have described, not through institutions embracing class interests. Furthermore, Publius perceives the duties and responsibilities of the separate institutions in our constitutional context to be different from those in a mixed regime.

Nor, we should add at this point, was Publius concerned that the system would evolve into a tool of specific social classes or orders. For instance, he could not conceive how, "by any possible means within the compass of human address" (63:388), it would be possible for the Senate to "gradually acquire a dangerous pre-eminence in the government and finally transform itself into a tyrannical aristocracy" (63:387). Such a transformation, he stresses, would require first that the Senate "corrupt itself" and then, in order, the state legislatures, the House, and finally "the people at large." By the same token, he could not envision the national government, as certain of the Antifederalists feared, ever regulating elections "in such a manner as to promote the election of some favorite class of men in exclusion of others." Any such effort, he argues, would in all likelihood lead to "an immediate revolt of the great body of the people, headed and directed by the State governments." Beyond this, he points out, "the dissimilarity in the ingredients which will compose the national government, and still more in the manner in which they will be brought into action in its various branches, must form a powerful obstacle to a concert of views in any partial scheme of elections" (60:367). In this respect, he writes that the different electoral foundations of the branches renders it highly unlikely that any "common interest" would exist "to cement" them "in a predilection for any particular class of electors" (60:368).

Whether the outgrowth of viewing the Founders' handiwork as a mixed regime or not, the equilibrium or balance framework of thought is conducive to thinking of the three branches as *equal* and coordinate. Though this view of the system has gained currency in relatively recent times, it is again difficult to see how the branches could be regarded as equal since their functions, as marked out in the Constitution, are of a different order. Whatever the problems with this modern conception, however, it is clear that Publius looked upon the Congress as the predominant institution, the most powerful of the branches. Nor, in this respect, can it be said that the policy of weakening the strong and strengthening the weak really puts the branches on more or less equal footing. What this policy does accomplish is to maintain the necessary partition of powers: to prevent that which Publius feared, namely, "the *whole* power of one department" being "exercised by the same hand which possess the *whole* power of another department" (47:302–3). Adequate protection against this, not a balance or equilibrium between the branches, was Publius's principal concern.

Republicanism and the Separation of Powers

The relationship between separation of powers and republicanism merits our special attention primarily because, as we have taken pains to note, this has become a focal point for critics of *The Federalist* and the constitutional system it attempts to justify. As we have shown, the compatibility of separation of powers with republicanism or the popular control of government has, since the turn of the twentieth century, been brought into question by various critics of the system. Many of these critics connect separation of powers with a mixed regime by maintaining that it was designed to protect the wealthy and wellborn from the ravages of majority rule. Still others look upon the separation of powers as intended to establish a passive and inactive government, one clearly biased in favor of the status quo and entrenched interests.[12] Virtually all see separation of powers as a manifestation of the Framers' (and Publius's) distrust of the people. And, largely because these critics overlook or choose to ignore Publius's position on the end or purpose of separation,[13] their interpretations do not, on the surface, seem at all implausible. For instance, it is a fact, as they contend, that Publius was much concerned about checking the legislature, which also happens to be that department closest to the people. Beyond this, as they also argue, he was most fearful of the House of Representatives, the most democratic of the branches. In fact, as we have seen, he even hoped that the executive might find sufficient support in the Senate for upholding his authority against legislative encroachments that would, in all probability, originate in the House.

Still other major aspects of his teachings deviate from the principles of classical republicanism that, as we noted in the last chapter, call for institutions and processes designed to allow the preferences of popular majorities to prevail. Bicameralism can be considered the most serious departure of all from these principles because it divides the representative branch of the government, a division that might well serve to blunt, obfuscate, or otherwise diffuse the will of popular majorities. Moreover, the upper branch represents the states equally, not the people—a clear departure from the republican standard of "one person, one equal vote." Then, too, there is the mode of appointment for judges and their tenure for good behavior which effectively isolates them from popular control. In sum, compared with the standards of classical republicanism, Publius's system rates low marks.

If we view the system with Publius's obvious concern to preserve the rule of law in mind, however, we can see why it takes the form it does. These deviations are necessary for maintaining the necessary partition of powers that he regarded as essential for the rule of law. For example, to insure that each department will have a will of its own—a condition indispensable for maintaining the necessary partitions—there must be different modes of election for the branches. Or, to take another example, without bicameralism the probability is that the legislature would soon absorb the executive and judicial powers, the very tyranny he sought to avoid. In sum, lacking adequate provisions for maintaining the separation of powers, Publius believed that the "perpetual vibration between the extremes of anarchy and tyranny" was unavoidable. Thus, he could hardly have supported a republican system that provided no checks against the legislature. From his vantage point, we may also say, a system comprised of three branches of government—a legislative, executive, and judicial—the members of which were all directly elected by the people, would be destined for a short and tumultuous life. So, too, would a system in which the people directly elect one branch that, in turn, was empowered to exercise complete control over the others. This much would seem to be clear from his remarks about revision of the Articles that we noted at the outset of this chapter.

What this points to is that republicanism, in the sense his critics conceive it, is incompatible with the rule of law and the values associated with it, not the least of these being liberty under the law. From Publius's vantage point, the principal source of this incompatibility is simply that the classical republican model provides no effective barriers that would prevent the legislature from assuming all the functions of government. At the same time, however, he does not regard the proposed Constitution as any the less popularly based because it does contain safeguards against the accumulation of powers. He does not suggest in his discourse that the values associated with the rule of law call for deviations from popular rule, that, for example, there must be some trade-offs between liberty on one side and popular government on the other.

We may attribute his silence on this score to two considerations. One, which we have already discussed at some length in the last chapter, relates to the impracticability of the classical republican form for the extended republic that he envisioned. The other, theoretical in nature, is that he believed the proposed system superior to one built on classical principles because it would simultaneously provide for popular rule and the ends associated with good government such as stability, energy, and the rule of law.[14] For instance, from what he does say we know that he thought that persistent majorities, though they might run into delays along the way, would eventually prevail and that the separation of powers would, in turn, serve to refine and improve the character of popular rule.

We can see this most clearly by turning our attention to the Senate, which plays such a pivotal role in the system of separation of powers and whose very existence has brought the republican character of the system into question. As we have seen, Publius believed that different channels of selection were indispensable for insuring the ends of separation of powers. Thus, the mode of election for the Senate would have to vary from that employed for the House—a theoretical requirement which, on its face, is not compatible with majoritarianism. The composition of the Senate, however, is still another matter that relates even more directly to the republican principle. In this regard, one of the few occasions where Publius openly voices displeasure with a constitutional provision arises in his discussion of the equality of state representation in the Senate. While he admits to seeing "some reason" why the government of a "compound republic . . . ought to be founded on a mixture of the principles of proportional and equal representation," he is quick to add that "it is superfluous to try, by the standard of theory, a part of the Constitution [i.e., the provision for equal state representation in the Senate] which is allowed on all hands to be the result, not of theory, but 'of a spirit of amity, and that mutual deference and concession which the peculiarity of our political situation rendered indispensable.' " He notes the need for a "common government, with powers equal to its object" and remarks that such a government would simply not be forthcoming without this provision, which represents a compromise between the larger and smaller states. Given this fact, the only alternative, he writes, was to heed "the advice of prudence" by embracing "the lesser evil" (62:377).[15] And, in conceding that equal representation in the Senate "would be more rational if any interests common to them [the smaller states] and distinct from those of the other states would otherwise be exposed to peculiar danger," we see that Publius could hardly have regarded this equal representation as having violated the essential characteristic of republicanism he sets forth in Federalist 39 since no particular class or interest benefits from it (62:378).

Despite his reservations, Publius could see one potential advantage to a Senate so constituted: since legislation could not be passed "without the concurrence, first, of a majority of the people, and then a majority of states," an "additional impediment" against "improper actions of legislation" and "the facility and excess of law-making," the "diseases to which are governments are most liable," would result. For these reasons, he concludes that "it is not impossible that this part of the Constitution may be more convenient in practice than it appears to many in contemplation" (62:378). In saying this, Publius directs our attention to two functions of the Senate, both of which to some extent take us beyond concerns directly connected with separation of powers, but which he regarded as critical for orderly and decent government: one as an "additional impediment" in the lawmaking process, the other as a barrier to excessive "law-making."

From the viewpoint of modern republican critics the "impediment" function of the Senate has drawn the most fire. However, if we enter into Publius's framework of thought, a good deal of this fire seems to be misdirected. In the first place, Publius regards the Senate as a "salutary check on the government" because it "doubles the security to the people by requiring the concurrence of two distinct bodies in schemes of usurpation or perfidy, where the ambition or corruption of one would otherwise be sufficient." In this context, the Senate is not blocking popular majorities, rather, it is a check against "usurpation or perfidy" on the part of a majority of the House members, who "may forget their obligations to their constituents and prove unfaithful to their trust" (62:378–79).

A related function of the Senate, in Publius's view, directly involves "the propensity of all single and numerous assemblies to yield to the impulse of sudden and violent passions and to be seduced by factious leaders into intemperate and pernicious resolutions" (62:379). As we have had occasion to note, he regarded the House, lacking effective barriers to the union of impulse and opportunity to prevent the formation of factious majorities among its members, as akin to the popular assemblies of pure democracies. Thus, it hardly comes as a surprise that he would look upon a well-constituted Senate—one whose members are fewer and have longer tenure than those of the House—as the principal impediment to stem "intemperate and pernicious resolutions" that might originate in the House. This is a check, however, not upon popular majorities but upon the representatives, who, though fit characters, are nevertheless susceptible to the same passions that actuate the multitude.

But beyond this, Publius clearly believes that the Senate should play a role in checking the passions of popular majorities. After surveying the "circumstances which point out the necessity of a well-constructed Senate only as they relate to the representatives of the people," he writes:

> To a people as little blinded by prejudice or corrupted by flattery as those whom I address, I shall not scruple to add that such an institution may be sometimes necessary as a defense to the people against their own temporary errors and delusions. As the cool and deliberate sense of the community ought, in all governments, and actually will, in all free governments, ultimately prevail over the views of its rulers; so there are particular moments in public affairs when the people, stimulated by some irregular passion, or some illicit advantage, or misled by the artful misrepresentations of interested men, may call for measures which they themselves will afterward be the most ready to lament and condemn. In these critical moments, how salutary will be the interference of some temperate and respectable body of citizens, in order to check the misguided career and to suspend the blow mediated by the people against themselves, until reason, justice, and truth can regain their authority over the public mind? [63:384].

In answering this question he alludes to the "bitter anguish" which "the people of Athens [would] have often escaped if their government had contained so provident a safeguard against the tyranny of their own passions." As if by way of reminding us of the observations he makes in Federalist 9 concerning the relationship between liberty and republicanism, he writes that with such a safeguard "popular liberty" might have avoided "the indelible reproach of decreeing to the same citizens the hemlock on one day and statues on the next" (63:384).

Publius is mindful that this position would seem to contradict what he has said about controlling the effects of faction in Federalist 10. Immediately after this passage, he turns his attention to a logical question that arises in light of his extended republic theory: why is it necessary for the Senate to perform this function, if, as he contended in Federalist 10, the extended republic provides a remedy for the problem of factions? Has he not already told us, to use his own words, "that a people spread over an extensive region cannot, like the crowded inhabitants of a small district, be subject to the infection of violent passions or to the danger of combining in pursuit of unjust measures"? While he acknowledges the importance of this "distinction"—a distinction he has "endeavored in a former paper to show" as "one of the principal recommendations of a confederated republic"—he does not regard "this advantage . . . as superseding the use of auxiliary precautions." In this vein, he continues, the "extended situation" of the United States that protects the people against "those dangers incident to lesser republics" also results in "the inconveniency of [their] remaining for a longer time under the influence of those misrepresentations which the combined industry of interested men may succeed in distributing among them" (63:385).

What can be said of this function of the Senate with respect to the principle of majority rule? First, we should note that in light of what Publius writes in both Federalists 51 and 10, it seems most unlikely that the Senate would be called upon to perform this function very often because, after all, the members of the House would "seldom" find themselves forced to respond to factious majorities. In this sense, the "auxiliary precaution" is also quite secondary to those inherent in the extended republic. Its distinctly secondary nature becomes more evident when we look at what Publius conceives to be its purpose and potential effectiveness. At one level it is designed to provide a delay to give the people an opportunity to reconsider. We may say that it acts as a check on factious measures that upon further examination and reflection the people would themselves reject.

This, of course, represents a republican remedy to the problem of factions, the most interesting aspect of which is Publius's suggestion that majorities might restrain themselves after delay and deliberation—that they are capable of self-restraint after due reflection. This would mean that Publius believed that majorities caught up in the heat of passion, just like individuals in like circumstances, might cool off if given the opportunity, thereby avoiding precipitous behavior. More important, from a theoretical viewpoint, it also suggests that he believed that the people would, after due deliberation, exhibit sufficient virtue to back away from factious measures, even if this meant foregoing the realization of their immediate wants. This solution to the problem of majority factions, suffice it to note, is of a different order than that set forth in Federalist 10. And from the context in which Publius discusses it, it would seem to be particularly effective in curbing majority factions actuated by passion, as distinct from interest. As such we may look upon it as complementing the remedies presented in Federalist 10, it would check factions growing out of passions that may rapidly and spontaneously sweep the nation, relatively unaffected by the obstacles associated with extensiveness.

What we have said to this point would suggest that the efficacy of this auxiliary precaution would be greatest with respect to factious majorities that are hastily formed under circumstances that were not conducive to sober, second thoughts. But the question arises, what if, on the contrary, the position of the majority represents their deliberative will? And what if, moreover, after being rebuffed by the Senate, this majority gives the measure in question a hard second, third, or even fourth look and still decides it wants to press ahead? Under these conditions will the Senate still be able to function as an impediment?

The answer that Publius provides is a qualified "no." "Against the force of the immediate representatives of the people," he writes, "nothing will be able to maintain even the constitutional authority of the Senate, but such a display of enlightened policy, and attachment to the public good, as will divide with that branch of the legislature the affections and support of the entire body of the people themselves" (63:390). Just as he had suggested in Federalist 51 that stronger factions might "be gradually induced" to realize the benefit of a government that protects both the weak and strong with an even hand, so he believes the Senate might build up a reservoir of good will and respect that might serve to stay the hand of a factious majority. Interestingly enough, it is the majority itself that must come to realize the virtues of the Senate, which again suggests that Publius placed some faith in the capacity of the people to recognize enlightened behavior. But if the majority persists, if the stock of "affection and support" is not sufficient or deep enough to produce this forbearance, he is clear that it will get its way; the constitutional authority of the Senate is not, in his view, itself sufficient to block determined majorities.

This would lead us to believe, as we noted in our discussion of republicanism in the preceding chapter, that Publius felt the republican genius of the people renders it very difficult for officeholders, even those who are not directly accountable to the people, to resist majorities. Or, to put this somewhat differently, an intangible, but nevertheless powerful, moral force attaches to a position backed by a majority simply because it is the majority's position. And those who would resist it by exercising their constitutional prerogatives do so at the risk of incurring public condemnation and the loss of prestige and status. That he must have entertained some such view is evident when he writes that "the most *popular* branch of every government partaking of the republican genius, by being generally the favorite of the people, will be as generally a full match, if not an overmatch, for every other member of the government" (66:403).

While Publius seems to believe that the Senate might have some success in blocking majority factions, and this principally through delay that might bring the majority back to its senses, he apparently sees little danger in the Senate ever blocking nonfactious majorities. To this very point, he considers what would happen if a coalition of the smaller states in the Senate were to attempt to block "the just and constitutional views of the other branch" by refusing to go along with a measure to augment the size of the House with the end of depriving the larger states of increased representation. He points out that despite the "equal authority" of the two branches "on all legislative subjects," the majority of the House, "when supported by the more powerful States, and speaking the known and determined sense of a majority of the people," would have "no small advantage in a question depending on the comparative firmness of the two houses." And what is significant in light of what we have said immediately above is that "this advantage must be increased by the consciousness, felt by the same side, of being supported in its demands by right, by reason, and by the Constitution; and the consciousness, on the opposite side, of contending against the force of all these solemn considerations" (58:357–58). But if this does not prove to be sufficient, Publius points to the power of the purse, which, he contends, "may, in fact, be regarded as the most complete and effectual weapon with which any constitution can arm the immediate representatives of the people, for obtaining a redress of every grievance, and for carrying into effect every just and salutary measure" (59:359).

Writing in a more general vein to the question of which branch is most likely to yield when there is a serious confrontation between them, Publius sees the House with a distinct advantage and this principally due to the character of the Senate: senators, being fewer in number and holding more prominent offices in the system, will have stronger individual interests in the proper operations of government. Moreover, because they "represent the dignity of their country in the eyes of other nations," they "will be particularly sensible to every prospect of public danger, or of a dishonorable stagnation in public affairs" (58:359). The firmness of the Senate or the president in resisting the House, in his judgment, can never be any stronger than the degree to which its foundations rest upon "constitutional and patriotic principles" (58:360).

In sum, we may say that Publius identifies three relatively distinct situations in which the Senate might act to block factious measures. And from what he does indicate the likelihood of its success in this role will depend upon the circumstances surrounding these measures. First, factious measures that originate in the House but lack popular support would be the easiest for the Senate to block. In this case, the Senate would not have to contend with the pressures of popular majorities, and the weight of the argument would, so to speak, be on their side. Second, the Senate would also have some success with factious measures that, though backed by majorities, have been hastily concocted or that, for one reason or another, have been insufficiently examined. By delaying the passage of the measure—as well, we might add, by pointing up the deficiencies—Publius holds out the prospect that the people might come to their senses. And third, the prospects of the Senate blocking factious measures supported by persistent and, we must assume, deliberative majorities are far slimmer and depend not only upon the merits of the case, but also upon the respect and goodwill the Senate has cultivated among the people.

As we have noted above, Publius also viewed the Senate as a barrier to excessive lawmaking. Indeed, it is probable that he regarded this function as the most important performed by the Senate because it played such a key role in avoiding "the mischievous effects of a mutable government." In this respect, he looked upon the Senate as a stabilizing force that could counteract the profusion of laws and "change of measures" that might well arise from the "rapid succession of new members" in the House (62:380).

Now these "mischievous effects" could, on Publius's showing, be "calamitous." He is outspoken regarding the consequences of "mutable policy." In the first place, he writes, "it poisons the blessings of liberty itself." The laws may be "so voluminous that they cannot be read" or they may be "so incoherent that they cannot be understood." More, they may "be repealed or revised before they are promulgated, or undergo such incessant changes that no man, who knows what the law is today, can guess what it will be tomorrow." And, in this connection, he asks rhetorically: "Law is defined to be a rule of action; but how can that be a rule, which is little known, and less fixed?" Beyond this, mutability itself accords an "unreasonable advantage . . . to the sagacious, the enterprising, and the moneyed few over the industrious and uninformed mass of the people." Those who keep track of all the changes in the law, noting how they affect the varying interests in the society, reap "a harvest, reared not by themselves, but by the toils and cares of the great body of their fellow citizens." Where mutability of policy prevails, Publius declares, there is some truth to the proposition that the "laws are made for the *few*, not for the *many*" (62:381).[16]

But the mischiefs of "unstable government" would not stop with merely enriching the sagacious few: mutable laws serve to curtail long-term commitments by the honest and enterprising individuals who, not without justification, fear that their "plans may be rendered unlawful before they can be executed." "In a word," he remarks, "no great improvement or laudable enterprise can go forward which requires the auspices of a steady system of national policy." However, the "most deplorable effect of all," in his estimation, is the "diminution of attachment and reverence which steals into the hearts of the people towards a political system which betrays so many marks of infirmity, and disappoints so many of their flattering hopes." Echoing the theme he touched upon in Federalist 49, he adds, governments, like individuals, will not "long be respected without being respectable" and to be "truly respectable" requires "a certain portion of order and stability" (62:381–82).

Publius's concern over "unstable government" and "mutable policy" ran very deep. To the critics of the proposed system who contended that the presidential veto power could be used to prevent "good laws" as well as "bad," Publius responds: "this objection will have little weight with those who can properly estimate the mischiefs of that inconstancy and mutability in the laws, which form the greatest blemish in the character and genius of our governments." A conservative strain of his thought emerges at this point when he writes that institutions that "restrain the excess of lawmaking" and preserve the status quo are "much more likely to do good than harm." The harm resulting from the defeat of a "few good laws," he continues, will be "amply compensated by the advantages of preventing a number of bad ones" (73:444).

As we might expect from this, Publius perceived the president playing a role vis-à-vis Congress analogous to that which the Senate plays vis-à-vis the House with respect to excessive lawmaking and factious measures. For instance, he conceives that a "secondary" function of the president's veto power is to increase "the chances in favor of the community against the passing of bad laws, through haste, inadvertence, or design." To this point he adds: "The oftener [a] measure is brought under examination, the greater the diversity in the situations of those who are to examine it, the less must be the danger of those errors which flow from want of due deliberation, or of those missteps which proceed from the contagion of some common passion or interest. It is far less probable that culpable views of any kind should infect all the parts of government at the same moment and in relation to the same object than that they should by turns govern and mislead every one of them." But the use of the veto in this context is not directed against popular majorities. Rather, it constitutes a check against factious or misguided majorities in the legislative branch. As he put it, the veto is "a salutary check upon the legislative body, calculated to guard the community against the effect of faction, precipitancy, or of any impulse unfriendly to the public good, which may happen to influence a majority of that body" (73:443). Even if one thinks that the executive is bound to comply with the "inclinations of the people," he writes, "we can with no propriety contend for a like complaisance to the humors of the legislature. The latter may sometimes stand in opposition to the former, and at other times the people may be entirely neutral. In either supposition, it is certainly desirable that the executive should be in a situation to dare to act his own opinion with vigor and decision" (71:433).

This is not to say he did not think that the veto should be used to thwart factious measures backed by popular majorities. But he fashions his argument here along lines he used with regard to the Senate acting in this capacity. "The republican principle," he readily grants, "demands that the deliberate sense of the community should govern the conduct of those to whom they intrust the management of their affairs." But the operative words for Publius are "deliberate sense," so that the executive is not bound to bend "to every sudden breeze of passion, or to every transient impulse which the people may receive from the arts of men, who flatter their prejudices to betray their interests." On the contrary:

> When occasions present themselves in which the interests of the people are at variance with their inclinations, it is the duty of the persons whom they have appointed to be the guardians of those interests to withstand the temporary delusion, in order to give them time and opportunity for more cool and sedate reflection. Instances might be cited in which a conduct of this kind has saved the people from very fatal consequences of their own mistakes, and has procured lasting monuments of their gratitude to the men who had courage and magnanimity enough to serve them at the peril of their displeasure [71:432].

Again we must note, as Publius puts the matter, this use of the veto does not constitute a violation of the republican principle. Rather, it provides the majority an opportunity to regain its reason.

As we have remarked, impeding factions, whatever their source, is a distinctly "secondary" function of the veto. Consonant with his general theory outlined in Federalist 51, Publius points out that the "primary inducement to conferring the power in question [the qualified veto] is to enable him [the president] to defend himself." The need for such a defense, as he sees it, is undeniable: in "purely republican" regimes, he writes, "the tendency of the legislature" to draw all powers on to itself is "almost irresistible." In this respect, he observes that the representatives "sometimes fancy that they are the people themselves" and take umbrage "at the least sign of opposition from any other quarter." Thus, he continues, "they often appear disposed to assert an imperious control over the other departments; and as they commonly have the people on their side, they always act with such momentum as to make it very difficult for the other members of the government to maintain the balance of the Constitution" (71:433). And, remarking once again on the inefficacy of paper barricades to keep the departments in their proper orbit, he maintains that without the qualified veto the president "might gradually be stripped of his authorities by successive resolution or annihilated by a single vote" (73:442).

The fact that the executive would be disinclined to engage in a "trial of strength" with the legislature constitutes for Publius "satisfactory security" that the veto "would generally be employed with great caution; and that there would oftener be room for a charge of timidity than of rashness in the exercise of it." On this matter, he alludes to the reluctance of the King of Great Britain "to put a negative upon the joint resolutions of the two houses of Parliament," a reluctance he feels is rooted in the fear of "risking the displeasure of the nation by an opposition to the sense of the legislative body." And, he asks rhetorically, "if a magistrate so powerful and so well fortified as a British monarch would have scruples about the exercise of the power under consideration, how much greater caution may be reasonably expected in a President . . . clothed for the short period of four years with the executive authority of a government wholly and purely republican?" (73:444). These observations, of course, bring us back around to the notion that seems to underpin Publius's thinking about the republican character of the proposed Constitution, a legitimacy attaches to the will of the majority that renders it irresistible for any length of time. What the president and the Senate can do with their constitutional powers is to help insure that the will of the majority is a deliberative one, and that the people are fully apprised of the possible consequences of their decision.

Despite the reluctance of the executive to challenge the legislature, Publius can see two types of situations where a president possessing only a "common share of firmness" (or "tolerable firmness") would exercise the veto. The first would be "in the case for which it is chiefly designed, that of an immediate attack on the constitutional rights of the executive." In such instances, he believes—again quite in keeping with his general theory—that the president's "fortitude would be stimulated by his immediate interest in the power of his office." The second situation he envisions would be one "in which the public good was evidently and palpably sacrificed." With regard to measures of such a description, Publius feels the executive would be motivated "by the probability of the sanction of his constituents, who, though they would naturally incline to the legislative body in a doubtful case, would hardly suffer the partiality to delude them in a very plain case" (73:445). In this latter case, the executive, far from thwarting a majority, would be acting with its acquiesence.

Additionally, Publius can see how the mere provision for the veto might serve to restrain Congress from "unjustifiable pursuits." In his words, its members "will often be restrained by the bare apprehension of opposition from doing what they would with eagerness rush into if no such external impediments were to be feared" (73:446).

The role and significance of an independent executive is scarcely confined to the judicious use of the veto power. Publius writes that "energy in the executive is a leading character in the definition of good government" (70:423). And when we look closely at leading features of his "good government," leaving to one side those connected with the veto power, we find that they are intimately related to the elements of the rule of law—uniformity, equality, and predictability. Among the chief benefits of unity in the executive, in his view, is a coherency and steadiness in the execution of policies that probably would not be the case with multiple executives. "Duration," still another element of good government, he regards as necessary "to the stability of the system of administration" (70:436). In this connection, the arguments he presents for the indefinite reeligibility of a president are all, some more directly than others, related to preserving and advancing the rule of law. An "avaricious" president excluded from another term, for instance, might "make the best use of his opportunities while they lasted, and might not scruple to have recourse to the most corrupt expedient to make the harvest as abundant as it was transitory" (72:437). A more direct consequence would be the "variable policy" and "mutability of measures" that would needlessly arise by "*necessitating* a change of men." To this point he writes: "It is not generally to be expected that men will vary and measures remain uniform. The contrary is the usual course of things" (72:439). On still another level, he even sees Senate approval "in the business of appointments" to be another factor that lends "to the stability of the administration." "A steady administration," he writes, is promoted by Senate confirmation because of "the greater permanency of its own composition" that "will in all probability" render it "less subject to inconstancy than any other member of the government" (77:459).

Constitutional Republicanism

What we see from Publius's discussion is that, save for equality of state representation in the Senate (which was, as he points out, an unavoidable compromise), every deviation from the principles of classical republicanism is designed to maintain the necessary partition of powers, and not—as his critics are wont to contend—to entrench minorities. In fact, one of the major purposes of separation of powers is to keep the republican processes open by preventing a select minority, the rulers, from oppressing the ruled.

Nor will it do to suggest, as certain modern critics have, that Publius was disingenuous—that he sought to camouflage his real purpose. Not only is he straightforward in contending that the representatives of the people are the major potential problem in maintaining the separation, he is consistent throughout regarding the need for checks on these representatives. In other words, his approach follows logically from his articulated concerns—eminently reasonable and widely shared concerns with both theoretical and empirical foundations. Such consistency certainly is not what we should expect if his purposes were other than those he sets forth. Indeed, if Publius were activated by antirepublican motives, such as those suggested by his critics, we must conclude that it is a foolish consistency: not only are its theoretical foundations far too elaborate for this purpose, it is illsuited for the end of entrenching identifiable minorities of status and wealth. What is equally revealing, as we have already intimated, is that he is forthright in discussing issues that his critics acknowledge are central to the relationship between republicanism and separation of powers. Aside from justifying the need for checks on the legislature, perhaps the most significant of these is his recognition of the effect the partition of powers will have on majority rule. But clearly these and other matters—e.g., whether the Senate would be able to transform itself into a "tyrannical aristocracy" —would be among those he would want to avoid bringing to the attention of his readers, if, indeed, his purpose was to beguile them.

More important, what does stand out from our analysis of separation of powers and republicanism is Publius's concern to provide institutions and procedures that will prevent the "perpetual vibration between tyranny and anarchy" that has plagued republics in the past. We could see from Federalist 9 that the principle of separation of powers would play an important role in rendering republicanism both defensible and respectable among the "enlightened friends of liberty." Certain of its key elements such as "legislative balances and checks" were among the new or improved principles of "political science." But only later, when he discusses expedients for maintaining the separation and the relationship of the branches to one an-

other, can we see how he envisioned the separation of powers operating to secure these ends.

In this context, the real challenge facing Publius was to show how
constitutionalism—understood in terms of the values to be served
by separation of powers such as freedom from governmental oppression, stability, liberty, a steady and impartial execution of the laws
with regard to both ruler and ruled—could be combined with his
conception of republicanism, which, off at the end, involved rule by
deliberative majorities. And it is in this endeavor that he shows how
separation of powers can be used to complement the extended republic solution to the problem of majority factions—how, in other
words, separation might serve to improve the quality of republicanism by forcing further deliberation. In this synthesis, he also presents
us with implicit constitutional moralities of sorts: the Senate should
act to inspire the confidence and respect of the people so that it
can effectively dissuade factious majorities; the House, for its part,
would do well to show restraint and forbearance toward the other
branches; and, among others, presidents might do well to show a
boldness in using their veto power to protect the interests of the
people from legislative designs.

But this complementary function of separation of powers is, we
would do well to remember, a bonus of sorts; even if the separation
of powers did not perform these functions, it would still be necessary,
in Publius's estimation, to provide the constitutionalism without which
republican government would not long survive.

NOTES

1. This position was first set forth by Elmer Schattschneider in the following
form: "Madison's defense of federalism [his presentation in Federalist 10 of the
extended republic theory] annihilates his defense of the separation of powers.
If the multiplicity of interests in a large republic makes tyrannical majorities
impossible, the principal theoretical prop of the separation of powers has been
demolished." *Party Government*, p. 9. James McGregor Burns puts this same
concern in different terms: "If, as Madison said, the first great protection against
naked majority rule was the broader diversity of interests in a large republic
and hence the greater difficulty of concerting their 'plans of oppression,' why
was not this enough? . . . Why was it necessary to have what Madison called
'auxiliary precautions' of checks and balances built right into the frame of
government?" *Deadlock*, p. 21. The puzzlement for both Burns and Schattschneider results from their failure to draw the distinction between the problems

of factionalism and tyranny. On this issue see George W. Carey, "Separation of Powers and the Madisonian Model: A Reply to the Critics," *American Political Science Review* 72 (Mar., 1978).

2. To this point Publius writes in Federalist 84 that "men of sense of all parties now with few exceptions agree" that "a single body" is "an unsafe depositary of such ample authorities" (518).

3. See, for example, Robert Dahl's *Preface*, pp. 22–29. Dahl holds that Madison's definition of tyranny is operationally meaningless. For a rejoinder to Dahl see Garry Wills, *Explaining*, chap. 12. See also the text below.

4. We use here a classification of separation of powers according to purposes set forth by William B. Gwyn, *The Meaning of Separation of Powers* (New Orleans: Tulane University Press, 1965). On Gwyn's showing, there have been various versions of the separation of powers doctrine advanced. For example, some theorists have advanced an "accountability" version on grounds that separation enables the people to determine more readily who is responsible for official actions. Others have stressed "efficiency" that is presumably the product of a division of governmental functions. Still others have set forth a "balancing" version, wherein the end is to insure an equilibrium between the branches by insuring one branch cannot operate beyond its prescribed authority. The "rule of law" construct is to provide for liberty under law. As Gwyn points out, some theorists actually combine one or more of these versions in their theories. For another excellent work that explores this doctrine in detail see M. J. C. Vile, *Constitutionalism and the Separation of Powers* (Oxford: Clarendon Press, 1967). For an interesting account of how this rule-of-law conception developed from medieval English roots see Roscoe Pound, *The Development of Constitutional Guarantees of Liberty* (New Haven: Yale University Press, 1957).

5. We dub this a "glass house" line of argument because he seems to be characterizing his critics as people in glass houses who do throw stones. He employs this technique in a wide variety of concerns: the bill of rights, the terms of office, the size of the representative assembly, and, among others, the separation of powers. Such critics must have riled Publius, for he writes in Federalist 85: "a man must have slender pretensions to consistency who can rail at the latter [the proposed Constitution] for imperfections which he finds no difficulty in excusing in the former [the New York Constitution]. Nor indeed can there be a better proof of the insincerity and affectation of some of the zealous adversaries of the plan of the convention among us who profess to be the devoted admirers of the government under which they live than the fury with which they have attacked that plan, for matters in regard to which our own constitution is equally or perhaps more vulnerable" (521).

6. The crucial passage relating to the status of the branches to settle such disputes is a bit ambiguous. It reads: "The several departments being perfectly co-ordinate by the terms of their common commission, neither of them, it is evident, can pretend to an exclusive or superior right of settling the boundaries between their respective powers" (314). Why he uses the word *neither* rather than, say, *none* is an interesting question. However, the logic of his position would seem to hold that none of the branches, including the courts, can have

the final say in controversies of this nature. In any event, that he does not designate the courts for this function in at least certain circumstances is noteworthy.

7. In this vein, commenting on how jealousies and passions have prevented reform of the Union of Utrecht to eliminate its "fatal evils," he calls upon his "fellow-citizens" to "pause . . . for one moment over this melancholy and monitory lesson of history; and with the tear that drops from the calamities brought on mankind by their adverse opinions and selfish pasison, let our gratitude mingle an ejaculation to Heaven for the propitious concord which has distinguished the consultations for our political happiness" (20:137).

8. As he puts this in Federalist 71: "The same rule which teaches the propriety of a partition between the various branches of power teaches likewise that this partition ought to be so contrived as to render the one independent of the other. To what purposes separate the executive or the judiciary from the legislature, if both the executive and the judiciary are so connected as to be at the absolute devotion of the legislature? Such a separation must be merely nominal, and incapable of producing the ends for which it was established" (433).

9. In discussing this aspect of the "pure doctrine," M. J. C. Vile writes: "It is perfectly possible to envisage distinct agencies of government exercising separate functions, but manned by the same persons; the pure doctrine here argues, however, that separation of agencies and functions is not enough. These functions must be separated in distinct hands if freedom is to be assured." *Constitutionalism*, p. 17.

10. Publius was quite aware that there would be a reciprocal influence between the constitutional provision relating to powers, terms of office, qualifications, and the behavior of the officeholders. These provisions would, he felt, serve, at least by indirection, to elicit the kind of behavior appropriate for the ends of the proposed system. Notable in this regard are his arguments for the indefinite reeligibility of the president.

For instance, he maintains, it is best that individuals be "permitted to entertain a hope of *obtaining*, by *meriting*, a continuance" in office. "This position," he argues, "will not be disputed so long as it is admitted that the desire of reward is one of the strongest incentives of human conduct; or that the best security for the fidelity to mankind is to make their interests coincide with their duty." And, he points out, "the love of fame, the ruling passion of the noblest minds," will not spur an individual to "undertake extensive and arduous enterprises for the public benefit, requiring considerable time to mature and perfect" unless there is "the prospect of being allowed to finish what he had begun" (72:437).

11. In his "*The Federalist* and Human Nature," James P. Scanlan notes the propensity of analysts to equivocate regarding Publius's view of human nature. However, he goes on the note that there is a well-developed theory of human nature or, more accurately, of human motivation to be found in *The Federalist*. Scanlan's analysis reveals in part that Publius believed "on the whole the stronger forces which affect human action are antagonistic passions and immediate and personal interests; the weaker are amicable passions, true and common interests, and motives of reason and virture . . . In general . . . men [will follow] the lines

of their immediate and personal interests" (p. 669). And, as Scanlan points out, one of the "problems which may be considered absolutely fundamental in *The Federalist*'s analysis" is that "the immediate and personal interests of the rulers may be opposed to the interests of the ruled, and may motivate the rulers to use their power for oppression" (p. 673).

12. Burn's *Deadlock of Democracy* is titled to reflect this position. However, of all the arguments concerning the intentions surrounding the separation of powers, this is by far the weakest. The whole point of the Philadelphia Convention was to establish a more powerful and energetic government. Throughout *The Federalist* Publius argues the need for a government *at least* as strong as that the proposed Constitution would establish.

13. On this matter, James Allen Smith seems to have set the example for those who followed. As Strout remarks, "The system of 'checks and balances' was . . . not designed, as Smith claimed, to protect the minority against popular majorities *among the ruled*; it was meant instead to protect citizens from the possible tyranny of their officials. Smith (like his conservative enemies) stood Madison's argurment on its head." *Spirit*, pp. xlvii–xlviii.

14. As odd as such a position my seem to modern critics of the system, James Wilson, an avowed majoritarian, believed that the separation of powers would perfect majority rule while, at the same time, securing liberty and the rule of law. See Ralph Rossum, "James Wilson and the 'Pyramid of Government': The Federal Republic," *Political Science Reviewer* 6 (Fall, 1976) and George W. Carey, "James Wilson's Political Thought," *Political Science Reviewer* 17 (Fall, 1987).

15. In Federalist 37 he couches similar observations in a more detached manner: "To the difficulties [facing the Convention] already mentioned may be added the interfering pretensions of the larger and smaller states. We cannot err in supposing that the former would contend for a participation in the government, fully proportioned to their superior wealth and importance; and that the latter would not be less tenacious of the equality at present enjoyed by them. We may well suppose that neither side would entirely yield to the other, and consequently that the struggle could be terminated by compromise. It is extremely probable, also, that after the ratio of representation had been adjusted, this very compromise must have produced a fresh struggle between the same parties to give such a turn to the organization of the government and to the distribution of its powers as would increase the importance of the branches, in forming which they had respectively obtained the greatest share of influence. These are features in the Constitution which warrant each of these suppositions; and as far as either of them is well founded, it shows that the convention must have been compelled to sacrifice theoretical propriety to the force of extraneous considerations" (229–30).

16. "Bill of attainder, *ex post facto* laws, and laws impairing the obligation of contracts" he regards as "contrary to the first principles of the social compact and to every principle of sound legislation." The reasons he advances for this all relate to his weariness with "the fluctuating policy which has directed the

public councils." "The sober people of America," he writes, have witnessed "with regret and indignation that sudden changes and legislative interference" have benefited "enterprising and influential speculators" at the expense of "the more industrious and less informed part of the community" (44:282).

3
·
Federalism

The proposed Constitution . . . even when tested
by the rules laid down by its antagonists, is, in
strictness, neither a national nor a federal Constitution, but a composition of both [39:246].

*T*HE ISSUE OF state-national re-
lations, in so many ways central to the controversies both past and
present concerning the nature and purposes of the Constitution,
posed difficulties for Publius that went well beyond those associated
with either his extended republic theory or separation of powers.
Indeed, these difficulties are manifest in his less than systematic
treatment of these relationships, his blurring of certain important
points, and his failure to answer certain critical questions that logically arise from his presentation. Largely for these reasons, we are
forced to piece together Publius's views toward state-national relations—that is, insofar as possible to superimpose a coherence on the
varied aspects of these relationships. This is no easy task because it
involves relating disparate aspects of his thinking about the relative
roles of the national and state governments under the proposed
Constitution.

These difficulties, it should be remarked, are not entirely of Publius's doing. The proposed Constitution did call for a significantly
altered relationship between the states and the national government—this, after all, was the main purpose of the Philadelphia Convention—but this new relationship was without precedent or parallel.
So much is candidly acknowledged in Federalist 37 where Publius,
in reflecting on difficulties confronting the Convention in its deliberations, remarks on the "novelty of the undertaking." What is known,
he writes, is that "the existing confederation is founded on principles

96

which are fallacious" and that "other confederacies" which might serve as "precedents" for establishing a new order "have been vitiated by the same erroneous principles." Thus, he continues, the experience of other confederacies "can . . . furnish no other light than that of beacons, which give warning of the course to be shunned, without pointing out that which ought to be pursued" (37:226).

Publius's problems can be put another way. It is not uncommon to hear our system described in terms of a cross between the unitary form (wherein the central government reigns supreme over the constituent units) and the confederal form (wherein the constituent units are sovereign). Over the decades this cross has come to be known as "federalism," which is generally considered to be—along with unitary and confederal—a third and distinct principle for the distribution of powers. For Publius, however, the word federal was synonymous with confederal and referred to systems which were "a *Confederacy* of sovereign states" (39:243).[1] Thus, in the very first sentence of *The Federalist* Publius can speak of the Articles of Confederation as the "subsisting federal government," that is, a government organized on confederal principles (1:33). Publius knew of the unitary form in terms of a "national" government characterized by a "*consolidation* of States." The system called for by the proposed constitution he called a "compound republic" because, as he viewed it, it was "a composition of both" the federal or confederal and national principles. What we come to see, then, leaving aside these semantical differences, is that Publius was obliged to explain and defend a new, hybrid principle for the distribution of sovereignty.[2] Given this situation, not only can we readily understand a major source of Publius's difficulties in dealing with the matter of state-national relations, we can also see why our history has been marked by complex and intense controversies over the proper division of sovereignty between these two jurisdictions.

We can also see a tension in Publius's discussion of state-national relations under the forms of the proposed Constitution. While stressing the imperative need for a stronger and more energetic government, Publius sought to downplay the extent to which the proposed system departed from federal or confederate principles. The most likely reason for this reluctance is that he wanted to blunt one of the more effective arguments against the new Constitution, namely, that it provided for a national, unitary, or consolidated system. But whatever the reason, the upshot of the tension is a kind of conflict avoidance: he is evasive, perfunctory, and even contradictory in answering certain sensitive questions, particularly those relating to the settlement of the disputes that were bound to arise between the state and national governments concerning their respective spheres of authority. For this reason the reader is left to fill in some very important gaps.

Publius's difficulties can best be seen by first examining his conception of the scope and nature of the powers of the proposed national government and then turning to the logical problems that arise from it.

The Confederate Republic

Publius's initial discussion of the "confederate republic" toward the end of Federalist 9 reflects his concern to answer charges that the confederal principle has been abandoned under the forms of the proposed system. After setting forth the advantages of this confederate republic, he turns his attention to a matter about which, judging from what he says in later papers, he had very strong feelings. He remarks that a "distinction, more subtle than accurate, has been raised between a *confederacy* and a *consolidation* of the States": that in confederations, as opposed to consolidated systems, the central government should only operate upon the "members in their collective capacities," not upon individual citizens; that it should have no control over "any object of internal administration"; and that the member states should have "equality of suffrage" in the common councils. But these distinctions, he argues, "are in the main arbitrary . . . supported" by neither "principle nor precedent." Indeed, by way of indicting the Articles, he goes on to say that where these arbitrary principles have been applied, they have been "the cause of incurable disorder and imbecility in government" (9:75–76).

Publius then proceeds to give an extremely broad definition of confederate republic, which he holds to be "simply . . . 'an assemblage of societies,' or an association of two or more states into one state." Moreover, he holds that "the extent, modifications, and objects of the federal authority are mere matters of discretion. So long as the separate organization of the members be not abolished; so long as it exists, by a constitutional necessity, for local purposes, though it should be in perfect subordination to the general authority of the union, it would still be, in fact and in theory, an association of states, or a confederacy" (9:76).

This definition is, we see at once, sweeping enough to embrace the system advanced in the proposed Constitution. And, as if to answer critics who contend that the system is not federal enough, Publius notes that under the proposed plan, the states, far from being abolished, are "constituent parts of the national sovereignty" with "direct representation in the Senate." On top of this, he maintains, the plan leaves the states "certain exclusive and very important portions of sovereign power." In other words, he has made it appear that the proposed system is well above the minimums required for a confederate republic, and that it conforms more closely than required with the allegedly distinctive characteristics of a confederacy which he has just dismissed as arbitrary. However, a second look at his argument shows that what he has in fact demonstrated is that the proposed government does not conform exactly with the national or unitary model. This is to say, his definition of confederate republic conforms with the definition of a unitary or national system save for the provision that subordinate units should exist "by a constitutional necessity." We see in his definition, for instance, that the component units, even in carrying out their "local" functions, "should be in perfect subordination" to the central government (9:76). In sum, through a selective use of Montesquieu, Publius has managed to turn the concept of confederacy on its head to embrace the unitary features of the proposed Constitution.

Publius's conception of the confederate republic foretells his general approach to the issues surrounding state-national relations: he is almost exclusively concerned in staking out and justifying far-ranging and broad authority for the national government along with the means necessary for the fulfillment of the duties and ends entrusted to it. Perhaps his basic concern in this respect, as we might expect from his discussion of the confederate republic, is the need for the national government to operate directly upon individuals, not upon the states in their corporate capacity. "The great and radical vice" of the Articles, he believes, consists in "the principle of LEGISLATION for the STATES or GOVERNMENTS, in their CORPORATE or COLLECTIVE CAPACITIES, . . . as contradistinguished from the INDIVIDUALS of whom they consist" (15:108). Under this principle, he remarks, uniform execution of the laws is hardly to be expected: the "love of power" is such that we cannot "expect that the persons intrusted with the administration of the affairs of the particular members of a confederacy will at all times be ready with perfect good humor and an unbiased regard to the public weal to execute the resolutions or decrees of the general authority. The reverse of this results from the constitution of man." Indeed, he argues, that national laws that require the "intervention of the particular administrations" for their execution are not likely to be executed at all because "the rulers of the respective members"—ignorant of "national circumstances and the reasons of state"—"will undertake to judge of the propriety of the measures themselves" on the basis of "immediate interests or aims" or "momentary convenience or inconveniences" (15:111). As this process would take place in the assemblies of every member state, "deliberating at a distance from each other, at different times and under different impressions," we can readily see why Publius despaired that a universal execution of the laws was possible under any such arrangement (15:112).

But his concern went beyond this. At the end of Federalist 20, the conclusion of a three essay survey of the defects of prior confederacies, he observes: "Experience is the oracle of truth; and where its responses are unequivocal, they ought to be conclusive and sacred. The important truth, which it unequivocally pronounces in the present case, is that a sovereignty over sovereigns, a government over governments, a legislation for communities, as contradistinguished from individuals, as it is a solecism in theory, so in practice it is subversive of the order and ends of civil polity, by substituting *violence* in place of the mild and *salutary* coercion of the *magistracy*" (20:138). As he remarks in Federalist 16, the only way to avoid the anarchy or civil war that these conditions inevitably produce is for the national government to operate directly upon individuals with "all the means" and "a right to resort to all the methods, of executing the powers with which it is intrusted, that are possessed and exercised by the government of the particular States" (16:116).

Moreover, and fully consonant with his conception of the confederate republic, Publius is equally adamant in insisting that the national government must possess the "requisite powers" for the objectives of the union. At various points in *The Federalist* he sets forth these objectives, but his formulation in Federalist 23 is the most succinct and comprehensive: "The principal purposes to be answered by union are these—the common defense of the members; the preservation of the public peace, as well against internal convulsions as external attacks; the regulation of commerce with other nations and between the States; the superintendence of our intercourse, political and commercial, with foreign countries" (153).[3] While these ends clearly relate to those traditionally associated with confederacies, Publius goes to great lengths to show that they require extensive means for their realization. Notable in this regard is the brace of essays (41–44) wherein he inquires into "whether any part of the powers transferred to the general government be unnecessary or improper?" (41:255). In answering this question, he has little difficulty in showing how the varied delegated powers serve as means clearly related to the objectives of union.

The most important part of Publius's exposition on this matter, however, involves his discussion of the "necessary and proper" clause because he is keenly aware that without the "substance of this power, the whole Constitution would be a dead letter." And again, consonant with his conception of the confederate republic, it seems evident that he wanted this clause to be interpreted broadly or liberally. We see this in his explanation of why the Framers did not follow the strict and narrow approach to the question of implied powers, the approach embodied in the Articles which forbade the Congress from exercising any power not "expressly" delegated. Such a constrictive approach, he contends, simply would not do because the new government, with powers "more extensive" than the government under the Articles, would "find itself still more distressed with the alternative of betraying the public interests by doing nothing, or of violating the Constitution by exercising powers indispensably necessary and proper, but, at the same time, not *expressly* granted" (44:284). In this context, the word *indispensably* is revealing because it suggests that he did not look upon the word *necessary*, taken by itself, as embodying the notion of indispensability—a view which John Marshall shared and later relied heavily upon in *McCulloch* v. *Maryland* to give a broad or liberal interpretation to the "necessary and proper" clause.

There are other evidences that he sought a broad interpretation. In setting forth the futility of a "positive enumeration of the powers necessary and proper," he stresses the need for flexibility: not only must the means accommodate "to all the possible changes which futurity may produce"[4] and to "every new application" of a delegated power, they must also "be properly varied whilst the object remains the same." This view would suggest that he could perceive various means to the same end, not simply those that could pass the indispensability test. But we need not speculate about his belief that the "particular powers" necessary for the exercise of a "general powers" do not derive from an explicit grant of authority. In the absence of any constitutional provision "on this head," he writes, these powers "would have resulted to the government by unavoidable implication." This position he readily adduces from a more fundamental proposition: "No axiom is more clearly established in law, or in reason, than that wherever the end is required, the means are authorized; wherever a general power to do a thing is given, every particular power necessary for doing it is included" (44:284–85).

Finally, in this connection, we should note that he offers up no means, criteria, standards, or principles that can be employed to determine whether the national government has exceeded its authority in the use of its implied powers. Put otherwise, he offers us no morality in this regard, a fact which would lead us to believe that he did not want to lend any support for a constrictive view of the extent of these powers. Moreover, on this score, it seems obvious that if he was concerned to limit implied powers in any significant way, the entire thrust of his commentary would have been far different from what it is, one concerned with the need for and nature of restrictions on the "particular powers." This view of Publius's stance is further supported by the fact that, as we shall see, he regards the people as the ultimate judges of whether the national government has overstepped its bounds, a solution most inappropriate if he believed the "necessary and proper" clause was meant to convey the notion of indispensability.

Still another aspect of Publius's thought, not entirely unrelated to the foregoing and quite in keeping with the spirit of his confederate republic as well, is his insistence that the national government should have the full power to achieve its objectives. In his words, "not to confer . . . a degree of power commensurate to the end would be to violate the most obvious rules of prudence and propriety, and improvidently to trust the great interests of the nation to hands which are disabled from managing them with vigor and success" (23:155). Or, at another point, "a government ought to contain in itself every power requisite to the full accomplishment of the objects committed to its care, and to the complete execution of the trusts for which it is responsible, free from every other control but a regard to the public good and the sense of the people" (31:194). And in discussing the power of taxation, he goes even further. Here he writes: "Of the same nature [as the "maxims of geometry"] are these other maxims in ethics and politics, that there cannot be an effect without a cause; that the means ought to be proportioned to the end; that every power ought to be commensurate with its object; that there ought to be no limitation of a power destined to effect a purpose which is itself incapable of limitations" (31:193).[5]

It is the last of these maxims concerning limitations on power that Publius takes great care to emphasize in his discussions of the national defense. For instance, he notes that "to raise armies; to build and equip fleets; to prescribe rules for the government of both; to direct their operations; to provide for their support" are all essential powers for the national defense. As such, he emphasizes, "these powers ought to exist without limitation, *because it is impossible to foresee or to define the extent and variety of national exigencies, and the correspondent extent and variety of the means which may be necessary to satisfy them*" (23:153). In Federalist 41, he wonders "with what color of propriety could the force necessary for defense be limited by those who cannot limit the force of offense?" And he answers that only if the "Constitution could chain the ambition or set bounds to the exertions of all other nations," would it be sensible to limit "the discretion of its own government and set bounds to the exertions for its own safety." In sum, as he puts it, "the means of security can only be regulated by the means and danger of attack" (257).

Nor is this all. He views any attempt to limit the means of defense as not only "vain" because it runs counter to the "impulse of self-preservation" but also, and what is worse, as implanting "in the Constitution itself necessary usurpation of power, every precedent of which is a germ of unnecessary and multiplied repetitions" (41:257). He makes the same point in a more general way toward the end of Federalist 25: "Wise politicians will be cautious about fettering the government with restrictions that cannot be observed" because every "breach" of these restrictions, though "dictated by necessity," weakens "that sacred reverence which ought to be maintained in the breast of rulers towards the constitution of a country" and constitutes "a precedent for other breaches where the same plea of necessity does not exist at all, or is less urgent and palpable" (167).

Finally, by way of assuring that the national government can stand on its feet, Publius sees a compelling need to anchor it on the firmest possible foundations. The government under the Articles of Confederation, he notes, "resting on no better foundation than the consent of the several legislatures . . . has been exposed to frequent and intricate questions concerning the validity of its powers, and has in some instances given birth to the enormous doctrine of the right of legislative repeal." Even so "gross a heresy . . . that a *party* to a *compact* has a right to revoke that *compact*," he writes, has "respectable advocates." Thus, he holds, "the foundations" of the new system must be "deeper than . . . the mere sanction of delegated authority. The fabric of American empire ought to rest on the solid basis of THE CONSENT OF THE PEOPLE. The stream of national power ought to flow immediately from that pure, original fountain of all legitimate authority" (22:152).[6]

The Compound Republic

The position and authority of the national government that Publius has staked out fully accords with his conception of the confederate republic—a conception, as we have remarked, broad enough to embrace the consolidated, national, or unitary forms of government. In doing this, he has set forth a proposition that is of some consequence in light of the provisions and nature of the proposed Constitution (e.g., state representation in the Senate, residual state sovereignty): both the general and particular powers needed to achieve the objectives of union are what might be termed nonnegotiable, whereas, it seems clear, the residual powers of the states are. For instance, to take the easy case, to promote the national defense, the national government may constitutionally reach out and take over functions traditionally regarded as within the realm of the states' residual powers.[7] Or, to put this otherwise, in Publius's confederate republic the residual powers of the state are not sacrosanct: they are potentially and perpetually subject to national assimilation since, as he sees it, the constitutional powers of the national government are incapable of definition.

In these terms it is understandable why Publius would turn his attention to examining and answering the contentions of critics who argued that instead of preserving " 'the *federal* form, which regards the Union as a *Confederacy* of sovereign states,' " the Founders " 'have framed a *national* government, which regards the Union as a *consolidation* of States.' " This he proceeds to do in Federalist 39, wherein we find the most systematic and comprehensive analysis of the proposed union from the vantage point of state-national relations. His purpose is "to ascertain the real character of the government in question," and to this end he sets forth five tests: (a) "the foundation on which it is to be established;" (b) "to the sources from which its ordinary powers are to be drawn;" (c) "to the operation of those powers;" (d) "to the extent of them;" and (e) "to the authority by which future changes in the government are to be introduced" (39:243).

In these tests we cannot help but notice that Publius now uses the "arbitrary" distinctions (i.e., those of the opponents of the proposed Constitution) that he rejected in Federalist 9 as the basis for distinguishing between the federal or confederal and national or unitary forms—a rejection which cleared the way for the development of his confederate republic. For example, in test a, he notes that the founding might be considered a "national" act since it involves "the assent and ratification of the people of America, given by deputies elected for the special purpose." However, he maintains, it is clearly a "*federal* act" for interrelated reasons. The "assent and ratification is to be given by the people, not as individuals composing one entire nation, but as composing the distinct and independent States to which they respectively belong. It is to be the assent and ratification of the several States, derived from the supreme authority of each State—the authority of the people themselves." As further evidence of this federal character, he observes that ratification will result "neither from the decision of a *majority* of the people of the Union, nor from that of a *majority* of the States." Rather, it requires "the *unanimous* assent of the several States that are parties to it." Put otherwise, the individual states are not bound by the "will of the majority of the whole people of the United States," nor are they bound by the "will of the majority of States": "Each State, in ratifying the Constitution, is considered as a sovereign body independent of all others, and only to be bound by its voluntary act" (39:243–44).

That Publius would describe the founding as federal is somewhat misleading and indicates, perhaps, his desire to make it appear that the proposed Constitution is less national than it is. In any event, it is not difficult to see how his description of the ratifying process could be construed to support the doctrine of "states' rights" from which have flowed the related practices of "nullification" and "interposition."[8] More specifically, labeling the founding as "federal" and stressing the sovereignty of the states in the ratification process lends some weight to the view that the Constitution is actually a compact between sovereign states—a position which, as we have seen, Publius expressly repudiates in Federalist 22.

Whether intended or not, the confusion on this point arises because Publius sees fit to fix upon the means or mode of ratification as the basis for categorizing the foundation of the proposed system. But as John Marshall was obliged to point out in *McCulloch* v. *Maryland*, the mode of ratification in no way alters the fact that the foundations of the system are national, and that the people, not the states, ratified the Constitution.

> They [the people] acted upon it [the Constitution], in the only manner in which they can act safely, effectively, and wisely, on such a subject, by assembling in convention. It is true, they assembled in their several states; and where else should they have assembled? No political dreamer was ever wild enough to think of breaking down the lines which separate the states, and of compounding the American people into one common mass. Of consequence, when they act, they act in their states. But the measures they adopt do not, on that account, cease to be the measures of the people themselves, or become the measures of the state governments.[9]

Marshall concedes that "the assent of the states, in their sovereign capacity, is implied in calling a convention, and thus submitting that instrument to the people." "But," he adds, it was "the people," not the states, who "were at perfect liberty to accept or reject it; and their act was final."

In the last analysis, Publius—somewhat obliquely, to be sure—does hold to the position he has outlined in Federalist 22 in his discussion of the foundations test. In the relevant passages of Federalist 39, that is, he does acknowledge that the Constitution, if ratified, will rest upon "the authority of the people themselves."

Tests b, c, and e pose no real problems. As for b, the sources of ordinary power, he regards the system as "mixed," partaking of both the national and federal principles. The House, for example, representing the people as a whole, is based on the national principle, whereas the Senate, in which the states are represented equally, is founded on the federal principle. The executive power is "derived from a very compound source," the allocation of electoral votes to the states being based "partly as distinct and coequal societies, partly as unequal members of the same society"—the federal and national principles, respectively. If the election of the president should fall to the House, he describes the process as "mixed": the House is national in character but the voting procedure would be federal, each state delegation voting as a unit (244).

The "operations of government," test c, is the simplest of all. Even though in certain kinds of legal controversies "to which the States may be parties, they must be viewed and proceeded against in their collective and political capacities only," the national government "in its ordinary and most essential proceedings" will operate on "the people in their individual capacities." Thus, the system is national in this respect. If it were federal, he remarks, the national government would operate upon the "political bodies composing the Confederacy in their political capacities" (245).

As for e, the means of change, he finds the amendment procedure "neither wholly *national* or wholly *federal*." If it were national, a "*majority* of the people of the Union" would possess the power "to alter or abolish" the government. If it were federal, the consent of each state would be necessary to amend. But the Constitution adopts neither principle in its pure form: "In requiring more than a majority, and particularly in computing the proportion by *States*, not by *citizens*, it departs from the national and advances towards the *federal* character; in rendering the concurrence of less than the whole number of States sufficient, it loses again the *federal* and partakes of the *national* character" (246).

Test d, which concerns the extent of powers, is clearly the most troublesome of all simply because, primarily for reasons already set forth, it involves the question of the proper division of authority between the two jurisdictions, state and national. Unlike the other tests, this issue admits of no definite or clear-cut answer by reference to the confederal or national principles. Nor, for that matter, is the answer to be found, as with the other tests, by reference to specific constitutional provisions. Indeed, unlike the other tests, this test involves a dynamic relationship whose configurations were bound to change over time.

Publius begins his discussion of extent by again noting the character of a "national government": besides operating directly on "individual citizens," it involves "an indefinite supremacy over all persons and things, so far as they are objects of lawful government." "Among a people consolidated into one nation," he continues, "this supremacy is completely vested in the national legislature." He contrasts this national system not with a confederacy but with "communities united for particular purposes," where supremacy "is vested partly in the general and partly in the municipal legislatures." In a consolidated system, "all local authorities are subordinate to the supreme," but in unions for "particular purposes," "the local or municipal authorities form distinct and independent portions of the supremacy, no more subject, within their respective spheres, to the general authority than the general authority is subject to them, within its own sphere." "In this relation," he concludes, "the proposed government cannot be deemed a *national* one; since its jurisdiction extends to certain enumerated objects only, and leaves to the several States a residuary and inviolable sovereignty over all other objects" (245). But it is equally obvious that the proposed system is not federal, even though—surprisingly enough—Publius does label it such when, in the summary last paragraph of this essay, he writes: "in the extent of them [powers of the national government] . . . it [the proposed system] is federal, not national" (246). In characterizing this important dimension of the proposed system as "federal," he may well have sought to downplay its national character. In any event, we do know that he was dealing with a new distribution of authority for which no word as yet had been coined.

Publius, having declared the proposed government "not national," concedes that in disputes "between the two jurisdictions" over their boundaries, "the tribunal which is ultimately to decide is to be established under the general government." But this, he argues, does not render it any less federal because "the decision is to be impartially made, according to the rules of the Constitution; and all the usual and most effectual precautions are taken to secure this impartiality." He concludes by observing that such a tribunal is "clearly essential to prevent an appeal to the sword and a dissolution of the compact," and that its establishment under the aegis of the national government, "rather than under local governments . . . is a position not likely to be combated" (246).

Publius completes his survey by noting that "even when tested by the rules laid down by its antagonists," the proposed system "is, in strictness, neither a national nor a federal Constitution, but a combination of both" (246). In this assessment, we should note, he is referring to the tests taken as a whole. In this regard, the range of the relevant factors involved in assessing the federal character of the system is considerably wider for Publius than for more modern commentators who focus almost entirely on the matter of extent.

Drawing the Proper "Line": A Second Look

The extent test brings us to the heart of the difficulties surrounding the division of powers between the state and national governments. Publius informs us here that the states, under the proposed Constitution, possess "a residuary and inviolable sovereignty over all other objects," i.e., those not enumerated in the Constitution. This is consistent with what he writes elsewhere and coincides with his depiction of the distribution of authority set forth in his discussion of the confederate republic: "the proposed Constitution . . . leaves in their possession [the states] certain exclusive and very important portions of sovereign power" (9:76). In short, the proposed system, as he pictures it, provides for a division or partition of sovereign powers conceived of in relation to the objectives or functions of government.

Given this theoretical partition or division, an obvious question is whether a line can be drawn between the two realms in order to delineate between their respective spheres of authority—a line that would at least mark out the realm of inviolable state sovereignty and that might even serve to prevent collisions between the two jurisdictions. From what Publius does say at various points the answer is clear: drawing any hard and fast line is simply out of the question. To begin with, as he writes in Federalist 37, the same kind of difficulties encountered in defining the boundaries between the legislative, executive, and judicial provinces ("indistinctiveness of object, imperfection of the organ of perception, inadequateness of the vehicle of ideas") must have been fully experienced by the Founders

"in delineating the boundary between the federal and State jurisdictions" (229). The "task of marking the proper line of partition
between the authority of the general and that of the State governments," he remarks, was certainly no less "arduous" for the Framers
than that of providing for the proper mixture of "energy and stability" in the government (227). Beyond this, of course, drawing a
rigid line would call for foreknowledge of the scope and extent of
the powers that the national government might need to fulfill its
objectives, in other words, an enumeration of the implied powers is
an obviously impossible task. But this suggests as well that it might
be impossible, if not imprudent, to even delineate the "exclusive"
or "inviolable" realm of state sovereignty. In other words, Publius's
argument to the effect that it is impossible to foretell what powers
might be needed, for instance, in defending the nation would suggest
that there really can be no such realm.

Despite these insurmountable difficulties, Publius does offer general guidelines that he believes do serve to mark out the proper
concerns and objectives of the two spheres. In Federalist 10 he envisions "the great and aggregate interests being referred to the national [legislature], the local and particular to the State legislatures"
(83). He provides much the same formula in Federalist 14 where he
writes that the national authority only extends to "certain enumerated objects, which concern all the members of the republic, but
which are not to be attained by the separate provisions of any," while
"the subordinate governments" will retain the authority to tend to
those concerns "which can be separately provided for" (102). The
most comprehensive formulation in terms of the states' realm occurs
in Federalist 45 where he writes that the powers of the national
government "will be exercised principally on external objects, as
war, peace, negotiation, and foreign commerce," while those reserved to the states "will extend to all the objects which, in the
ordinary course of affairs, concern the lives, liberties and properties
of the people, and the internal order, improvement, and prosperity
of the State" (292–93). And he offers some relatively specific examples of the states' concerns. He maintains, for example, that "the
administration of private justice between the citizens of the same
State, the supervision of agriculture and of other concerns of a
similar nature . . . are proper to be provided for by local legislation"
and "can never be desirable cares of a general jurisdiction" (17:118).

For the most part, as we have noted, Publius confines himself to setting forth the national goals and showing how the delegated powers relate to them. Indeed, as he puts it at one point, an examination of the states' residual powers would be "too tedious and uninteresting for the instruction it might give" (17:120). Nevertheless, he takes pains to indicate the wide scope of these powers within the broader context of the language and purpose of the proposed Constitution. For instance, because the proposed Constitution "aims only at a partial union or consolidation," he maintains that "the State governments . . . clearly retain all the rights of sovereignty which they before had, and which were not, by the act *exclusively* delegated to the United States." In this respect, he can see "only three cases" where the states have alienated their sovereignty or, put otherwise, where the national government possesses exclusive jurisdiction: "where the Constitution in express terms granted an exclusive authority to the Union; where it granted in one instance an authority to the Union, and in another prohibited the States from exercising the like authority; and where it granted an authority to the Union to which a similar authority in the States would be absolutely and totally *contradictory* and *repugnant*" (32:198). This last case, of course, does allow for concurrent jurisdiction or the exercise of the same powers, such as taxation, when there is no absolute and total contradiction or repugnance in the sense he describes. "The necessity of a concurrent jurisdiction in certain cases," he acknowledges, "results from the division of the sovereign power; and the rule that all authorities, of which the States are not explicitly divested in favor of the Union, remain with them in full vigor is not only a theoretical consequence of that division, but is clearly admitted by the whole tenor of the instrument which contains the articles of the proposed Constitution" (32:201).

Now Publius is aware that his general formulation, though helpful in describing the general contours of the proposed system, certainly will not provide a fine, straight line that can be used to divide the realms of the two jurisdictions, but rather one that is somewhat blurred and wavy. This is why, we may assume, when discussing the matter of extent of powers, he turns to the means for resolving controversies. Evidently, that is, he sees a procedural solution to the problem of a proper delineation. However, as sensible as this approach is, he offers not one solution but two. What is worse, the solutions he does offer differ in important respects, even to the extent of being incompatible with one another.

To see this we can best begin with the solution that he provides in Federalist 39. At this juncture, he informs us that "the tribunal which is ultimately to decide is to be established under the general government." While over the years this has been taken to mean that the Supreme Court is to be the final arbiter, this is by no means clear from the way he puts it. That is, he writes of "the tribunal . . . to be established," which would lead one to believe that it is to be constituted after the adoption of the Constitution. In any event, the Supreme Court is established by the Constitution and we can only speculate why, if he meant for the Court to be this "tribunal," he did not say so. His vagueness, perhaps, is an indication that he wanted to skirt a sensitive issue raised by certain Antifederalists, whether the Supreme Court, an agency of the national government, would be an impartial tribunal in such matters. In fact, even if the Antifederalists had not raised this issue, the very principles of Publius's own teachings would serve to do so. Will not members of the judiciary, like the members of the political branches, develop an attachment to the government that they serve? Will they not seek indirectly to expand their powers by broadening the powers of the national government whenever possible? Cannot the Supreme Court, as a branch of the national government, be considered a party to the cause it is judging? Are we to regard them as exempt from Publius's proposition advanced with regard to senators, namely, "the more permanent and conspicuous the state of men in power, the stronger must be the interest which they will individually feel in whatever concerns the government"? (58:359). Or might it not, as the weakest branch, simply go along with Congress for fear of antagonizing it? In short, what at first glance seemed to be a reasonable solution to a crucial and perplexing problem turns out, after some consideration, to be fraught with some very serious difficulties.

Even more puzzling is his reference to "the rules of the Constitution" according to which the decision is to be made. To be sure, certain "rules" are to be found in the Constitution, but they are of little use in settling controversies that might arise. For instance, perhaps the most important rule of all is to be found in the "supreme Law of the Land" clause, which accords supremacy to national laws passed pursuant to the Constitution. But the controversies between the states and national governments, as Publius knew full well, would center around whether the national government did or did not act pursuant to the Constitution. And the fact is that the Constitution does not provide any "rules" for a determination of this nature.[10] Consequently, the claims he makes for "impartiality" on this account are certainly not well grounded.

Publius's solution in essay 39 would seem to be a bit disingenuous. It is not, however, his only solution. He provides another that is at once straightforward and more conformable with his general approach. Faced with the question of who should "judge of the *necessity* and *propriety*" of laws passed by the national government, he answers "that the national government, like every other, must judge, in the first instance, of the proper exercise of its powers, and its constituents in the last" (33:203). After speculating on the issue of which government is more likely to encroach upon the other and concluding that such "conjectures . . . must be extremely vague and fallible," he writes that the "safest course" is "to lay them altogether aside and to confine our attention wholly to the nature and extent of the powers as they are delineated in the Constitution." "Everything beyond this," he continues, "must be left to the prudence and firmness of the people; who, as they will hold the scales in their own hands, it is to be hoped will always take care to preserve the constitutional equilibrium between the general and the State governments" (31:197). In Federalist 46, he contends that the "adversaries of the Constitution" have come to view the state and national governments "as mutual rivals and enemies . . . uncontrolled by any common superior." And, he adds, these adversaries "must be told that the ultimate authority, wherever the derivative may be found, resides in the people alone, and that it will not depend merely on the comparative ambition or address of the different governments whether either, or which of them, will be able to enlarge its sphere of jurisdiction at the expense of the other. Truth, no less than decency, requires that the event in every case should be supposed to depend on the sentiments and sanction of their common constituents" (46:294). Drawing the proper line, then, between the two spheres falls to the people according to this solution.

Three comments are in order concerning this mode of resolution. First, while it does not necessarily exclude the Court from playing a role in the resolution of conflict,[11] it is clear that the common constituents have the final say. And given Publius's aversion to frequent changes in the Constitution, it seems evident that the common constituents are to exercise their sovereign authority, not through the amendment or constituent process, but through the ordinary political processes. Put otherwise, we can hardly envision him supporting a solution that, in effect, requires that every time there is substantial controversy over the proper boundary, recourse must be had to the amendment process. On the contrary, he is quite explicit in saying that the first line of defense against Congress overstepping its authority in the exercise of implied powers would be the "executive and judiciary departments, which are to expand and give effect to legislative acts." But, "in the last resort," he writes, "a remedy must be obtained from the people, who can, by the election of more faithful representatives, annul the acts of the usurpers" (44:286).

Viewed in this manner, there is an evident incompatibility between the solution proffered in Federalist 39 and that set forth elsewhere, an incompatibility that has created serious tensions in the actual operations of the system.[12] Specifically, the will of the common constituents on matters pertaining to the relative authority of the two domains expressed by the people through the political processes may run counter to the will of the Supreme Court. When this occurs, the solution set forth in Federalist 39 would require that the issues in question be settled through constitutional amendment—by the people acting in the constituent capacity—rather than in the political capacity, principally, through Congress. This is another reason why Publius's remarks in Federalist 39 concerning the resolution of state-national controversies are puzzling and something of an aberration.

This leads to a second observation. Because Publius was willing to allow the people to "hold the scales in their hands," the issues and controversies arising from the vertical distribution of powers between the state and national government were not, so it seems, regarded as constitutional questions like those arising from the horizontal distribution of powers between the legislature, executive, and judiciary. Whereas Publius sought to avoid appeals to the people to resolve the disputes between these branches, he seems to embrace the notion that the common constituents ought to be entrusted with maintaining the proper equilibrium between the state and national governments. And this proper equilibrium turns out to be whatever the people declare it to be. As we shall see, in this connection, he did believe that the states would enjoy a decided advantage over the national government in the affections of the people. But if, he writes, "the people should become more partial to the federal than to the State governments," the people "ought not . . . to be precluded from giving their confidence where they may discover it to be most due" (46:295).

And third, as we might expect, Publius is clear in both his solutions that the controversies over the proper line must be settled in the national arena. Obviously, if a state or combination of states were empowered to follow their own lights in such controversies, this would have constituted a reversion to "the political monster of an *imperium in imperio*" which had plagued the Articles (15:108). What we come to see, however, is that the only national forum through which the common constituents can register their will is the Congress. This, in turn, means that a presumptive legitimacy would be accorded to whatever decision Congress—the very institution most likely to encroach upon the states' domain—may make concerning the extent of national powers vis-à-vis the states. On Publius's own terms, the coincidence of impulse and opportunity for congressional aggrandizement at the expense of the states posed questions and concerns that he was obliged to face.

The States and Limited Government

The essence of his answer to these concerns is found in Federalist 51 where, after setting forth the means by which the legislative authority can be held in check, he writes: "In the compound republic of America, the power surrendered by the people is first divided between two distinct governments, and then the portion allotted to each subdivided among distinct and separate departments. Hence a double security arises to the rights of the people. The different governments will control each other, at the same time that each will be controlled by itself" (323). In other places, he indicates how the states will not only be able to resist the encroachments of the national government but also, and more important, how they will serve to inhibit the Congress from encroaching upon the liberties of the people.

That Publius believed the states possessed the potential to thwart schemes of aggrandizement by the national government is beyond question. One theme that permeates *The Federalist* is that the states will enjoy a natural advantage over the national government in any confrontation between the two. Indeed, Publius suggests at various places that he believes the states are far more likely to encroach upon the prerogatives of national government than the national government on those of the states. In Federalist 45, for example, he again refers to the experiences of "ancient and modern confederacies" and remarks upon "the strongest tendency continually betraying itself in the members to despoil the general government of its authorities." And though he concedes that the proposed system is so different from these confederacies "as greatly to weaken any inference," he cautions that "the inference ought not to be wholly disregarded" because the states, under the proposed forms, still retained "a very extensive portion of active sovereignty" (45:290). Part of this conviction, no doubt, also rested on his view that those matters "which are proper to be provided for by local legislation, can never be desirable cares of a general jurisdiction," and that any "attempt" on the part of the general government "to exercise" them "would be as troublesome as it would nugatory" so that their "possession . . . would contribute nothing to the dignity, to the importance, or to the splendor of the national government" (17:118–19).

Nevertheless, apparently aware that this line of argument would not allay the fears of the Antifederalists, Publius in Federalists 45 and 46 systematically details the reasons why he believes that states will enjoy an advantage over the general government. In this undertaking he compares them "in respect [a] to the immediate dependence of the one on the other; [b] to the weight of personal influence which each side will possess; [c] to the powers respectively vested in them; [d] to the predilection and probable support of the people; [e] to the disposition and faculty of resisting and frustrating the measures of each other" (45:290–91).

The first three of his reasons are straightforward enough: the fact that the very existence of the national government—e.g., the election of senators and the president—depends on the states should serve to "beget a disposition too obsequious than too overbearing toward them [the states]"; the state employees will be more numerous than those of the national government and their "influence would lie on the side of the state"; and "the powers of the national government are few and defined," whereas residual powers of the states extend to a variety of concerns affecting the "lives, liberty, and property of the people" as well as the states' internal concerns (45:291–92).

As for d, the attachment of the people, he remarks:

> Into the administration of these [the state governments] a greater number of individuals will expect to rise. From the gift of these a greater number of offices and emoluments will flow. By the superintending care of these, all the more domestic and personal interests of the people will be regulated and provided for. With the affairs of these, the people will be more familiarly and minutely conversant. And with the members of these will a greater proportion of the people have the ties of personal acquaintance and friendship, and of family and party attachments; on the side of these, therefore, the popular bias may well be expected most strongly to incline [46:294–95].

Still another reason for this natural inclination, he believes, derives from the "known fact of human nature that its affections are commonly weak in proportion to the distance or diffusiveness of the object." For this reason, he observes, attachment to family is stronger than attachment to neighborhood, attachment to neighborhood stronger than to "the community at large." Thus, he holds, "the people of each State would be apt to feel a stronger bias towards their local governments than towards the government of the Union." Moreover, he points out that the state governments will bear the responsibility for "the ordinary administration of criminal and civil justice," a responsibility that renders them "the immediate and visible guardian of life and property." The regulation of "all those personal interests and familiar concerns to which the sensibility of individuals is more immediately awake, contributes more than any other circumstance to impressing upon the minds of the people affection, esteem, and reverence toward government." In contrast, because the national government will regulate more "general interests," which have a less immediate impact upon the people, it is "less likely to inspire an habitual sense of obligation and an active sentiment of attachment." It is, he concludes, a "natural propensity of the human heart" that attaches the common constituents to the states (17:119–20).

How decisive Publius really believed these factors would be in the resolution of differences between the two governments is open to serious question. At other places in the essays, he contends that the common constituents will come down on the side of that government that provides the best administration. And, as we shall see shortly, he gives us good reason to believe that the national government will be better administered, at least in those spheres where national administration is practicable.

It is with respect to e, "the disposition and faculty of resisting and frustrating the measures of each other," that Publius sets forth what must be considered the major restraints on the national government in light of his basic assumptions. To begin with, he maintains that "the prepossessions, which the members of Congress will carry into the federal government, will generally be favorable to the States." He offers two reasons for this view. First, the experience of the state legislatures has shown that their members were inclined to sacrifice the general interest of the state to the narrow interests of their "counties or districts." This propensity to put local or particular concerns above the general welfare, he believes, will also manifest itself in the national legislature or, more exactly, "the members of the federal legislature will be likely to attach themselves too much to local objects." And second, the experience under the Articles shows that "an undue attention [has been paid] to the local prejudices, interests, and views of the particular States", that its "members have but too frequently displayed the character rather of partisans of their respective States than of impartial guardians of the common interest." And while he sees every prospect that the new national government "will . . . embrace a more enlarged plan of policy," its members, he feels, will certainly "be disinclined to invade the rights of the individual States, or the prerogatives of their governments." Yet he does not believe that the "motives on the part of the State governments to augment their prerogatives by defalcations from the federal government will be overruled by . . . reciprocal predispositions" (46:296–97).

But what if the national government were to "feel an equal disposition with the State governments to extend its power beyond the due limits"? Publius answers this question at some length and provides still another, though distinctly nonconstitutional, solution to national-state controversies. He observes that "should an unwarrantable measure of the federal government be unpopular in particular States, which would seldom fail to be the case, or even a warrantable measure be so, which may sometimes be the case, the means of opposition to it are powerful and at hand." "The disquietude of the people; their repugnance, and perhaps, refusal to cooperate" coupled with "the frowns of the executive magistracy of the State" and "embarrassments created by legislative devices" would pose difficulties "in any State" and "in a large state, very serious impediments." And if, he continues, "several adjoining States" were to act "in unison," they would "present obstructions which the federal government would hardly be willing to encounter" (46:297–98).

The situation, from Publius's perspective, could only worsen if the federal government were to undertake "ambitious encroachments . . . on the authority of the State governments." Such encroachments, he writes,

> would be signals of general alarm. Every government would espouse the common cause. A correspondence would be opened. Plans of resistance would be concerted. One spirit would animate and conduct the whole. The same combinations, in short, would result from an apprehension of the federal, as was produced by the dread of a foreign, yoke; and unless the projected innovations should be voluntarily renounced, the same appeal to a trial of force would be made in the one case as was made in the other.

But Publius can scarcely envision this occurring: "Who," he asks, "would be the parties" in such a showdown? He answers: "A few representatives of the people would be opposed to the people themselves; or rather one set of representatives would be contending against thirteen sets of representatives, with the whole body of their common constituents on the side of the latter" (46:298).

Publius, not content to rest his case on these grounds alone, turns to the "visionary supposition that the federal government might over time set out to accumulate a military force for the projects of ambition." Aside from arguing that the national government could not conceivably raise an army large enough for this purpose, he ridicules the notion that "the people and the States should, for a sufficient period of time, elect an uninterrupted succession of men ready to betray both; that the traitors should, throughout this period, uniformly and systematically pursue some fixed plan for the extension of the military establishment; that the governments and the people of the States should silently and patiently behold the gathering storm and continue to supply the materials, until it should be prepared to

burst on their own heads" (46:298–99). In sum, he holds, "the federal government" under the forms of the proposed Constitution
"will be restrained" by a dependence on the people from undertaking "schemes obnoxious" to them (46:300).

In this vein, at another place, Publius contends that the people
will be able to exercise "that original right of self-defense" with
"infinitely better prospect of success" against the "national rulers"
than against those of the states. The absence of "distinct governments" in the subordinate "parcels, subdivisions, or districts" of the
states, he observes, render "regular measures for defense" impossible: "The citizens must rush tumultuously to arms, without concert,
without system, without resource; except in their courage and de-
spair." But in the compound republic, he goes on to say, "the people,
without exaggeration, may be said to be entirely the masters of their
own fate." The state and national governments will jealously watch
each other, ready to check any usurpation by the other; and the
people, by throwing their weight one way or the other, will provide
the decisive force in any contest between them. Moreover, if the
people's "rights are invaded by either" government, "they can make
use of the other as the instrument of redress" (26:180–81).

Publius regards it "as an axiom of our political system that the
State governments will, in all possible contingencies, afford complete
security against invasions of the public liberty by the national authority." In this he sees the state legislatures playing a dominant
role. The reasons for this are multiple: "Projects of usurpation cannot be masked under pretense so likely to escape the penetration
of select bodies of men, as of the people at large. The legislature
will have better means of information. They can discover the danger
at a distance; and possessing all the organs of civil power and the
confidence of the people, they can at once adopt a regular plan of
opposition, in which they can combine the resources of the community. They can readily communicate with each other in the different States, and unite their common forces for the protection of
their common liberty" (28:181).

Beyond any question, a good deal of what Publius writes about
the capacity of the states to resist obnoxious or oppressive national
measures is prompted by his desire to show that the fears of the
Antifederalists over standing armies are without foundation. In large
part, this accounts for the attention he devotes to the probable

outcome of any military confrontation between the two jurisdictions. Nevertheless, far short of any such showdown we can see reasons why the mere existence of the states as relatively self-sufficient political entities serves to limit the national government, not only with regard to encroaching on the states' domain but in the exercise of its delegated powers as well. The states do represent organizations around which opposition to national measures may organize and through which this opposition can be aired. Certainly, on Publius's showing, the national government would be loathe to undertake measures or programs which a number of adjoining states might find highly objectionable, not so much perhaps because of the civil-war potential inherent in this kind of cleavage, but rather because of the difficulties and expense surrounding enforcement in the face of a substantial, organized, articulate, and highly visible opposition. Moreover, we should expect the national government to be reluctant to undertake such measures even if they were backed by national majorities, unless these majorities were sufficiently intense to force the matter. But such majority insistence would hardly constitute the normal state of affairs. What Publius's analysis points to, then, is that at least in some instances the national government, in order to act effectively, will have to rely on something more than the support of mere majorities of the common constituents. Because it is obliged to take into account the reaction that will be fueled by the adversely affected states, it is more or less forced on such matters into consensual politics—a politics that, among other things, seeks accommodation with the affected interests to help assure, as far as possible, that its policies can achieve the desired ends.

Publius presumes in his analysis that the state interests will find outlets in the political processes of the proposed system far short of recourse to arms—e.g., the multiplicity of offices that give the states an advantage in any appeal to the common constituents, the predisposition toward the states of those who serve in the national councils, the equality of state representation in the Senate that could be regarded, in Publius's words, as "a palladium to the residuary sovereignty of the States" (43:279). Even the potential for resistance must be reckoned with in Congress. In sum, the picture he paints for the resolution of conflict between the state and the national governments is a far cry from any "tribunal" impartially applying the "rules of the Constitution."

Federalism in Perspective

To assess accurately the role Publius felt federalism—the vertical
distribution of powers—would or should play in the proposed system
in securing the liberty and rights of the citizenry, it is necessary to
view it in the context of other principles he advances. For example,
although Publius surely makes a good case that the states would
protect the people against the potential tyranny of the national government, we can readily see that it would be a mistake to suppose
that he therefore thought the compound system—or federalism, as
we have come to understand it—vital to the preservation of the liberty
and rights of the citizens. Contrary to what is widely believed today,
Publius did not look upon the states as citadels of liberty. As we have
seen from his discussion of the extended republic, he regarded them
as far more prone than the national government to the ills of majority
factions. On his showing, then, the states would be relatively useless
in combating the evils of majority factions. Such factions, by definition, would have the backing of the common constituents so that
resistance by the states would be unlikely, unless the matter was
regional in nature. But, more important, given their own propensity
to succumb to factions, they would scarcely constitute reliable barriers.

However, Publius was not concerned about the states' role with
regard to factions. Rather, his remarks are directed almost exclusively to the states' role in preventing tyranny by the national government. Yet here again, the state's role can hardly be considered
significant because, as we have seen, the primary protection against
tyranny is the separation of powers. For Publius, a key consideration
in this respect was not the extent of the powers vested in the national
government but whether the "internal structure of the proposed
government" rendered it a safe repository of these powers (23:156).
In this regard he writes: "Whatever may be the limits or modifications of the powers of the Union, it is easy to imagine an endless
train of possible dangers; and by indulging an excess of jealousy and
timidity, we may bring ourselves to a state of absolute skepticism
and irresolution. . . . all observations founded upon the danger of
usurpation ought to be referred to the composition and structure
of the government, not to the nature or extent of its powers" (31:196).

Equally, if not more important, Publius believed the republican
character of the proposed system would serve to check and control

the exercise of power. To this point he observes "the whole power of the proposed government is to be in the hands of the representatives of the people. This is the essential, and, after all, the only efficacious security for the rights and privileges of the people which is attainable in civil society" (28:180). Toward the end of essay 46, he summarizes the points he has made to show the capacity of the states to resist oppressive and unwarranted national encroachments in what he considers a manner "altogether conclusive":

> Either the mode in which the federal government is to be constructed will render it sufficiently dependent on the people, or it will not. On the first supposition, it will be restrained by that dependence from forming schemes obnoxious to their constituents. On the other supposition, it will not possess the confidence of the people, and its schemes of usurpation will be easily defeated by the State governments, who will be supported by the people (300).

And there can be no question about which of these suppositions Publius entertained.

Finally, there is no escaping the fact Publius thought the common constituents would and should draw the line between the two jurisdictions. But what is significant is the ground upon which he felt they would ultimately make their decision, a factor that, as we remarked above, seems to contradict what he argues in Federalist 46 and elsewhere about the advantages the states would enjoy with the common constituents in any confrontation with the national government. After remarking that "it may be laid down as a general rule that their [the people's] confidence in and obedience to a government will commonly be proportioned to the goodness or badness of its administration," he goes on to observe that there are "various reasons" having to do with the interior structure of the proposed system and its extensiveness to believe "that the general government will be better administered than the particular governments" (27:174). Accordingly, it seems, he believed that superior administration would overcome those natural affections that give the states an advantage over the national government among the common constituents.[13] And so much he expressly declares in Federalist 46: "If . . . the people in future become more partial to the federal than to the State governments, the change can only result from such manifest and irresistible proofs of a better administration as will overcome all their antecedent propensities." And, to repeat what we noted earlier, he sees no reason why the people "ought . . . to be precluded from giving most of their confidence where they may discover it most due" (295).

In this regard, Publius "hazard[s] the observation" that as the operations of the national goverment "are intermingled with the ordinary exercise of government," thereby rendering it a familiar part of their ordinary political life, "the greater will be the probability that it will conciliate the respect and attachment of the community." He even goes further than this in suggesting "that the authority of the Union and the affections of the citizens toward it will be strengthened, rather than weakened, by its extension to what are called matters of internal concern" (27:176).

His posture toward federalism, then, differs markedly from that which he assumes toward the separation of powers. After we strip away his arguments designed to allay the fears raised by the Antifederalists and look carefully at his basic position, we see that he can perceive no harm to the basic values associated with constitutionalism—stability, constancy of policy, liberty, the rights and privileges of the citizenry, and the like—resulting from consolidation so long as it is backed by the common constituents. Put otherwise, he would not be disturbed—and this because the internal structure of the proposed system merited such confidence—if the line between the state and national spheres eventually turned out to be heavily biased in favor of the national government. But, above all, given his overriding concern that the national government possess the means to accomplish its ends, we can say that what he wanted at a minimum was a wide and inviolable sphere of sovereignty for the national government—a sphere free from interference or control by the states.

If Publius looked to any value that should determine where the line should be drawn between the state and national authority, it would revolve around efficiency, which government could provide better administration. But he conceded that, even if the national government were to gain the confidence of the people, "the State governments would have little to apprehend, because it is only with a certain sphere that the federal power can, in the nature of things, be advantageously administered" (46:295). Thus we see that Publius only painted a broad, and somewhat ambiguous, picture of state-national relations. He was, it would seem, content to let time and experience determine what distribution of authority would prove most suitable for the common constituents. As he observes at the outset of Federalist 82, no matter how wise or careful its framers, "the erection of a new government . . . cannot fail to originate questions of intricacy and nicety; and these may, in a particular manner, be expected to flow from the establishment of a constitution founded upon the total or partial incorporation of a number of distinct sovereignties." To this he adds, " 'Tis time only that can mature and perfect so compound a system, can liquidate the meaning of all the parts, and can adjust them to each other in a harmonious and consistent WHOLE" (491).

NOTES

1. See Martin Diamond, "What the Framers Meant by Federalism," in George C. S. Benson, ed., *Essays on Federalism* (Claremont, Calif.: Institute for Studies in Federalism, 1962).

Diamond's analysis must be modified to a certain extent. The word *federal* at the time of ratification carried with it still another connotation: those who favored strengthening the existing confederation of states were called "federalists," those opposed, "antifederalists." The term *federalist* is, hence, appropriate for Publius's undertaking because he is urging the people to adopt a stronger union. See W. B. Allen and Gordon Lloyd, eds., *The Essential Antifederalist* (Lanham, Md.: University Press of America, 1985), pp. viii-xiv. This terminology has persisted over the decades. We commonly use the term *federal government* when referring specifically to the national government.

2. Probably the most introspective work dealing with the concept of federalism is S. Rufus Davis, *The Federal Principle* (Berkeley: University of California Press, 1978). Davis does discuss the distinctly American experience with this concept.

3. In Federalist 41, Publius offers up another list of objectives and ends similar to this. "1. Security against foreign danger; 2. Regulation of the intercourse with foreign nations; 3. Maintenance of harmony and proper intercourse among the States; 4. Certain miscellaneous objects of general utility; 5. Restraint of the States from certain injurious acts; 6. Provision for giving due efficacy to all these powers" (256). These are the categories or classes of ends Publius employs in discussing the appropriateness of the delegated powers.

4. This point he makes at other places with reference to the objectives of the national government. "Constitutions of civil government are not to be framed upon a calculation of existing exigencies, but upon a combination of these with the probable exigencies of ages, according to the natural and tried course of human affairs. Nothing, therefore, can be more fallacious than to infer the extent of any power proper to be lodged in the national government from an estimate of its immediate necessities. There ought to be a CAPACITY to provide for future contingencies as they may happen; and as these are illimitable in

their nature, so it is impossible safely to limit that capacity" (34:207). In this vein, he writes that "a system of government meant for duration" ought to be able "to accommodate itself" to "revolutions" in the areas of "manufacturing and commerce" (41:256).

5. This is almost but not identical to the "axiom" he advances in Federalist 23: "the *means* ought to be proportioned to the *end*; the persons from whose agency the attainment of any *end* is expected ought to possess the *means* by which it is to be attained" (153).

6. Publius addresses this same issue in Federalist 43: "It has been heretofore noted among the defects of the Confederation that in many of the States it had received no higher sanction than a mere legislative ratification." He again remarks that the Articles—quite unlike the proposed system—were merely "a compact between independent sovereigns, founded on ordinary acts of legislative authority" that could "pretend to no higher validity than a league or treaty between the parties" (279).

7. For instance, in order to provide for the national defense it has been argued that the national government should exercise control over education in order to secure the needs of the defense establishment. Beyond this, it could be argued that the national government, for a variety of reasons, should assume the function of zoning. See Harry V. Jaffa, "The Case for a Stronger National Government" in Robert A. Goldwin, ed., *A Nation of States* (Chicago: Rand McNally, 1961).

8. For example, John C. Calhoun could maintain: "The great and leading principle is, that the General Government emanated from the people of the several States, forming distinct political communities, and acting in their separate and sovereign capacity, and not from all of the people forming one aggregate political community; that the Constitution of the United States is, in fact, a compact, to which each State is a party . . . and that the several States, or parties, have a right to judge of its infractions; and in case of a deliberate, palpable, or dangerous exercise of power not delegated, they have the right, in the last resort, to use the language of the Virginia Resolutions, '*to interpose for arresting the progress of the evil, and for maintaining, within their respective limits, the authorities, rights, and liberties appertaining to them.*' This right of interposition, thus solemnly asserted by the State of Virginia, be it called what it may,—State-right, veto, nullification, or by any other name,—I conceive to be the fundamental principle of our system, resting on facts historically as certain as our revolution itself, and deductions as simple and demonstrative as that of any political or moral truth whatever; and I firmly believe that on its recognition depend the stability and safety of our political institutions." "The Fort Hill Address" (Richmond: Virginia Commission on Constitutional Government, 1960), pp. 2–3.

9. 4 L. Ed. 403 (1819)

10. This is not to say that the Constitution is completely silent about limits to state or national authority. But these limits relate to such matters as ex post facto laws, bills of attainder, obligation of contract and are of a different order than those that would arise in the controversies to which Publius alludes.

11. The Court, for instance, might be called upon to interpret the provisions of the laws in dispute in order to settle a controversy. But the Court would not make the "strategic" decisions involving where the line should be drawn, i.e., whether the Congress has exceeded its constitutional authority. The matter of constitutionality is left to Congress and the common constituents. This view is reinforced by the fact that in setting forth the Court's power of judicial review, Publius makes no mention of this power extending to matters such as confining the national government to its constitutional sphere—a matter he most certainly would have mentioned had he believed it should be handled by the Court.

12. The "Court packing" controversy of the 1930s arose from this very tension. On one side, there were the "common constituents" represented by the Congress and president, who backed certain New Deal measures; on the other, the Court, which regarded these measures as an unconstitutional invasion of the residual powers of the states. This episode also provides an excellent illustration of how the system, consonant with Publius's conception of republicanism, eventually moves whither the greater force carries it.

13. See also in this regard Federalist 3, where he maintains that the best talent, once "an efficient national government is established," will naturally be drawn to the national government. "Hence," he argues, "it will result that the administration, the political counsels, and the judicial decisions of the national government will be more wise, systematical, and judicious than those of individual States, and consequently more satisfactory with respect to other nations, as well as more *safe* with respect to us" (43).

4

·

Limited Government

> Until the people have, by some solemn and au-
> thoritative act, annulled or changed the estab-
> lished form, it is binding upon themselves
> collectively, as well as individually; and no
> presumption or even knowledge of their senti-
> ments, can warrant their representatives in a
> departure to it prior to such an act [78:470].

*I*T MAY SEEM odd that we now
turn to the principle of limited government when, in fact, we have
already examined the principal protections against oppression and
injustice, whether by the people or by their rulers. There is, to put
this otherwise, no gainsaying Publius's reliance on the extended republic to control the effects of faction and the separation of powers
to prevent tyranny—two evils normally associated with unrestrained
or unlimited government. But there is a third dimension to limited
government that, though tacitly understood in much of his previous
discussion and argumentation, is only articulated fully toward the
end of *The Federalist*: the Constitution must be regarded as the fundamental law that contains limitations on the authority of the national and state governments.

Now the enforcement of these limitations calls for means of a
different order than those which control the effects of faction or
prevent tyranny. The solutions to the problems of faction and tyranny are largely self-executing: the conditions of the extended republic, provided a modicum of public virtue, are sufficient to control
factions; likewise prevention of tyranny, in the last analysis, depends
upon the interests and natural ambitions of officeholders to counteract one another. But the situation with regard to enforcing constitutional prohibitions is markedly different: the prohibitions are

relatively specific, they are in the body of the Constitution as limitations on the authority of Congress (by indirection as well on the executive as a participant in the lawmaking process), and, as such, some agency or body is required to guarantee their observance.

The major reason Publius does not get around to this matter until a relatively late date is that, as we shall see shortly, he believed the courts would play an indispensable role in the observance of these limitations, and it is only after a thorough examination of the legislative and executive branches that he turns to the judiciary. In fact, the first essay devoted exclusively to the judiciary is the famed Federalist 78, in which he outlines and offers theoretical justification for the courts' power to declare legislative acts contravening the Constitution null and void. We can perhaps best comprehend Publius's position with respect to the importance of the limited Constitution and the role of the courts by first surveying Federalist 78 and then returning to the problems and questions it raises.

The Judiciary: Independence and Tenure

Federalist 78 starts off innocently enough. Publius informs us that he is not going to inquire into "the utility and necessity" of an independent judiciary because this matter has already been covered in connection with pointing out the shortcomings of the Articles and "the propriety of the institution in the abstract is not disputed." What remains to be considered, he writes, are "only questions" relating "to the matter of constituting it, and to its extent." The first of these, "the manner of constituting it," he discusses under three general heads: "1st. The mode of appointing the judges. 2nd. The tenure by which they are to hold their places. 3rd. The partition of the judiciary authority between different courts and their relations to each other" (78:464).

The first of these considerations Publius deals with summarily. In the two preceding essays, he comments, he has thoroughly discussed and answered objections to the mode of nomination and appointment of "officers of the Union in general" so that he feels any further remarks would be "useless repetition." However, certain of his observations on this matter are of interest because, as we noted earlier, the mode of appointment to the judiciary does deviate from the strict requirements of the separation of powers doctrine. To begin with, Publius is convinced that it is best that only one person, rather than "a body of men of equal or perhaps of superior discernment," be charged with the responsibility of nominating officers, because the provision for "sole and undivided responsibility" will "beget a livelier sense of duty and a more exact regard to reputation." What is more, an individual will have "*fewer* personal attachments" than an "assembly of men," each *member* of which will have personal preferences. To this concern, he writes that because "there is nothing so apt to agitate the passions of mankind as personal considerations," an assembly would in all likelihood display "all the private and party likings and dislikes, partialities and antipathies, attachments and animosities." Thus, he maintains, the choice, whether through compromise or dictation by the dominant party, would too often be based on considerations other than the "intrinsic merit of the candidate" (76:456).

However, Publius observes that the concurrence of the Senate in the selection process should "have a powerful, though, in general, a silent operation" by serving "to prevent the appointment of unfit characters from State prejudice, from family connection, from personal attachment, or from a view to popularity." It more or less obliges the president to use great care and discretion in selecting his nominees because the "propriety of his choice" will be determined by a "different and independent body . . . whose opinion would have great weight in forming that of the public." Hence, the president's "own reputation" and even his "political existence" might be on the line. These considerations, Publius concludes, go a long way toward insuring that he would not nominate for the "most distinguished and lucrative stations" those who possess "no other merit than that of coming from the same State . . . or of being . . . personally allied to him, or of possessing the necessary insignificance and pliancy to render them the obsequious instruments of his pleasure" (76:457–58). This, of course, provides further assurance that the judges would be truly independent of the executive.[1]

To return to Federalist 78, we find that Publius is preoccupied with the second consideration, "the tenure by which judges are to hold their places." Under this broad heading he sees three related concerns: "their [the judges'] duration in office, the provisions for their support, the precautions for their responsibility" (78:465). He deals with only the first of these concerns in this essay. In so doing, however, he ranges outward to a discussion of the nature of the proposed Constitution and the courts' role in upholding its limitations.

Publius begins his treatment by noting that the proposed Constitution conforms with the practice of most states in providing that the judges "are to hold their offices *during good behavior.*" He remarks further: "The standard for good behavior is certainly one of the most valuable of the modern improvements in the practice of government. In a monarchy it is an excellent barrier to the despotism of the prince; in a republic it is no less an excellent barrier to the encroachments and oppressions of the representative body. And it is the best expedient which can be devised in any government to secure a steady, upright, and impartial administration of the laws" (78:465). What we see here is that Publius is expanding upon his observations in Federalist 9 by telling us why he believes this standard of "good behavior" represents an improvement in the "science of politics." The answer he gives, in effect, is that it ties in with and contributes to the ends of the separation of powers: it acts as a barrier to legislative encroachments, Publius's primary concern with maintaining the partition of powers; it secures the impartial application of the laws, which goes a long way toward curbing oppressive legislation; and it contributes to stability and constancy in the adjudication of the laws, which promotes ordered liberty.

Publius is concerned to allay fears that the independence of the judiciary, resulting from its constitutionally prescribed tenure, will pose a threat to the liberties of the people. In language that is often quoted in controversies surrounding the role of the modern courts, he maintains that "the judiciary from the nature of its functions, will always be the least dangerous to the political rights of the Constitution; because it will be least in a capacity to annoy or injure them." And he continues: "The executive . . . holds the sword of the community. The legislature not only commands the purse, but prescribes the rules by which the duties and rights of every citizen are to be regulated. The judiciary, on the contrary, has no influence over either the sword or the purse; no direction either of the strength or of the wealth of society, and can take no active resolution whatever." In sum, as he puts it, the judicial branch possesses neither "FORCE nor WILL"—presumably the prerogatives of the executive

and legislature, respectively—"but merely judgment; and must ultimately depend upon the aid of the executive arm even for the efficacy
of its judgments" (465).

"This simple view of the matter," according to Publius, "suggests
several important consequences" among the more important being
"that the judiciary is beyond comparison the weakest of the three
departments of power; that it can never attack with success either
of the other two; and that all possible care is requisite to enable it
to defend itself against their attacks." He cites Montesquieu to the
effect that the judicial power, when compared to that of the legislature and the executive, is "next to nothing." Thus, the "general
liberty of the people can never be endangered" by the judiciary
provided, he is quick to add, that it "remains truly distinct from
both the legislature and the executive." Harkening back to Montesquieu and the message of Federalist 51, he holds that there can
be "no liberty" if there is a union of the judicial power with either
the executive or legislative powers. But its "natural feebleness," he
points out, places it in "continual jeopardy of being overpowered,
awed, or influenced by its co-ordinate branches," rendering "permanency in office . . . an indispensable ingredient in its constitution,
and, in a great measure, as the citadel of the public justice and the
public security" (465–56).

In emphasizing the inherent weakness of the judiciary, Publius is
simply pointing up the imperative need for permanent tenure. In
terms of his general strategy outlined in Federalist 51, the provision
for tenure during good behavior strengthens the judiciary by rendering it far less vulnerable to being swallowed up by the other
branches—a state of affairs that would constitute the tyranny he
dreaded. Yet having shown that tenure during good behavior would
effectively maintain the necessary constitutional partition of powers,
he could easily have stopped and proceeded to another concern.
Instead he goes on to point out why he believes the "complete independence of the courts of justice is peculiarly essential in a limited
Constitution." He puts his general position in the following terms:
"By a limited Constitution, I understand one which contains certain
specified exceptions to the legislative authority; such, for instance,
as that it shall pass no bills of attainder, no *ex-post-facto* laws, and
the like. Limitations of this kind can be preserved in practice no
other way than through the medium of courts of justice, whose duty
it must be to declare all acts contrary to the manifest tenor of the

Constitution void. Without this, all the reservations of particular
rights or privileges would amount to nothing" (466). This would
suggest that the power of judicial review derives not from the provisions of the Constitution taken in conjunction with one another,
but from the inherent logic of a written Constitution that contains
limitations. So much Publius seems to acknowledge in Federalist 81,
where he writes that the "doctrine" that "the Constitution ought to
be the standard of construction for the laws" for the courts "is not
deducible from any circumstance peculiar to the plan of the convention, but from the general theory of a limited Constitution" (482).

By way of explaining the theoretical character and status of "American constitutions," Publius raises the issue of whether the power
of the courts to declare "legislative acts void, because contrary to
the Constitution" does not "imply a superiority of the judiciary to
the legislative power." "It is urged," he remarks, "that the authority
which can declare the acts of another void must necessarily be superior to the one whose acts may be declared void." But, he insists,
this is not the case. Rather, and a matter he will elaborate on in due
course, the courts' authority derives from a position that rests upon
the clearest of principles: "that every act of a delegated authority,
contrary to the tenor of the commission under which it is exercised,
is void." Thus, "no legislative act" that contravenes the Constitution
is valid. "To deny this," he contends, "would be to affirm that the
deputy is greater than his principal; that the servant is above the
master; that the representatives of the people are superior to the
people themselves; that men acting by virtue of powers may do not
only what their powers do not authorize, but what they forbid" (467).

Having asserted the fundamental law status of the Constitution,
Publius then turns to examine the contentions that the "legislative
body" should be the "constitutional" judge of its own powers and
that its judgment should also be binding on the other departments.
This, he holds, "cannot be the natural presumption where it is not
to be collected from any particular provisions of the Constitution.
It is not otherwise to be supposed that the Constitution could intend
to enable the representatives of the people to substitute their *will*
to that of their constituents." He writes that "it is far more rational
to suppose that the courts were designed to be an intermediate body
between the people and the legislature in order, among other things,
to keep the latter within the limits assigned to their authority" (467).

Publius sheds more light on this particular aspect of his argument when, in Federalist 81, he rejects the idea of "vesting the ultimate power of judging in a *part* of the legislative body." While such a provision, he recognizes, would not technically violate the maxim of separation of powers—i.e., the part would not possess the whole legislative power—it comes too close for comfort: "From a body which had had even a partial agency in passing bad laws we would rarely expect a disposition to temper or moderate them in the application. The same spirit which had operated in making them would be too apt to operate in interpreting them; still less could it be expected that men who had infringed the Constitution in the character of legislators would be disposed to repair the breach in the character of judges" (483). Instead, he contends, an independent judiciary is the fit branch for these determinations: "Every reason which recommends the tenure of good behavior for judicial offices militates against placing the judiciary power, in the last resort, in a body composed of men chosen for a limited period." The members of the judiciary, in contrast to the legislators, are "of permanent standing"; the judges, well versed in the law through "long and laborious study," are far better equipped than the legislators to perform the task of final "revision and control"; and the legislators are seldom "chosen with a view to those qualifications which fit men for the stations of judges," which increases the possibility that "the pestilential breath of faction may poison the fountains of justice" (483–84).

In Federalist 78, Publius is content to note that "the interpretation of the laws is the proper and peculiar province of the courts." Thus, because the Constitution "is, in fact, and must be regarded by the judges as, a fundamental law," ascertaining its meaning, "as well as the meaning of any particular act proceeding from the legislative body," falls within the province of the judiciary. Consequently, if there is an "irreconcilable variance between the two, that which has the superior obligation and validity ought, of course, to be preferred; or, in other words, the Constitution ought to be preferred to the statute, the intention of the people to the intention of their agents" (467).

This is a theme Publius stresses in pointing out how the resolution of a conflict between two "contradictory laws" differs from that involving a conflict between statutory and fundamental law. In the former case, the "rule of construction" derived from "the nature and reason of the thing" holds "that between the interfering act of an *equal* authority that which was the last indication of its will should have the preference." But with regard to the latter, "the interfering acts of a superior and subordinate authority of an original and derivative power, the nature and reason of the thing indicate the converse of that rule": "the prior act of a superior ought to be preferred to the subsequent act of an inferior and subordinate authority" (468).

But if it is a legitimate function of the courts "to regulate their decisions by the fundamental laws rather than by those which are not fundamental," to void those statutes that contravene the Constitution, may not the courts "substitute their own pleasure to the constitutional intentions of the legislature"? This is an important question that Publius really does not answer or explore. Such a charge he regards as having "no weight" since it could be leveled as well against the acknowledged and routine functions of the courts: the courts could as easily step out of line "in the case of two contradictory statutes; or . . . in every adjudication upon any single statute." "The courts," he continues, "must declare the sense of the law; and if they should be disposed to exercise WILL instead of JUDGMENT, the consequence would equally be the substitution of their pleasure to that of the legislative body." He suggests that what this proves, if anything, is "that there ought to be no judges distinct from that body"—i.e., that if the judges are disposed to exercise "WILL," they should be members of the legislature, not the judiciary (468–69).

Publius concludes this section of his discussion of constitutionalism and the role of the courts by reemphasizing the need for the "permanent tenure of offices." In his words, "nothing will contribute so much as this [permanent tenure] to that independent spirit of the judges which must be essential" for their "arduous" task of preserving the "limited Constitution against legislative encroachments" (469).

Up to this point in his presentation Publius has centered his attention on the courts' role in upholding the Constitution against violations by the legislature. But, quite in keeping with the differentiation he employs throughout his discussion of the separation of powers, he realizes that popular majorities may be the impetus behind *unconstitutional* measures. What he has to say about the function of the courts in this respect is somewhat reminiscent of his discussion of the role of the Senate: "The independence of the judges is equally requisite to guard the Constitution and the rights of individuals from the effects of those ill humors which the arts of designing men, or the influence of particular conjunctures, sometimes disseminate among the people themselves, and which, though they readily give place to better information, and more deliberate reflection, have a tendency, in the meantime, to occasion dangerous innovations in the government, and serious oppressions of the minor party." But unlike the Senate, which can only delay a measure, the courts have a responsibility to nullify the measure. In no way, he argues, does this represent an abrogation or infringement of "the fundamental principles of republican government which admits the right of the people to alter or abolish the established Constitution whenever they find it inconsistent with their happiness." Rather, it is to say that the people can only make such changes by acting in their constituent capacity, "by some solemn and authoritative act," presumably through the amendment process. "It is not to be inferred from [the republican] principle," he maintains, "that the representatives of the people, whenever a momentary inclination happens to lay hold of a majority of their constituents incompatible with the provisions in the existing Constitution would, on that account, be justifiable in a violation of those provisions." In other words, the *constituent* will of the people as expressed in the Constitution is superior to the *political* will of the people that finds expression through Congress. In any event, he sees the role of the courts the same whether the infractions arise from "momentary inclinations" of majorities or "wholly from the cabals of the representative assembly." The difference, as he sees it, "is that it would require an uncommon portion of fortitude in the judges to do their duty as faithful guardians of the Constitution, where legislative invasions of it had been instigated by the major voice of the community" (469–70).

Publius is also careful to draw a distinction between unconstitutional laws and laws that are unjust or factious but not necessarily unconstitutional. In this regard, he writes, the courts may also be "an essential safeguard against the effects of occasional ill humors in society" that "sometimes extend no farther than to the injury of the private rights of particular classes of citizens, by unjust and partial laws." "Here," he holds, "the firmness of the judicial magistracy is of vast importance in mitigating the severity and confining the operation of such laws." It would seem that he envisions the courts interpreting the laws either broadly or narrowly, as the case may be, to achieve these ends. No doubt, in light of the more general ends or purposes of separation of powers, Publius could also envision an independent judiciary, simply because of its independence, posing very real problems for legislative majorities bent on drafting partial legislation that would discriminate unfairly against certain sectors or classes of society. For instance, the legislators would have to make sure that such discriminatory provisions of the law were carefully crafted so its provisions could not, under any circumstances, be interpreted to extend beyond the targeted group to their family, friends, or political allies. In any event, it is clear that he believes that the "obstacles to the success of an iniquitous intention [which] are to be expected from the scruples of the courts" will force legislators "to qualify their attempts." "This is a circumstance," he continues, "calculated to have more influence upon the character of our governments than but few may be aware of." The experience in certain states, he remarks, clearly illustrates the "benefits" to be derived from "the integrity and moderation of the judiciary" (470).[2]

By way of linking these observations to the subject of this essay, he observes that the benefits—"adherence to the rights of the Constitution, and of individuals"—are not to be expected "from judges who hold their offices by a temporary commission," because such judges would seek to curry the favor or avoid the displeasure of those vested with the power of appointment. For instance, he contends that selection of the judges by the people or their agents would result in "too great a disposition to consult popularity to justify a reliance that nothing would be consulted but the Constitution and the laws" (470).

Publius concludes this essay by offering up still another and "weighty" reason for permanent tenure: the "qualifications" that are required for judges. A knowledge of "rules and precedents," he points out, is "indispensable" in order to "avoid arbitrary discretion in the courts." And, because of the "variety of controversies which grow out of the folly and wickedness of mankind," he continues, "the records of those precedents must unavoidably swell to a very considerable bulk" so that "a competent knowledge of them" can be attained only after "long and laborious study." Publius concludes from this that the number of individuals in society "who will have sufficient skill in the laws to qualify them for the stations of judges" will be small. If the "proper deductions for the ordinary depravity of human nature" are made, he adds, the number is reduced even further. In the last analysis, by his reckoning, "the government can have no great option between fit characters" who would be hard to lure away from "a lucrative line of practice" if the appointments were only temporary (471).

Judicial Review and Republicanism

Publius manages to pack a good deal of constitutional morality into his argument for judicial tenure during good behavior: he finds the opportunity to go well beyond the text or obvious import of the proposed Constitution to set forth what he conceives to be the appropriate powers, duties, and responsibilities of the courts for the proper operation of the system. Moreover, most of what he has to say in this regard can be viewed as gratuitous because, as we have already commented, the case for permanent tenure can be convincingly made in the context of his position regarding the separation of powers and the imperative need to maintain a separation between the branches. In other words, permanent tenure, quite simply, is a necessary defense against "attacks" or domination by either the legislative or executive branches. That Publius is not content to rest his case on these grounds, that he goes beyond them to argue that this defense is also needed for other purposes, can understandably be taken to mean, as it has in relatively recent times by both liberal and conservative commentators, that he wanted the judiciary to play a crucial, if not decisive, role in policing and refining legislative output.

More generally, as the Antifederalists perceived, to place the judiciary, as Publius did, in what can be called a "preferred position" with respect to the interpretation of the fundamental law may potentially render it the supreme branch of the system, more powerful than even the Congress. As "Brutus," one of the more insightful and prolific opponents of ratification, put it:

"The supreme court under this constitution would be exalted above all other power in the government, and subject to no control." The court, he contended, "will give the sense of every article of the constitution, that may from time to time come before them. And in their decisions they will not confine themselves to any fixed or established rules, but will determine, according to what appears to them, the reason and spirit of the constitution."[3] And, he reasons, as the courts develop rules and principles over the years concerning what is and what is not conformable with the Constitution, the legislature "will not go over the limits . . . which the courts may adjudge [it is] confined." In short, as Brutus concluded, "the judgement of the judicial, on the constitution, will become the rule to guide the legislature in the construction of [its] powers."[4]

That Publius was aware of the thrust of this line of argument is apparent from Federalist 81, wherein he presents his understanding of the Antifederalist position in the following terms: "'The authority of the proposed Supreme Court of the United States, which is to be a separate and independent body, will be superior to that of the legislature. The power of construing the laws according to the *spirit* of the Constitution will enable that court to mould them into whatever shape it may think proper; especially as its decisions will not be in any manner subject to the revision or correction of the legislative body. This is as unprecedented as it is dangerous. . . .the errors and usurpations of the Supreme Court of the United States will be uncontrollable and remediless' " (482).

To this specific charge Publius writes: "there is not a syllable in the plan under consideration which *directly* empowers the national courts to construe the laws according to the spirit of the Constitution, or which gives them any greater latitude in this respect than may be claimed by the courts of every state." He reiterates his position that the courts are bound by the Constitution and "that wherever there is an evident opposition" between the statutory laws—i.e., laws enacted through the political processes—and the Constitution, which embodies the constituent will of the people, the statutory law must give way. But even this position, which is far short of authorizing the courts to interpret the spirit of the Constitution, cannot, as we have already remarked, be deduced "from any circumstance peculiar to the plan of the convention, but from the general theory of a limited Constitution." And, he goes on to say, once again using his "glass house" technique, "as far as it [the general theory] is true [it] is equally applicable to most if not all the

State governments" whose constitutions also attempt "to set bounds
to the legislative discretion" (482).

In addition, we learn from Federalist 78 that Publius conceives
the power of judicial review extending only to specific constitutional
prohibitions on legislative authority. Put another way, the constitutional limitations on the legislature seem to form the raison d'être
for the courts' power to void legislation. On this score, particularly
in light of our previous discussion of federalism, it is interesting to
note that he does not mention any role for the courts in limiting
the implied powers of Congress even when, such as in Federalist 80,
the subject matter—the "proper objects" of the federal judiciary—
presents an open invitation to do so. In fact, one of the major thrusts
of Publius's discussion concerning the national judiciary is to show
its utility for keeping the state governments in line. At one level he
notes that the need for "one court of supreme and final jurisdiction
is a proposition that has not been, and is not likely to be contested"
(81:481), and this is true, he intimates, for reasons that he sets forth
in Federalist 22. In that essay he details the difficulties that arose
under the Articles because of the lack of a judiciary. "If there is in
each State a court of final jurisdiction, there may be as many different
final determinations on the same point as there are courts. . . . To
avoid the confusion which would unavoidably result from the contradictory decisions of a number of independent judicatories, all
nations have found it necessary to establish one court paramount
to the rest, possessing a general superintendence and authorized to
settle and declare in the last resort a uniform rule of civil justice"
(22:150). Significantly, he deems this general superintendence as even
more imperative "where the frame of the government is so compounded that the laws of the whole are in danger of being contravened by the laws of the parts." The "bias of local views and prejudice
and . . . the interference of local regulations" can serve to undermine
the "general laws" simply because "men in office naturally look up
to that authority to which they owe their official existence" (150–
51).

Not surprisingly, Publius holds it as axiomatic that "the judicial
power of a government" ought to be "coextensive" with "its legislative" in order to avoid "a hydra in government from which nothing but contradiction and confusion can proceed." In other words,
the federal judicial authority should extend over the full range of
legislative authority. Publius advances this proposition not, it would

seem, to guarantee that the courts, if called upon, might be able to review the constitutionality of all laws passed by Congress, but to insure "uniformity" of interpretation and application. When, in elaborating on these matters, he does speak to the issue of the courts exercising their power of judicial review —i.e., "giving efficacy to constitutional provisions"—his concern is with possible encroachments by the states. "The States, by the plan of the convention, are prohibited from doing a variety of things"—e.g., issuing paper money and imposing duties on imports—which, he claims, "no man of sense will believe . . . would be scrupulously regarded without some effectual power in the government to restrain or correct the infractions of them." As he sees it, these prohibitions could only be enforced either by "a direct negative on State laws, or an authority in the federal courts to overrule" those state laws that "might be in manifest contravention of the articles of Union" (475–76).

"Will" versus "Judgment"

There is other and more compelling evidence to indicate that Publius, far from believing that the courts should be free to interpret the spirit of the Constitution, thought that the courts' power of judicial review, at least with regard to national legislation, should be highly circumscribed. It is important to recall that Publius, in discussing the role of the courts, differentiates between the legislative, executive, and judicial prerogatives. More precisely, he contends that the judiciary possesses "neither FORCE [the major constitutional power of the executive] nor WILL [the constitutional prerogative of the legislature], but merely judgment." As he remarks, the courts are obliged to exercise "judgment," not "will," because the exercise of "will" would be to encroach upon the legislative domain—a usurpation of functions that could lead to the judicial supremacy that was so much feared by certain of the Antifederalists.

The critical question in this framework is, of course, how to distinguish between will and judgment. While their meanings do overlap, we do find in ordinary usage a distinction between them that would seem to convey the differences between the judicial and legislative realms Publius had in mind. Judgment, for instance, has a more passive connotation: a judgment is an opinion about something or a state of affairs rendered after reflection. Frequently this re-

flection involves weighing, juxtaposing, and measuring various factors against known and accepted standards or criteria. Thus, for
example, we judge of performances in sports, in the arts, or on
examinations. On the other hand, an exercise of will—most certainly
in the sense Publius seems to think of it—is not passive but active
in nature. It involves a choice among a variety of legitimate alter-
natives or goals with the concomitant capacity to achieve, implement,
or move toward them. As such, will can be more arbitrary than
judgment; the valuation of goals in the exercise of will may depend
upon a wide variety of inherent human emotions, wants, or desires.

While much more can be said in general about will and judgment
in order to differentiate between them, Publius does provide us with
relatively specific criteria that help us to judge when the courts have
overstepped their bounds. To begin with, as we have already emphasized, he advances the doctrine of judicial review as a device to
enforce the "specified exceptions to the legislative authority" marked
out in the Constitution. That this is a narrow or restricted scope for
judicial review is attested to by the examples he offers: prohibitions
on "bills of attainder . . . *ex-post-facto* laws and the like." Both restrictions are easily definable and, what is more, both are designed
to prevent practices which, in the course of the common law tradition, have come to be regarded as the hallmarks of arbitrary and
tyrannical governments. And when he writes "and the like," we may
assume that he is referring to provisions of an equivalent category
or type—an assumption that seems entirely warranted when he declares immediately thereafter that the courts' "duty . . . must be to
declare all acts contrary to the *manifest tenor* of the Constitution void"
(78:466, emphasis added).

Still another standard for determining whether the courts are following the straight and narrow is suggested in his remarks concerning the need to attract qualified individuals. It is "indispensable,"
he writes, that the judges "should be bound down by strict rules
and precedents" to "avoid an arbitrary discretion [an exercise of
"will"] in the courts." Here the words and phrases *bound down, strict
rules and precedents,* and *indispensable* all serve to narrow the range
of judicial discretion.

Perhaps the most demanding standard of all that Publius offers
for the legitimate exercise of judicial review is the "irreconcilable
variance" test, which embodies, but goes beyond, the unwritten rule

that the courts should presume the constitutionality of legislation. By the terms of this test, only after searching and failing to find a compatibility between any reasonable interpretation of a disputed statute and the constitutional provision in question are the courts entitled to declare the statute void. This is a stringent requirement that, if rigorously followed, would virtually insure that only rarely would the courts find it necessary to void a statute.[5]

It is infrequently remarked that the logic of the fundamental law doctrine applies to the executive and judiciary as well as to the legislature. But it does, and so the question arises, what if the courts overstep their legitimate boundaries? Suppose, as some of the Antifederalists feared, the members of the Supreme Court were, in effect, to usurp the legislative function? Publius answers these concerns as we might expect. He regards "the supposed danger of judiciary encroachments on the legislative authority" as "a phantom." To be sure, he admits, "misconstructions and contraventions of the will of the legislature may now and then happen." However, in his judgment, "they can never be so extensive as to amount to an inconvenience, or in any sensible degree to affect the order of the political system." This he contends can be "inferred with certainty" from the "nature of the judicial power" as well as from the "objects to which it relates" and "its total incapacity to support its usurpations by force." This "inference," he writes, "is greatly fortified by the consideration" that the Congress possesses the power to impeach and remove "members of the judicial department." "This alone," he maintains, "is a complete security" against judicial encroachment: "There never can be danger that the judges, by a series of deliberate usurpations on the authority of the legislature, would hazard the united resentment of the body intrusted with it, while this body was possessed of the means of punishing their presumption by degrading them from their stations" (81:484–85).

While, in Publius's view, the courts are clearly indispensable to the integrity of the proposed system, their role in giving positive direction to the system, even in a negative way through their authoritative interpretations of the Constitution, would seem to be minuscule. His composite portrait of the judiciary would indicate as much: it is feeble and weak compared with the legislature and executive; it can take no "active resolution whatever"; it is to be a passive institution, "bound down by strict rules and precedents,"

exercising only "judgment," not "will"; its powers to declare acts
of the legislature unconstitutional should be exercised only when
they are contrary to the "manifest tenor" of the Constitution and
this only after determining that there is an "irreconcilable variance"
between the statute and the Constitution.

Quite apart from these rules and tests, there are other major
considerations, all of which derive from Publius's broader theory,
that would serve to render it quite unlikely that the courts would
be called upon to exercise their power of judicial review. Given
separation of powers, and the morality Publius urges upon the president and the Senate, how likely is it that an unconstitutional measure
from the House of Representatives, the most likely source of such
a measure, would make it all the way to the courts? And how likely
is it that the House would pass a bill that contravenes the "manifest
tenor" of the Constitution? Moreover, Publius anticipated that settlement of major controversies arising from both the separation of
powers and the division of powers between the national and state
governments would be achieved through distinctly nonconstitutional
means. This is not to say the courts would play no role with regard
to state-national relations. But their primary function in this regard,
as marked out by Publius, would seem to be that of enforcing the
national laws and the Constitution against the states.

What Publius offers, then, primarily in Federalist 78, is a positive
constitutional morality with regard to the proper role of the judiciary
in preserving the integrity of the constitutional system. The cures
for the excesses or abuses of government that might arise from either
popular factions or the rulers are to be found in the conditions,
forces, and factors associated with the extended republic or the
constitutional provisions for the separation of powers. Nevertheless,
the fundamental law doctrine places a very special twofold obligation
on the judiciary: it must interpret the laws and enforce the constitutional limitations without, at the same time, overstepping its legitimate boundaries and encroaching upon either the constitutional
prerogatives of the other branches or of the people. Publius's remarks to this concern can appropriately be viewed as "instructions"
on how the judiciary is to negotiate this narrow path. Moreover, we
may surmise that the chief reason he stresses the courts' role in this
respect is not that he feared Congress passing ex post facto laws,
bills of attainder, or conferring titles of nobility. Rather, given the

thrust of his remarks, he wanted to lay solid foundations for the national judiciary to exercise authority over the states: in pointing up that the courts, theoretically at least, have the authority to curb the Congress, he scarcely leaves any doubt about their authority relative to the states.

The Bill of Rights

If there is any doubt that Publius envisioned the courts playing a limited and passive role vis-à-vis the legislature, his opposition to a bill of rights should dispel them. Put otherwise, if Publius had looked upon the courts as the guardians of individual and minority rights against the encroachments of the legislature, it seems likely that he would have favored a bill of rights, particularly one formulated to give the courts wide discretionary latitude in reviewing the acts of Congress. Instead, he adamantly opposes an addition of rights beyond those specified in the Constitution on grounds that it is unnecessary and even dangerous.

Now in this connection it should be remarked that Publius opposed the idea of amendments to the proposed Constitution with the end of establishing a more "perfect" system. The reasons for this opposition varied: he despaired of ever seeing "a perfect work from imperfect man," the more so as any plan intended "to embrace thirteen distinct States in a common bond of amity and union must . . . be a compromise of . . . many dissimilar interests and inclinations"; the proposed plan was "superior to any the revolution has produced" and "the best that the present views and circumstances of the country will permit"—one which "promises every species of security which a reasonable people can desire"—and, *inter alia*, the "extreme . . . imprudence of prolong[ing] the precarious state of our national affairs." But perhaps the most important of all is that such amendments would require another constitutional convention "under circumstances" less "favorable to a happy issue" than "those in which the late convention met, deliberated, and concluded" (85:523–24). Publius certainly could not have been unmindful of the fact that even convening such a convention would probably signify the demise of the proposed plan.

In Federalist 84 we find Publius's response to the particular objection "that the plan of the convention contains no bill of rights."

But, in this response, he advances lines of argument against the incorporation of rights that are of a different character than those he employs against amendments in general. These arguments present us with the clearest picture we have of the major theoretical and practical difficulties Publius perceived in attempting to provide for limited government in a republican regime.

Publius's disdain toward a bill of rights is evident in the first paragraph of this essay. He writes that he has tried in the preceding eighty-three essays to take "notice of" and "answer most of the objections which have appeared against" the proposed Constitution, but, he continues, "there . . . remain a few which either did not fall naturally under any particular head or were forgotten in the proper places." These objections he proceeds to describe as "miscellaneous points," though he does acknowledge that the absence of a bill of rights is the "most considerable" of them (84:510).

Publius uses the "glass house" technique to launch his argument against a bill of rights. He notes that the constitutions of "several of the states" contain no bill of rights with New York among this number. He then takes up the arguments advanced by those who simultaneously "profess an unlimited admiration for its [the New York] constitution" but who, as "among the most intemperate partisans of a bill of rights," attack the proposed Constitution for its presumed shortcomings in this regard. With respect to the contention that the New York constitution "contains, in the body of it, various provisions in favor of particular privileges and rights which, in substance," constitute the same thing as a bill of rights, Publius responds that the proposed Constitution also contains a number of such provisions (510). Among those he cites are the provisions for habeas corpus, the prohibitions against ex post facto laws, bills of attainder, and titles of nobility, trial by jury in criminal cases, and the delimitation of punishment for treason and through the impeachment process.

After citing these provisions, Publius observes that "upon the whole," they may be "of equal importance with any which are to be found" in the New York Constitution. In this regard, he singles out the habeas corpus, ex post facto, and titles of nobility provisions in the proposed Constitution—"*to which*," he adds gratuitously, "*we have no corresponding provision in our* [New York] *Constitution*"—as "perhaps greater securities to liberty and republicanism than any" contained in the New York Constitution. Protection against ex post facto laws and provision for the writ of habeas corpus he points out, do away with "the practice of arbitrary imprisonments [which] have been, in all ages, the favorite and most formidable instruments of tyranny." He accords special attention to the habeas corpus provision by quoting from Blackstone, who regarded the habeas corpus act to be " 'the BULWARK of the British Constitution' " (84:511–12).

With this Publius turns to the second contention advanced by the admirers of the New York Constitution: though it does not contain a bill of rights, it "adopts, in their full extent, the common and statute law of Great Britain, by which many other rights not expressed in it are equally secured" (510). This line of argument poses little difficulty for Publius. He notes that this "common and statute law" is by express provision of the same constitution "made subject to such alterations and provisions as the legislature shall from time to time make concerning the same." As such, he points out, it possesses "no constitutional sanction"—i.e., is not part of the fundamental law—and cannot rightly be considered any "part of a declaration of rights, which under our constitutions must be intended as limitations of the power of the government itself" (512).

Having said this much, he goes on to contend that bills of rights so understood really have no place in republican regimes. As he sees it, "bills of rights are, in their origin, stipulations between kings and their subjects, abridgments of prerogative in favor of privilege, reservations of rights not surrendered to the prince." Such, he maintains, describes the Magna Charta, the *Petition of Right*, and the Declaration of Right, which was later transformed by a parliamentary act into the Bill of Rights. Thus, he holds, given this "primitive signification" of bills of rights, they "have no application to constitutions, professedly founded upon the power of the people and executed by their immediate representatives and servants" because "the people surrender nothing; and as they retain everything they have no need of particular reservations." Thus, he regards the Preamble to the Constitution, which declares that " 'WE, THE PEOPLE of the United States . . . do *ordain* and *establish* this Constitution for the United States of America," as "a better recognition of popular rights than volumes of those aphorisms which make the principal figure in several of our State bills of rights and which would sound much better in a treatise of ethics than in a constitution of government" (512–13).

Publius concludes the "glass house" segment of Federalist 84 by pointing out that a "minute detail of particular rights" is not as appropriate or necessary for the proposed Constitution, which is "intended to regulate the general political interests of the nation," as it is for constitutions which regulate "every species of personal and private concerns." Consequently, by his standards, if the proposed Constitution is deficient with regard to the specification of rights, "no epithets of reprobation will be too strong" for the New York Constitution. Nevertheless, "the truth is," he believes, "that both of them contain all which, in relation to their objects, is reasonably to be desired" (513).

There are some seeming inconsistencies in Publius's argument. He contends, for instance, that the proposed Constitution does contain those rights essential for liberty and republican government, but he also contends that rights are inappropriate for republican regimes. Some of this apparent inconsistency, however, can be satisfactorily explained away by paying close attention to the language he uses when he turns to the rights that the opponents of the proposed Constitution champion. At this juncture, he makes clear that his concern transcends the issue of appropriateness, by canvassing the dangers associated with the addition of "bills of rights, in the sense and to the extent in which they are contended for." His obvious concern in this regard is with both the nature and extent of the rights being advanced as necessary for the liberty and well-being of the people. To begin with, he maintains, these bills of rights "would contain various exceptions to power which are not granted" and for this reason "would afford a colorable pretext to claim more than were granted." In this regard, he asks rhetorically, "For why declare that things shall not be done which there is no power to do?" His concern here goes beyond the obvious one that a complete listing of rights is impossible and that a listing of some rights would create a presumption that government can infringe upon those not listed. Rather, his point is that in listing rights, "the doctrine of constructive powers" might be employed to give the government authority over the very concerns the rights were designed to protect. For example, while a declaration that "the liberty of the press shall not be restrained" would not, in his view, "confer a regulating power," he believes it "evident that it would furnish, to men disposed to usurp, a plausible pretense for claiming that power." Such men "might urge with a semblance of reason that the Constitution ought not to be charged with the absurdity of providing against the abuse of an authority which was not given, and that the provision against restraining the liberty of the press afforded a clear implication that a power to prescribe proper regulations concerning it was intended to be vested in the national government" (513).

Publius also uses the provision for liberty of the press as an example to illustrate the character of the dangers and problems associated with other rights being advanced for incorporation into the proposed Constitution. After observing that there is no such provision for this liberty in the New York Constitution, he declares "that whatever has been said about it in that of any other State amounts to nothing." "What," he asks, "signifies a declaration that 'the liberty of the press shall be inviolably preserved'? What is the liberty of the press? Who can give it any definition which would not leave the utmost latitude for evasion?" Because it is incapable of such a definition, he infers "that its security, whatever fine declarations may be inserted in any constitution respecting it, must altogether depend on public opinion, and on the general spirit of the people and of the government" (514).

In an extended footnote, Publius takes up the contention of those who argue that liberty of the press needs protection from the proposed national government because it might impose duties "upon . . . publications so high as to amount to a prohibition." In the first place, he cannot fathom how "it could be maintained that the declarations in the States constitutions, in favor of the freedom of the press, would be a constitutional impediment to the imposition of duties upon publications by the State legislatures." "It certainly cannot be pretended," he argues, "that any degree of duties, however low, would be an abridgment of the liberty of the press" since Great Britain, which enjoys liberty of the press to a greater degree than any other nation, taxes its newspapers. Thus, he points out that protection of the press from this quarter "must depend on legislative discretion, regulated by public opinion" and that "general declarations, respecting the liberty of the press will give it no greater security than it will have without them." In the last analysis, he writes, "it would be quite as significant to declare that government ought to be free, that taxes ought not to be excessive, etc., as that the liberty of the press ought not to be restrained" (514–15).

Publius concludes his discussion of the bill of rights by urging upon his readers another "view of this matter": "The truth is, after all the declamations we have heard, that the Constitution is itself, in every rational sense, and to every useful purpose, a BILL OF RIGHTS." He offers up two basic reasons for this view; both relate to what he regards as the fundamental purposes of a bill of rights. First, the proposed plan, "in the most ample and precise manner," declares and specifies "the political privileges of the citizens in the structure and administration of the government." In so doing, it comprehends "various precautions for the public security which are not to be found in any of the State constitutions." Second, the plan "in a variety of cases" also defines "certain immunities and modes of proceeding . . . relative to personal and private concerns." "Adverting therefore to the substantial meaning of a bill of rights," he claims, "it is absurd to allege that it is not to be found in the work of the convention" (515).

Rights: An Overview

Publius's arguments against a bill of rights do leave something to be desired. At one level, as we have remarked, they are not entirely consistent. If, for instance, there is, as he contends, no need to declare "that things shall not be done which there is no power to do," then what are we to make, for example, of his assertion that the prohibition of title of nobility "may truly be denominated the cornerstone of republican government"? Are we to assume from this that without this prohibition the national government would possess the authority to confer such titles? Still another and related matter is this: if the rights already embodied in the proposed Constitution serve, as he suggests, a good purpose, why would not the enumeration of still more rights be beneficial? At another level, and in a more general vein, Publius chooses to ignore the question of how the implied powers of the national government might serve to infringe upon acknowledged rights. As he emphasizes at various places, it is not really possible to define a priori the limits of the implied powers of the national government, a fact that weakens his position that a bill of rights would be dangerous because it "would contain various exceptions to powers which are not granted."

The outline of Publius's answers to these concerns is not hard to come by in light of his general conception of the proposed plan and what he says elsewhere about related matters. We can begin by observing that he would be loathe to add rights to the fundamental law that might conceivably limit the powers of the national government. In this regard, one of his central messages, particularly with regard to providing for the common defense, is the impossibility and futility of placing a priori limitations on the national government. Because the implied powers could not be spelled out, only "rights" that held out virtually no prospect of limiting the national government could safely be incorporated into the fundamental law. The provision against titles of nobility, we may say, constitutes a perfectly harmless "right" from this perspective. We can hardly imagine any circumstance when this right might hinder the national government in the performance of its duties. Likewise, it is difficult to see under what circumstances the national government would be impeded by the prohibitions relating to bills of attainder and ex post facto laws. Moreover, we should note, these particular rights are the product of the common-law tradition and, as such, their origins, foundations, and meanings are well established.

This view of Publius's position is bolstered if we look to the right of habeas corpus, which he regards at least as highly as the ex post facto prohibition. We can easily see how the habeas corpus provision might hamstring the national government if it were not qualified in the manner it is to provide for its suspension, i.e., "when in Cases of Rebellion or Invasion the public Safety may require." Though this right is not absolute, we can understand why it merits a place in the fundamental law: it is a traditional common law right, well established in the tradition, and, what is equally important, the reasons for which it may be legitimately suspended can be specified. Herein we also find a reason why Publius felt rights "in the sense and to the extent contended for" by the opponents of the Constitution were dangerous. To recur to the example Publius offers, liberty of the press, we can readily perceive that it does not lend itself to the same kind of qualifications as habeas corpus; that is, it could be interpreted to limit either the delegated or implied powers of the national government, but to specify what conditions would warrant its suspension or abridgment would be virtually impossible. Thus, as he puts it, the exercise of the right has to depend on the good sense of the people who will, as circumstances dictate, be called upon to make these decisions through the political processes. This right, in other words, could not easily be chiseled into stone. And, we may presume, the same could be said of the other rights being advanced that Publius does not discuss.

Publius's position toward the bill of rights is understandable in light of still other dimensions of his thought. We know, for instance, that he did not place much stock in parchment barriers. Consequently, he could hardly have viewed a bill of rights as an efficacious means of protecting individual or minority rights. The observance of the rights specified in the Constitution depends not on their constitutional sanction, but on their status as traditional and accepted limitations on governmental power very closely related to the ends associated with the separation of powers such as liberty and protection from arbitrary rule. In this sense, the proposed Constitution merely recognizes and codifies that which the people have long since come to recognize as a right against those possessed with governmental authority. However, from Publius's point of view, only positive harm could come about from incorporating rights whose status depended largely upon their constitutional sanction, and this because the more the observance of a right depends on constitutional sanction, the more it assumes the character of a parchment barrier.[6] And violations of the parchment barriers, as Publius tells us, would not only tend to disparage the very right in question, they would also serve to degrade the Constitution itself. In sum, Publius's sensitivity to the limitations of constitutional prohibitions or safeguards and his views on the potential damage of their repeated violations constitute another substantial reason, quite apart from his fears over the convening of another constitutional convention, for his antipathy toward a bill of rights.

Publius's discussion of the judiciary makes it clear that he would not have regarded it as strong enough to enforce those rights that did not have solid roots or whose meaning and scope were somewhat ambiguous. It would be all they could do, if the occasion were to arise, to block majority-inspired encroachments of those prohibitions already in the Constitution. Even if this were not the case, however, his argument is cast on theoretical grounds that would preclude this solution to the protection of rights. As he notes, employing such a means is foreign to the essence of republicanism wherein the people are sovereign. Thus, off at the end, the proper guardians of rights are the people—whose sovereignty constitutes the most basic right of all.

N O T E S

1. It should be noted that his remarks are directed to the appointment process in general, not specifically to the judiciary. As he pictures the process it is ideally suited for the selection of judges. However, it seems, Publius must have felt the relationships between cabinet officers and the executive would be considerably different from what they have turned out to be in practice.

2. Somewhat reminiscent of his position in Federalist 51, where he sees the successful operation of the proposed system leading stronger factions to forebear in the pursuit of their short-term interests out of consideration for their long term interests, he seems to envision that even losers in litigation will come to realize the "benefits of the integrity and moderation of the judiciary" because "no man can be sure that he may not be tomorrow the victim of a spirit of injustice, by which he may be a gainer today" (78:470).

3. Storing, ed., *The Complete Anti-federalist*, II, 420.

4. Ibid., pp. 423–24.

5. This test is similar to that set forth by Justice Brandeis in his concurring opinion in *Ashwander* v. *T.V.A.* (1936): "When the validity of an act of the Congress is drawn in question, and even if a serious doubt of constitutionality is raised, it is a cardinal principle that this court will first ascertain whether a construction of the statute is fairly possible by which the question may be avoided." 297 U.S. 346.

6. Such is clearly the case, for example, with regard to separation of powers. Here we find an interrelationship between constitutional provisions and human motivations. The efficacy of the constitutional provisions depends upon the rival ambitions and interests of the officeholders. In turn, the constitutional provisions, to be effective, must serve to reinforce and provide an outlet for these ambitions and interests. But, as Publius indicates in Federalists 47 and 48, a constitutional stipulation to the effect that the branches should remain separate and distinct would by itself be worthless.

Conclusion

*T*O THIS POINT we have explored in depth Publius's understanding of both the meaning and interrelationship of the basic principles embodied in the proposed Constitution. What emerges is a relatively comprehensive picture of a constitutional republic designed to provide for popular control of government, as well as for ordered liberty characterized by the rule of law. As we have remarked at various points of our analysis, however, these principles are not by themselves sufficient for achieving these conditions; they must be joined by an appropriate constitutional morality, if the system is to operate in the fashion anticipated by Publius. Yet Publius does not articulate, much less dwell upon, crucial elements of this morality. Indeed, at various points in his discourse, he simply assumes that the appropriate morality will find its way into the operations of the system. It is as if he believed the conditions or terms of this morality constituted givens so universally accepted that they needed no defense or elaboration. In some cases—as when, for example, he assumes that officeholders will defend their constitutional turf against encroachments—these givens take on the form of propositions more or less self-evident from his assumptions about human behavior. In others, however, they assume the form of moral commandments that are necessary for the constitutional system to operate in the fashion he envisions: the branches of government should show restraint toward one another; judges should exercise their judgment, not will; or the voters should fix their attention on fit characters.

The role of this constitutional morality gives rise to questions that require us to view Publius's teachings from a broader perspective. At one level, there is reason for concern about how this morality, necessary for the proper operations of the system, can be perpetuated over time so that the generations that follow the Founders will obey its injunctions. While, to be sure, we can say that *The Federalist* tacitly embodies its substance, thereby providing it a permanent place in our heritage, we find no discussion about how it is to be disseminated and transmitted over time. And this points to an even more basic problem: *The Federalist* is also silent about how that virtue, which Publius presupposes will operate to diminish the possibilities of factious rule, can be promoted, cultivated, or even preserved, once the proposed system is set in motion. This is no small matter because, as he intimates, "Republican government" requires a "higher degree" of virtue "than any other form of government" (55:356). Obviously he believes that the people whom he is addressing possess sufficient virtue for republican government. Thus the question becomes, what provisions are necessary to insure that the degree of virtue sufficient for self-government will be preserved over time?

The answers to these and like concerns, as we shall see, reveal still other dimensions of Publius's thought. Consequently, after surveying the "problem" of virtue, we will be in a better position to assess the lasting contributions of *The Federalist*, its character, and its status among the classics of political thought.

The Problem of Virtue

The problems associated with the cultivation and perpetuation of virtue are particularly interesting in the context of Publius's teachings. On one side, despite his emphasis on the difficulties and dangers associated with self-government, he writes with confidence about the capacity of the proposed system to survive. He claims to have identified cures, consonant with the spirit and substance of republicanism, for the fatal diseases and shortcomings of popular government that arise from the unreflective and unrestrained pursuit of immediate and partial interests. But what is noteworthy is that these remedies and cures deal with the symptoms, not the causes. Indeed, on this point, we need only recall *Federalist 10*, wherein he writes that it is "the protection" of "the diversity in the faculties of men from which the rights of property originate" that "is the first object of government" (78). In turn, he acknowledges that "the various and unequal distribution of property" that results from the protection of these faculties constitutes "the most common and durable source of faction" (79). In a broader vein, he warns of the undesirability and impracticality of eliminating liberty or attempting to give "every citizen the same opinion, the same passions, and the same interests" to avoid the fatal dangers of faction (78).

This aspect of Publius's approach is particularly significant because it reflects a strategic dimension of his thought about government, its proper role and scope. From the perspective of classical thought we see that he is endorsing a restricted or limited government, one that is to protect, not intrude upon, the domains that give rise to faction. Clearly, the functions of the proposed system he defends and advocates do not include nurturing opinions to promote a more cohesive and cooperative society, subduing or moderating passions to lessen the severity of conflict, or narrowing or refining interests to facilitate the task of advancing the common good. Moreover, he is not concerned that the proposed Constitution contains no provisions for educating or otherwise inculcating the citizenry with sufficient virtue to avoid or prevent the turmoil and conflicts caused by the pursuit of immediate and partial interests.[1] Nor, and only a slightly different matter, does he evince concern about the lack of an appropriate mechanism to develop the intellectual and moral potential of generations to come, so that at the very least they will be better equipped to protect and promote the "permanent and aggregate interests of the community."[2] On the contrary, his attention is riveted on another matter, the adequacy of the safeguards against the potential abuses of government. Measured against classical theory, then, Publius is seen by some as promoting a system that lowers the ends or goals of political society;[3] collective and individual liberty, rather than the intellectual and moral improvement of the citizenry, seems to be its paramount end.

There are ready answers for Publius's inattention to the problem of virtue. Perhaps the most obvious is that the major task confronting him was explaining and selling a new constitution in what he perceived to be a rapidly deteriorating political situation. In other words, his first order of business had to be securing ratification of the proposed Constitution, an act he believed would serve to remove

grave and immediate dangers to the very survival of the states. What
is more, as he viewed the situation, the principal shortcomings of
the existing confederation were attributable to the defects of its
structure and processes and not to unique, underlying conditions
relating to the moral character of the people. Given his views of the
source of these difficulties, the imperative need for immediate change,
and the political controversy surrounding ratification, we should
hardly be surprised that he does not raise complex and potentially
contentious issues necessarily connected with the cultivation of virtue.

In this vein we should also note that even if, consonant with classical teachings, Publius had regarded the intellectual and moral refinement of the citizenry to be among the primary ends of government, his most immediate concern would still have had to be securing
a stronger union. This, in turn, would have involved him with the
same problems and concerns with which he deals in *The Federalist*.
Nor, beyond this, does it appear that any likely transformation of
society would render his concerns irrelevant; that is, short of a society
of saints (or angels), there would still be problems associated with
the pursuit of short term and partial interests and the possibilities
of oppressive rule. From Publius's vantage point, even a society of
Socrateses—"as little to be expected as the philosophical race of kings
wished for by Plato" (49:315)—would not be entirely free of difficulties. But more to the point, his discussion of the causes and nature
of factions alone would scarcely lead us to believe that he thought
men could be elevated to a sufficiently high moral plateau to erad-
icate the problems with which he felt constrained to deal.

There do, however, appear to be more basic theoretical reasons
for Publius's relative silence on the problem of virtue. We can best
come to an understanding of them by recalling that Publius's con-
ceptual framework is not congruent with that of the Ancients. Consequently, to assess Publius's treatment of virtue by the standards
of classical theory is misleading, if not meaningless. As we know, the
Ancients conceived of the political community as an organic whole
wherein government and society were, conceptually speaking, inseparable. Yet Publius clearly embraces a distinction between society
and government, a distinction that by itself signifies that there is a
separate, somewhat distinct, and limited political realm in which
government is to operate—a realm that embraces only a part of
individual or social concerns. And though drawing comparisons be-

tween these modern and ancient conceptions is tricky business at best, it is safe to say that within Publius's conception, government exercises only a small portion of what the Ancients regarded to be the primary functions and responsibilities of the polis, among the most important of these being character formation or education in virtue.

This matter can be pictured in other terms. Publius viewed the Constitution as a deliberative, authoritative, and constituent act of the people. Thus, the Constitution and the government it establishes is a creature of the society over which it operates. In this view, emphasis is naturally placed on marking out the boundaries of government and placing limitations on its authority—a process that inherently presumes that a separation does and should exist between government and society. To put this otherwise, in Publius's view constitutions do not create a people or society, but rather they establish governments. And should the society find the constitution and the government it creates deficient, it can—again through a deliberative, authoritative, and constituent act—adopt a new constitution with a government to its liking. Abolishing government, then, in no way abolishes the society; the two are separate entities, the government being the creation of society. This mode of thinking, to go no further, only reflects the degree to which government and society were distinct in Publius's universe of thinking. It indicates as well why, within this universe, the notion of limited government is embodied in the very notion of constitutionalism.

From this point of view, a basic reason for his silence—and one that well illustrates the incongruity between the classical view and Publius's framework of thought—is that, for Publius, society, not government, is the source and generator of values. What is more, the government as an agent of society bears only that responsibility for education in virtue that the society places upon it. In this scheme of things two aspects of his thought are significant. First, Publius, and we may assume the society of which he was a part, would probably recoil at the prospects of government directing moral education along lines suggested by the classical models since this would involve a stringent curtailment of individual liberty.[4] And second, he also believed—along with, we must assume, the people whom he was addressing—that the state and local governments would bear the primary responsibility for any public education deemed necessary:

that education of the young was among the "residual" powers of the states. This, we may also assume, is an additional reason for his silence on the problem of virtue.

From still another perspective, it is evident that the problem of virtue was not a particularly pressing one for Publius. As our discussion of the role of representation in the extended republic (Chapter 2) indicates, from his vantage point it is enough that the people possess sufficient virtue to identify and elect fit characters. Put otherwise, so long as Congress—the engine of the proposed system—is composed of fit characters, and so long as its composition remains such that no party or interest can be the judge of its own cause, the system will render decisions within parameters acceptable to the people. For the most part, as we have already noted at some length, the system will perpetuate itself through the strategy of equipping rival and opposite interests with the constitutional means to protect their respective domains. In addition, he regarded the steady and impartial administration of the laws, which he felt would ensue once the proposed system was put into motion, as another powerful and positive force reinforcing a morality necessary for the perpetuation of the regime. Once established, popular confidence and trust in the processes and institutions of government could even serve to overcome the propensity of dominant interests to press their immediate demands at the expense of the long range interests of the community.

But Publius's lack of attention to the problem of virtue cannot be entirely explained away by the foregoing factors. Aside from his stress on the means for remedying the deficiencies traditionally associated with republican regimes, he also emphasizes the positive goals of a firmer union. He views the extended republic as protecting and promoting the "permanent and aggregate interests of the community" (10:78); he holds that both "justice and the general good" (51:325) will prevail under the proposed system; and he declares, as we noted at the outset, "the public good, the real welfare of the people, is the supreme object to be pursued" (45:289). Obviously the achievement of these ends under the republican form requires more than just keeping government within its proper bounds; it requires virtue in the citizenry as well.

That Publius did not concern himself with this matter can be explained on the tacit assumption, entirely consistent with his views concerning liberty and the separation of government and society, that the private sector—e.g., the family, churches, schools, communities—would cultivate and nourish the virtue necessary not only for the perpetuation of the regime, but for the pursuit of the collective good. In short, the intellectual and moral development of individuals falls primarily to society, with government assuming only that role which society assigns to it.

Publius's Teachings: An Overview

Our discussion thus far points to the obvious fact that *The Federalist* does not constitute a comprehensive and systematic discourse in political philosophy.[5] We should not conclude from this, however, that it does not deserve a place among the classics in political thought. What it does mean is that we are obliged to take into account the context within which it was written in order to appreciate both the order and nature of its contributions. To begin with, as we have intimated above, Publius is not out to refashion the society upon which the proposed system is to rest; he understands very well that government must be 'fashioned' to the society, as well as to the values and character of the individuals who comprise it. What is more, and a fact we have not dwelt upon, many of the significant features of the proposed Constitution are not new to those whom he is addressing. Indeed, the similarities in institutions and practices of government between most of the states were far greater and more significant than their differences. These similarities comprised the major elements of institutional framework similar in certain salient respects to the proposed Constitution. Thus, there existed a widespread understanding on the purposes and roles of institutions and procedures that Publius could take for granted. Where he does concentrate his attention, and where much is to be gleaned, is on the new or novel features of the new Constitution, as well as the changes embodied in it that are seen as improvements on the corresponding institutions and practices at the state level.

Nevertheless it is also clear that Publius is concerned about critical and perennial problems of political theory. He was, no less than Plato and Aristotle, concerned with the question of how to secure impartiality in the resolution of conflict within the society so that justice might prevail. For disparate reasons, some of which relate to his conception of the relationship between government and society, Publius simply could not embrace the likes of Platonic "Guardians" for achieving this end. Such a solution would clearly verge on employing "a power independent of the majority—that is of the society itself" (51:324). Above all, Publius was obliged to deal with existential reality by way of outlining how the elements of the proposed system— liberty, representation, and the multiplicity and diversity of interest— would serve to produce this impartiality consonant with republican principles. Nevertheless, as we have seen, Publius does rely upon "Guardian-like" qualities to prevail in the legislative assemblies in order to realize justice between competing interests.

Likewise, with Aristotle, he could perceive the dangers of conflict between the haves and have-nots, though, as we noted, he could also see far more complex patterns of conflict between multiple and diverse interests. For this reason, Publius's solution to the problem of resolving conflict between antagonistic interests is, in some respects, more involved than that envisioned by Aristotle in his discussion of the polity. Nevertheless, their end was essentially the same, that no group should be judge of its own cause for fear that this would allow it to advance its partial interests at the expense of the whole. In the same fashion, we can view Publius's defense of the separation of powers to insure the rule of law, not of men, as embracing elements of Aristotelian thought—not the least of which was an overriding fear of arbitrary and capricious rule.

That Publius wrote with the values and concerns of the better part of the Western political tradition in mind—and this would include the medieval and modern, as well as ancient—seems evident enough. The broad ends that he advances—e.g., ordered liberty, the "safety and happiness" of the people, "justice," the "permanent and aggregate interests of the community," "good government" —merely reflect this fact. To be sure, perhaps because he assumed his readers both understood and shared his vision, he does not enlarge on or refine certain of these goals to the satisfaction of many modern students. But whatever his deficiencies in this respect, he is clear about what he perceives to be the obstacles to their realization and why he believes the proposed system will operate to overcome them.

Viewed from this perspective, *The Federalist* reflects what can appropriately be termed a common-sense approach to politics—an approach that combines and employs experience, observation, and reason to achieve the desired ends. At one level, for instance, Publius clearly holds to certain fixed maxims regarding human motivation and behavior derived largely, it would seem, from his study of history and his observations of human behavior. That men are prone to pursue immediate self-interests at the expense of the long-range common good, that they are neither perfect nor perfectible, are certainly among the more basic of these. Certainly he regarded these as conditions that have to be taken into account to build an enduring political order. But there are others which serve to condition his teachings: "man will be interested in whatever he possesses, in proportion to the firmness or precariousness of the tenure by which he holds it" (71:431); "the reason of man, like man himself, is timid and cautious when let alone, and acquires firmness and confidence in proportion to the number with which it is associated" (49:315); or "it is a known fact in human nature that its affections are commonly weak in proportion to the distance or diffusiveness of the object" (17:119).

These and like observations merge both with experience—particularly his conclusions regarding the shortcomings of ancient republics, the existing confederacy, and the state governments—and with reason to yield a common-sense defense of the particulars of the proposed system. This much we see in his arguments and discussions surrounding numerous and disparate issues, such as the size of representative assemblies, the role and function of a second legislative chamber, presidential reeligibility, unity in the executive, the nominating procedures, the permanent tenure for judges, terms of office, the need for the national government to operate directly upon the people, and, *inter alia*, the futility of limiting the powers of government. While there is no grand theory in such an approach—the focus being, so to speak, on the nuts and bolts of the system—we should not minimize the significance of Publius's effort and its contribution to political thought. It points up the difficulties confronting the Framers in designing institutions and procedures of government to channel, control, and make use of the passions so that reason can prevail, while simultaneously embracing the values of liberty and self-government endemic to the American people. In so doing, it concretely illustrates both the complexities and potentialities of shaping institutions and procedures to achieve given ends.

From Publius's concern to show how the institutions and procedures of the proposed Constitution will use or employ the motives, instincts, and nature of man—at least as he views these characteristics—to produce the desired ends, we come to realize that institutions and procedures play a basic role in his political science. A properly constituted government, he maintains, can make up for deficiencies or shortcomings in the character of both the rulers and ruled. Furthermore, he even holds out prospects that such institutions and procedures may, in the long run, beneficially affect the character of a people.

In this respect, we must note that Publius was able to employ such a common-sense approach with its emphasis on means principally because, we may surmise, substantial agreement existed, even among the critics of the proposed system, about the meaning, priority, and desirability of the ends he emphasized. This is to say, for instance, that for the founding generation there was a consensus surrounding the value of liberty, as well as its meaning and character. Similarly, there must also have been a consensus about the evils or conditions—e.g., faction and tyranny—to be avoided. In sum, despite the difficulties confronting him, Publius did enjoy the luxury of advancing his positions in a society with shared moral foundations, convictions, and outlooks. He was not compelled, in other words, to engage in the kind of discourse or analysis that characterizes more philosophically oriented works.

Publius's preoccupation with means, however, should not blind us to the originality and enormous significance of his conception of and thoughts on republicanism, which served to give coherence to the Framers' undertaking. On one hand, as we have noted, he broke with traditional thinking and set forth the theoretical case for the feasibility, even the desirability, of republican government over an extensive territory. On the other, he provided a conception of republican government compatible with both the principles of political equality and the separation of powers. In this way, he tied republicanism to the procedures and institutions that would provide for the rule of law and ordered liberty.

Theory and Practice: An Appraisal

The nature of *The Federalist*, the fact that it does embody a common-sense approach in the sense we have indicated, means that we must evaluate it in terms appropriate to its nature and scope, not in terms normally employed for more comprehensive and systematic theoretical treatises. This is to say, for example, that the problem of virtue, while certainly not an irrelevant matter, was largely outside the scope of Publius's concern for reasons that are understandable in light of his purpose, approach, and assumptions. But, by the same token, other matters are quite germane to his undertaking, particularly those that form the foundations for his principal teachings. Not the least of these relate to questions that arise from the multiplicity and diversity of interests, the condition vital to his solution for majority factions.

As we have seen, Publius attempts to refute the traditional wisdom that a republican government is suitable only for a small, relatively homogeneous population within limited territorial confines. Nevertheless, he does acknowledge that the political union he envisions depends upon a sufficient degree of what we can call commonality—a shared heritage, religion, language, and so forth. In Federalist 2 he writes, in effect, that the proposed union is a natural and logical step because the people share common roots, speak "the same language," profess "the same religion," are "attached to the same principles of government," and are "very similar in their manners and customs" (38). Likewise, in Federalist 14 he invokes a common ancestry and shared past to argue for a stronger union: "the kindred blood which flows in the veins of American citizens, the mingled blood which they have shed in defense of their sacred rights, consecrate their Union and excite horror at the idea of their becoming aliens, rivals, enemies" (104).

Yet in setting forth and defending his extended republic theory, Publius writes as if there are no limits to the kind and number of interests that the extended republic can accommodate. Indeed, one might well conclude from reading Federalists 10 and the later part of 51 that the greater the multiplicity and diversity, the better. In any event, he does not squarely face up to the hard questions that arise from his stance, questions that were raised by the Antifederalists from the outset of the ratification struggle. Key among these was the Antifederalists' contention that a strong central government could enforce uniform laws for such a diverse people only through continual recourse to coercive measures that would eventually result in despotism.

Beyond this, Publius's teachings raise other, though similar, concerns. To begin with, he envisions the system promoting and encouraging diversity so that we are entitled to ask, Is it not possible that this diversity will undermine the commonality necessary for the regime to operate without continual recourse to coercion, so much feared by the Antifederalists? Are there not limits to the kinds of interests the system can accommodate, much less protect and cultivate, without experiencing severe internal tensions that could well serve to undermine its foundations or effectiveness?

One aspect of these concerns can be illustrated by recurring to Publius's example in Federalist 51 relating to how the multiplicity of religious sects forms the basis for their liberty. Certainly he could not have written so confidently to this effect if the country had contained substantial numbers of, say, devout Muslims and Hindus. The basis for the religious liberty in the context in which he writes would seem to derive from the fact that the sects are, in the main, Christian, and that the differences between them which cause their division are not of a sufficient magnitude or degree to constitute grounds for a restrictive or prescriptive majority coalition. Put otherwise, it is the absence of disagreement on fundamentals that allows for their peaceful coexistence, as well as for a genuine dialogue concerning what constitutes their general or collective welfare. But if this is so, then Publius's basic commitment to liberty and the diversity it nourishes poses a problem. This diversity may erode those elements of commonality that provide the basis for deliberation about the common good or help to secure the social unity and cohesion necessary for government to perform its delegated functions.

Still another, and not entirely unrelated, threat to the system would be a high degree of polarization of the people into relatively distinct and opposing camps. Now, to be sure, Publius did not conceive of the normal state of political affairs to be majorities pitted against minorities, nor, for the same reason, we may say, did he conceive of it in terms of relatively fixed or stable majorities, united by a coherent and interrelated set of shared principles, over against like-minded minorities—a situation wherein elections would obviously play the crucial role in the resolution of issues. But in his *Disquisition on Government*, John C. Calhoun—though it is clear he is writing with the distinct possibility of a civil war in mind— indicates how it could come to pass that the proposed system, as explained and defended by Publius, might be endangered by such a polarization: when a dominant party finds itself in control of all the branches of government.[5] In such a case, the potentialities for tyranny are present.

see note

Calhoun was wrong in predicting the collapse of the separation of powers because he extrapolated from the polarization or division arising over issues related to a single concern, namely, slavery. We may note in passing, however, that the conditions associated with the extended republic are effectively neutralized when intensity surrounds a polarization along the lines pictured by Calhoun. In such a case, not only are the contending parties firmly committed to their positions, there is no independent force that can serve to mediate between them. That Publius was not oblivious to this is indicated by his assurances that decisive majorities—the dominant party in this polarization—will rarely unite around a factious proposal.

The collapse of the separation of powers in the manner suggested by Calhoun—that is, through the control of all branches by one party— would, however, require more than polarization over a single issue. It would require as well the existence of a dominant party with a strong ideological commitment spanning a wide range of issues and concerns. Put another way, ideology—in the sense of a comprehensive, coherent, theoretical construct that determines one's view of the world and posture toward social, political, economic, and cultural concerns—is necessary in order to provide a unifying link between the personnel of the departments. The ideology, that is, must be comprehensive enough to insure the same outlook, mindset, or orientation on the part of the rulers. The commitment to the ideology would also have to be strong—strong enough, at least, to overcome the rulers' interest in maintaining the autonomy of their own offices or departments. In other words, ideological commitment must outweigh institutional commitment. Yet this alone would still not be sufficient: unless a majority of the people share the same ideology, the breakdown of separation could only occur through an unconstitutional usurpation of powers by the rulers. But with popular backing the system most surely would collapse: not only would the separation of powers be rendered ineffective, there would be no room for a mediating group, if one did exist, to prevail in the legislature.

The collapse of the system along these lines seems remote. Indeed, in fairness to Publius, his teachings are not entirely without answers to the difficulties to which we have alluded. As we have remarked, he perceived that the principal function of the national government would be to regulate economic interests whose differences could be compromised, not to resolve conflict between passion-based factions whose differences, more likely than not, would be intractable. Thus, it can be argued, the politics at the national level would be low key. Furthermore, with regard to the problems arising from diversity, it could well be that he thought the states, not the nation, would constitute the arenas of conflict, and that, moreover, the potential difficulties to which we alluded arising from the diversity spawned by liberty would also be best handled by the state and local governments.

But assuming this to be the case only highlights the degree to which we have departed from Publius's vision; a departure which, far from mitigating the potential problems associated with his teachings, has created new ones of very serious proportions. To begin with, particularly with the advent of the New Deal, it is clear that the logic of divided sovereignty could not be sustained. This much, as we have endeavored to show, could have been anticipated on a close reading of *The Federalist*. While this development, by itself, does not constitute a serious departure from Publius's design, its nature and direction does. Although Publius could write that the Congress's chief function would be the "regulation" of "various and interfering interests," we now have a positive government wherein the role of Congress has expanded well beyond mere regulation to include the dispensation of goods and services to varied interests. And there would seem to be no limits to the scope or size of this positive government. Inherent to its development has been coalitional politics marked by a high degree of complex horse-trading and logrolling among interests competing for governmental favors and goods. Because scarcely any interest can afford to stand outside of this ongoing coalitional process, there is no longer any substantial base for a sufficiently disinterested or distanced group of representatives to mediate among the competing interests. That is, to put this otherwise, because virtually all representatives have participated in this process, at best only a few are in a position to resist the process or to assert, with credibility, what its limits should be in terms of the long-range common good.[7]

The consequences of this lack of a mediating element are not particularly severe so long as the government possesses sufficient resources to placate the demands placed upon it, but acute problems arise with limited or diminishing resources in the absence of such an element. Extrapolating from Publius's assumptions—borne out, many would argue, by experience—we cannot expect the participants in this process to forebear and sublimate their immediate self-interests to the long-term common good. The problem, consequently, becomes that of somehow arresting processes that will eventually lead to insolvency, or, short of this, preventing highly intense confrontational politics that might endanger the stability of the system. Whether Congress can act to avoid these consequences is far from certain. Even assuming Congress can display the degree of fiscal responsibility when needed, there is still the question of what the reaction of the deprived groups would be, the more so as they may have come to look upon governmental dispensations as entitlements.

Not entirely unrelated to this development and to the potential problems it raises has been another, the acceptance of a new constitutional morality, one quite different from that set forth by Publius. Publius, we should recall, perceived Congress to be the predominant branch of the proposed system for reasons, as we have seen, that went well beyond its merely constitutional authority. To be sure, he viewed Congress as the most dangerous branch as well—a fact that some have taken to mean that he held an animus toward Congress. However, it would be a mistake to believe that he felt matters should be otherwise, that is, that Congress should be subordinated to the executive or judicial branches. Rather, his attitude toward Congress would seem to parallel his attitude toward republicanism; he sees legislative predominance necessarily linked to republicanism and, in much the same fashion as he acknowledges the faults of republicanism, he is frank in recognizing the potential dangers of this predominance. At the same time, in a more positive vein, he did believe that Congress would "refine and enlarge the public views."

Such a view, needless to say, is no longer widely held. Instead, another conception of the separation of powers—frequently, and without foundation, attributed to the Framers or to Publius—prevails: that the Constitution creates *equal* and coordinate branches. There are reasons that go well beyond the scope of our inquiry which partially account for this new morality. For instance, the emergence of political parties, a distinctly extraconstitutional development, has served to democratize the presidency, thereby providing the grounds for our chief executives to claim that they, not the Congress, reflect the authentic voice of the people. As important as this development has been for the growth of presidential authority, however, the extent to which it has altered the basic design envisioned by Publius is debatable. Certainly he wanted an executive who would be tough enough to stand up to Congress, when the occasion demanded. More important, while many might question the prudence of the Congress using the powers at its disposal to curtail presidential authority, few would regard this as unconstitutional. In short, though there has been and will continue to be heated debate about the proper relationship between the president and the Congress over their respective domains, the struggle between the two takes place within the parameters outlined by Publius.

The relationship between the Congress and the courts, however, is of a different order. The *equal* and coordinate version of the separation of powers, when taken in conjunction with a view of judicial review considerably beyond that which Publius argued for, actually renders the Supreme Court first among the presumed equals. Relying principally, though not exclusively, on the fourteenth amendment, the Supreme Court has seen fit to move beyond the relatively passive role marked out for it by Publius. It has taken on an active and positive role by, in effect, legislating to fulfill mandates it finds in the Constitution or by providing remedies to alleviate conditions contrary to its view of the principles or values embodied in the Constitution.

Our point here is not to rehash the lengthy and intense controversies that have arisen over the growth of judicial authority. Nevertheless, a few comments are in order in light of our remarks above. First, in this process the Court has contributed its share to centralization of powers by moving into areas long regarded as well within the realm of the state's authority. Thus, contrary to the manner envisioned by Publius, a good deal of centralization has come about, not through the political processes but through unilateral judicial action. And second, in this process the courts have introduced into the national arena highly divisive issues of opinion and passion. Put otherwise, the courts have boldly moved into areas where the Congress has been reluctant to enter. To the extent that Publius may have sought to avoid conflict at the national level over potentially divisive policies involving opinions and passions—issues which, perhaps, he believed would pose less danger if handled at the state and local level—his efforts have been undone by a new constitutional morality, which holds that the Court has as much, if not more, authority than the Congress to take positive action to remedy social wrongs.

Of course, this view of judicial power raises questions, which have also been extensively explored, about the republican character of this new morality. For our purposes, the controversy provides an excellent example of how the system goes awry once it strays too far from the constitutional morality Publius provided. Once, this is to say, the courts strayed from his injunction that they should exercise "judgment" and not "will," which he believed was the prerogative of the Congress, we find no ready answers about how to right the system. Because of his concern to maintain the independence of the judiciary, he seems to hedge on the question of remedies should the courts intrude upon the legislative domain. In the last analysis, to be sure, he does write that the impeachment and removal powers of Congress ought to be a "complete security" against this form of judicial behavior (81:485). Yet he also provides us with another morality which, over the decades, has assumed the status of an unwritten constitutional rule: that the impeachment process should not be employed for partisan purposes—individuals should only be removed from office for specified and substantial reasons after an impartial trial.[8] As a result, this process is, at best, an unwieldy check on the judiciary—or, for that matter, on the executive—save for the most blatant transgressions. And when the alleged transgressions are themselves the cause or at the center of partisan controversy, it is next to useless as a weapon.

Finally, this new morality—particularly with respect to the scope of judicial authority—perhaps more clearly than any other single concern reveals the gulf that exists between Publius's conception of the proposed system and the prevailing views and practices. Publius, to begin with, does not evince much concern about the potential intrusions by the judiciary or executive on legislative powers. Indeed,

his overriding concern was to prevent the legislature from drawing
all powers into its "impetuous vortex" (48:309). To be sure, he could
conceive that the courts might take "active resolutions," but it is
doubtful that he could envision the Congress feeling constitutionally
obliged to honor and support them. He would, that is, be surprised
at the extent to which Congress itself has even sanctioned judicial
intrusions upon its authority.

These and like divergences would appear to be merely manifes-
tations of a more fundamental difference between Publius's understanding of our system and that which has gained currency with the
increasing concentration of authority at the national level. To a great
extent, as we have seen, Publius was preoccupied with the organization and exercise of power to protect against faction, tyranny, and
mutability of the laws, while providing for good government which
would operate in accordance with the refined and deliberate will of
the nation. Recognizing the sovereignty of the people, his basic concerns centered on the adequacy of the institutions and processes to
render just and equitable solutions, primarily with respect to conflicts between economically based interests. In contrast, the newer
morality embraces a different set of concerns that revolve around
the realization of individual and collective rights—social, economic,
and political—through the agencies of government. This by itself
reflects the centralization of authority in the national government
over wide-ranging concerns far beyond the accommodation of merely
economic interests. More important, the newer morality focuses not
on processes, but on ends whose realization becomes the measure
of the democratic character of the system. Furthermore, framing
these ends in terms of rights and justice, as is often the case, opens
up avenues for their achievement through the courts. Conversely,
because these ends frequently involve complexities and issues over
which there are different opinions, sometimes passionately held, their
realization is not so readily achieved through the political processes.
In sum, the emergence of this new morality helps to account for the
major discrepancies we find between what Publius envisioned and
modern practice, particularly with regard to the decline of the Congress and the enhanced powers of the courts.

Finally, to the extent the system has changed along the lines we
have outlined, we may ask, what is the relevance of *The Federalist*?
If, that is, it does not even serve to explain the manner in which the

American system operates today, then of what use are its teachings? These are questions that can be answered at different levels. It is clear, for example, that *The Federalist,* in lending a coherency to the proposed Constitution and its underlying values, provides benchmarks against which we can measure both the direction and degree of change in our system and its underlying principles since the founding era. This in itself is revealing. From almost the outset we see that Publius, unlike many of his modern critics, presupposed an objective moral order that rendered the problem of factions very real for him and presumably for the Founders. Beyond this, by reading *The Federalist* with care, we are in a better position to identify the potential dangers and difficulties that accompany the evolution or alterations of the basic principles.

At still another level, Publius's teachings force us to ask questions about our system which we are out of the habit of asking. Are interests today increasingly the judges of their own cause? Is there a dangerous consolidation of powers or functions in the hands of any one branch? That is, are Publius's concerns about tyranny still pertinent? Are there still reasons for concern about the coincidence of "impulse and opportunity"? Is, in other words, the concern about "factious" rule passé? Does moving beyond limited government— one whose primary function is the regulation of interest—to positive government cause long-term difficulties that endanger the system? Can the federal principle be more judiciously used to defuse potentially divisive issues? Does the increasing ethnic, racial, cultural, and linguistic heterogeneity of the society, taken together with the expanded role of the national government, render the original concerns of the Antifederalists to the extended republic highly relevant?

Perhaps Publius's profoundest contribution is to be found in the substance and character of his approach, which reveals a good deal about the unique character of American political thinking. He understands the magnitude of the choice confronting the American people—indeed, he perceives their choice as one that could affect all of mankind—and we can only assume that he set upon a course he deemed best calculated to secure popular approval of the proposed Constitution. His appeals, this is to say, had to make sense to his readers. And what we find in his approach is an earthiness. There are no appeals to abstract rights or claims that the new system will lead to a utopia. Instead we find a realistic assessment of the tasks that will confront the new system, of the nature of the individuals who will comprise it, as well as of the potential dangers that might overtake it. The goals sought—order, self-government, rule of law, stability, ordered liberty—are, Publius recognizes, not easily attainable, nor are they entirely compatible with one another. But the goals are not abstractions; they have not only constituted, albeit imperfectly, the basic elements of the American heritage which, in turn, finds its roots in the broader Western tradition, they conform as well with the genius of the American people. In welding together a system that will simultaneously serve these ends, we gain from Publius an appreciation of the role of common sense, as opposed to abstract reasoning. Reason, of course, has its place in *The Federalist*. But it is reason more frequently than not closely linked to either experience or observation. Such may be said even with regard to his extended republic theory, perhaps the most original element of his teachings.

Finally, we should observe that Publius could promise his readers a new government that "upon the whole" would be "a good one," one that "promises every species of security which a reasonable people can desire." It would be "chimerical," he wrote, to ever expect a "perfect plan" (85:523). Such were the limitations he acknowledged to the capacities of "imperfect" man. Nor, he intimates at another point, would the capacity of man alone suffice to produce even a "good" constitution: "It is impossible for the man of pious reflection not to perceive in it [the deliberations of the convention] a finger of that Almighty hand which has been so frequently and signally extended to our relief in the critical stages of the revolution" (37:230–31). We may confidently say that one of Publius's lessons for generations yet to come is quite simply that founding constitutional republics is, indeed, a very "ticklish" business.

NOTES

1. Publius did not believe this true of all people, at all times. But the system, it would seem, is built with this general rule in mind, not its exceptions. See Scanlan, "*The Federalist* and Human Nature."

2. As Mayard Smith points out with regard to a related matter: "The fact is that *The Federalist* elaborates no educational system or directive and religious strictures; no training in the use of reason, in the kinds of problems accessible to it, in its potentialities; no interest in a morality sensitized by contemplation

of its source." "Reason, Passion and Political Freedom," *Journal of Politics* 22 (Aug., 1960), 543.

3. Martin Diamond pictures Publius (Madison) as a disciple of the "new science of politics" who was not concerned "to instruct and to transcend passions and interests," but rather with "directing man's passions and interests toward the achievement of those solid goods this earth has to offer: self-preservation and the protection of those individual liberties which are an integral part of that preservation and which make it decent and agreeable." This "new political science," according to Diamond, "gave a primacy to the efficacy of means rather than to the nobility of ends: The ends of political life were reduced to a commensurability with the human means readily and universally available. In place of the utopian end postulated by the ancients, the forced elevation of human character, the moderns substituted a lowered political end, namely, human comfort and security." "Ethics and Politics," p. 47.

4. Diamond notes the "harsh demands of the classical teaching: the general sternness of the laws; the emphasis placed on rigorous and comprehensive programs of education; the strict regulation of much that we now deem 'private'; the necessity of civic piety; the extremely limited size of the polis; and the severe restrictions on private economic activity." "Ethics and Politics," p. 45.

5. Because there are theoretical "interstices" in Publius's political thought, there is a temptation to fill them in by recurring to the writings of more systematic political thinkers whose thoughts and concerns are similar to Publius's. Likewise, because Publius may not be very expansive on certain concerns or points, it is tempting to use the thoughts or analyses of other theorists to provide a more comprehensive picture of what Publius was up to. Thus, it is not at all surprising that in most of the major works dealing with *The Federalist* a good deal of time is spent attempting to show the linkage or parallels between Publius's thoughts and those of other, more systematic, theorists. See, for example, Wills, *Explaining America*; Dietze, *The Federalist*; David F. Epstein, *The Political Theory of "The Federalist"* (Chicago: University of Chicago Press, 1984); and George Mace, *Locke, Hobbes, and "The Federalist Papers"* (Carbondale: University of Southern Illinois Press, 1979).

While it is beyond our purpose here to examine and evaluate the linkages that have been drawn, a few comments are in order. In the first place, the variety of theorists whose thinking presumably influenced Publius would suggest that if one looks hard enough, a linkage of some degree can be established between Publius and any number of major political thinkers of the past. For this reason, it is probably more accurate to say that the direct influence on Publius was negligible, that, as we say in the text, he was writing well within the mainstream of Western political thinking, whose major principles and ideas had, so to speak, become part of the landscape.

Moreover, linking Publius's thought to specific political thinkers is a very tricky business, the more so as this linkage is designed to render his teachings more comprehensive and coherent. For example, following Adair's lead, Gary Wills links Publius's teachings closely with those of David Hume and the Scottish Enlightenment. But others, on various points and for different reasons, dispute

Wills's depiction of this connection. See, for example, Epstein, *The Political Theory*.

The methodological difficulties of superimposing the more systematic efforts of other theorists onto *The Federalist* are also enormous. These can perhaps be illustrated by considering the difficulties of using John Locke for this purpose since his theory is probably the one most frequently linked to the Founders. The first major difficulty is interpreting Locke, that is, giving meaning to his theory. As matters stand we have at least two Lockes in our literature: one, the moderate, common-sense Locke who espoused the natural rights many take to be the foundation of our tradition; the other, a philosopher whose primary ends vary little, if any, from those of Hobbes. We have, in sum, the "good" Locke and the "not-so-good" Locke, both of whom have been credited with exercising enormous influence on Publius. The battle over the correct interpretation of Locke thus becomes, at one remove, a battle for the "correct" interpretation of the American political tradition and *The Federalist*. But the outcome of this contest—though it is quite unlikely given its nature that there ever can be a definitive resolution—cannot be decisive because we still would have to know how Publius looked upon Locke.

The problems encountered with showing single-author influence are obviously multiplied when attempting to show the impact of two or more theorists on Publius's thought. And these difficulties are further compounded if Publius is conceived of as three individuals, each with a significantly different viewpoint.

6. Speaking of the tendency of numerical majorities toward the abuse of power, Calhoun writes: "Nor would the division of government into separate departments . . . prevent this result. Such a division may do much to facilitate its operations, and to secure to its administration greater caution and deliberation; but as each and all the departments,—and, of course, the entire government,—would be under the control of the numerical majority, it is too clear to require explanation, that a mere distribution of its powers among its agents or representatives, could do little or nothing to counteract its tendency to oppression and abuse of power." *Disquisition on Government* (State College, Pa.: Bald Eagle Press, 1952), p. 50.

7. For a detailed discussion of the effects of positive government on Publius's solution to the problem of majority factions see George W. Carey, "Majority Tyranny and the Extended Republic Theory of James Madison," *Modern Age* 20 (Winter, 1976).

8. We see from Federalist 65 and 66 Publius's deep concern to render the impeachment process as impartial as possible, a task he acknowledges is most difficult because partisanship is so closely connected to the proceedings. The impeachment process is no small matter because, in his words, it "concerns the political reputation and existence of every man engaged in the administration of public affairs" (65:397).

Index

Adair, Douglass: on the Declaration and Constitution, xxxii*n*, 46*n*
Allen, William B., 125*n*
Antifederalists: arguments against extended republic, 7, 45*n*; concern over blending of powers, 51–52; fear of federal regulation of elections, 83; contend courts will usurp legislative powers, 138–39
Articles of Confederation: critical deficiencies of, xvii–xviii, 52, 92*n*

Beard, Charles A.: praise of *The Federalist*, xxx–xxxi*n*, 44*n*; on Publius as an economic determinist, 46*n*
Benson, George C. S., 125*n*
Bill of Rights: Publius's opposition to amendments, 145; Publius's disdain toward, 146; compares proposed and New York state constitution, 146–48; inappropriate for republican regime, 147; inconsistencies in Publius's argument against, 148, 150–51; would pose dangers, 148–150; Constitution as, 150, 152; basis for Publius's opposition to, 151–53
Blackstone: on habeas corpus, 147
Bourke, Paul F., 45*n*
Boyd, Julian F., xxx*n*
Brandeis, Justice: on presumption of constitutionality of legislation, 153*n*
"Brutus": on fear of judicial usurpation, 138–39
Burns, James McGregor: xxxii*n*; on inadequacy of constitutional system,

xxxii*n*, 44*n*; separation of powers unnecessary, 91*n*, 94*n*

Calhoun, John C.: concurrent majority principle, xiv, 30; Constitution as compact between states, 126*n*; on collapse of the separation of powers, 165–66, 175*n*
"Cato": argument against extended republic, 45*n*
Colbourn, Trevor, xxxii*n*, 46*n*
Compound republic: characteristics of, 104–5; foundation of, 105–6, 126*n*; means of change, 107; operations of, 107; extent of powers, 107–9; problems in delineating sphere of national and state authority, 109–11; Supreme Court versus common constituents as arbiter of national-state conflict, 112–15; Congress as arbiter of national-state conflict, 115; states advantage over national government, 115–18; potential state resistance to oppressive national government, 118–21, 122–23; need for consensus, 121; importance of good administration, 123–25, 127*n*. *See* Confederate Republic; Federalism
Confederate Republic: nature and advantages of, 7–8, 98–100; need for adequate powers, 100–104. *See* Compound Republic; Federalism
Congress: critical role in curbing factions, 32–35; as jury in mediating interest conflict, 41; as central council, 41–42;

177